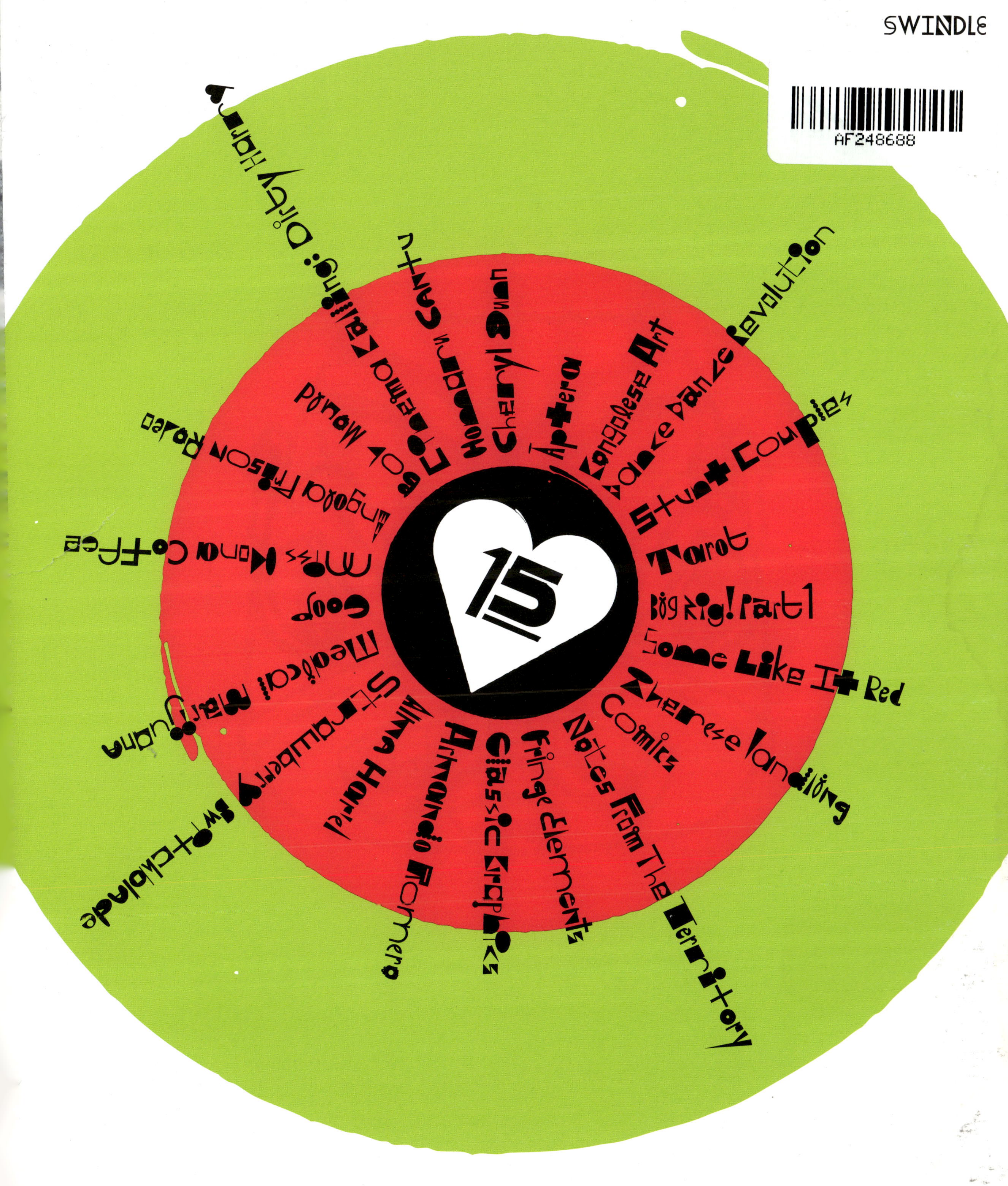

SWINDLE
AF248688
15
Dirty Harry
Homeschool Canby
Cheryl Sun
Aptera
Kongolese Art
Dance Dance Revolution
Stunt Couples
Tarot
Big Rig! Part 1
Some Like It Red
Therese Landing
Comics
Notes From The Territory
Fringe Elements
Classic Graphics
Armando Romero
Alina Harel
Strawberry Switchblade
Medical Marijuana
Goop
Mrs. Kona Coffee
Angola Prison Rodeo
Boy Monad
Erasmo Carlos

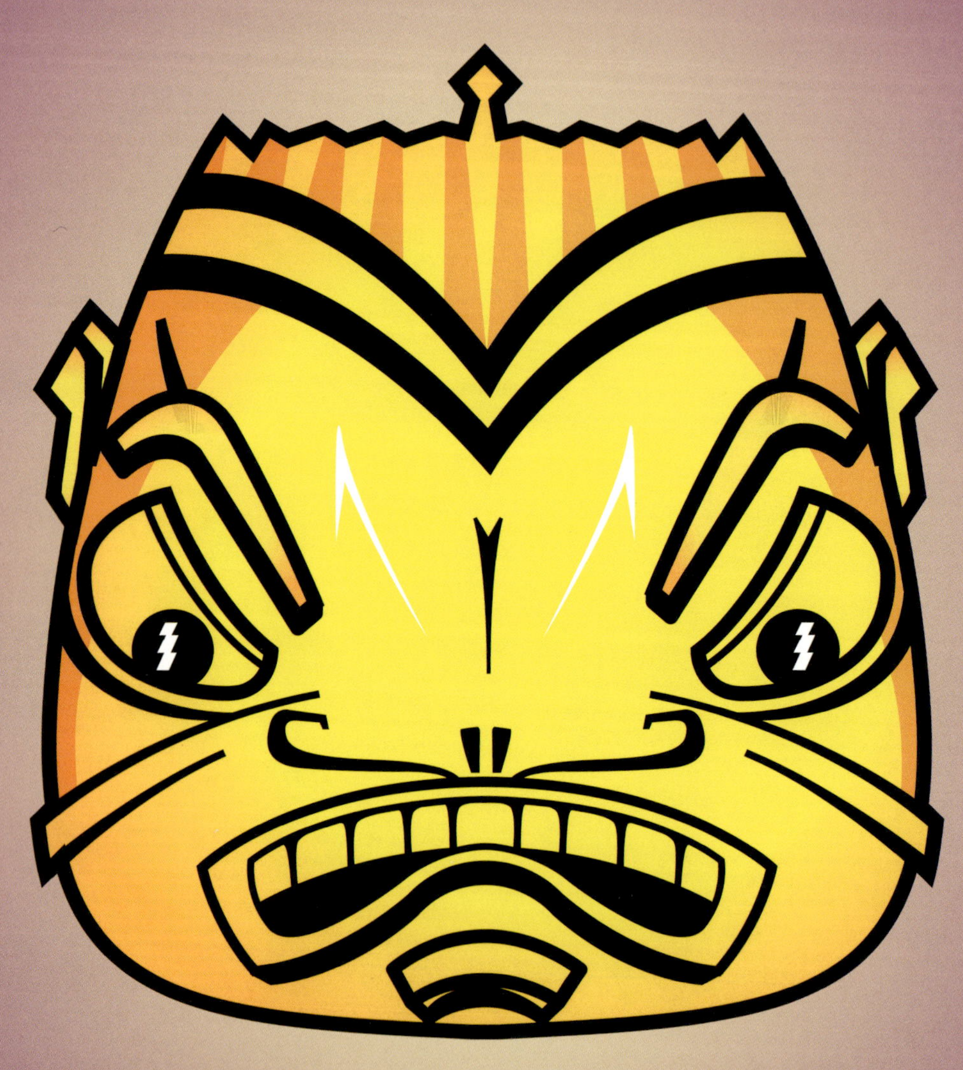

God of Efficiency!

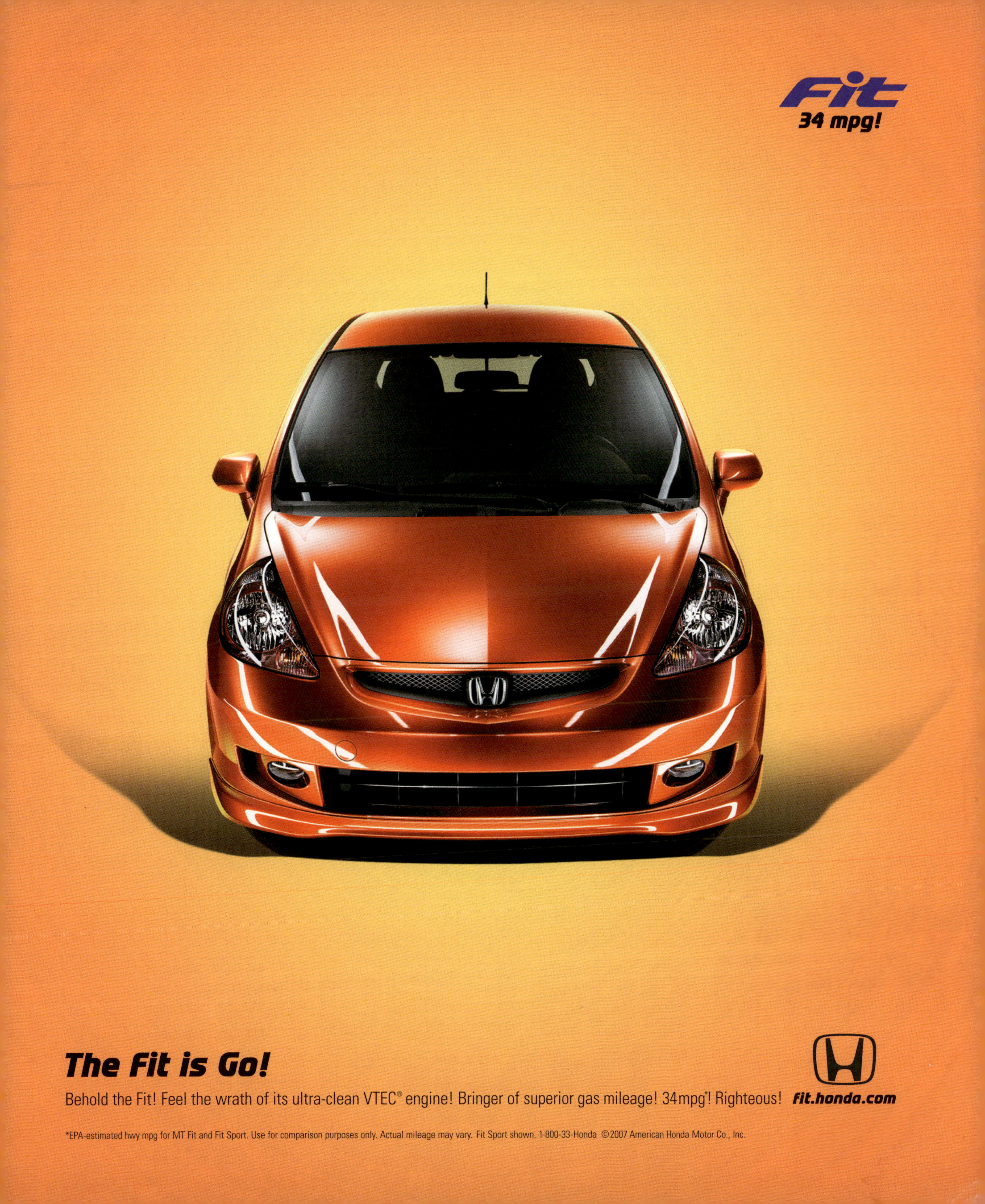

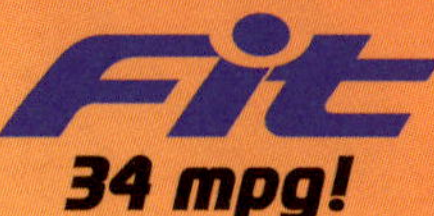

The Fit is Go!

Behold the Fit! Feel the wrath of its ultra-clean VTEC® engine! Bringer of superior gas mileage! 34 mpg*! Righteous!

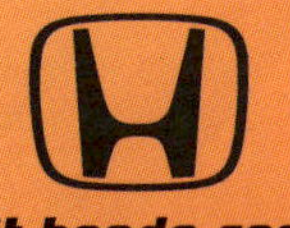

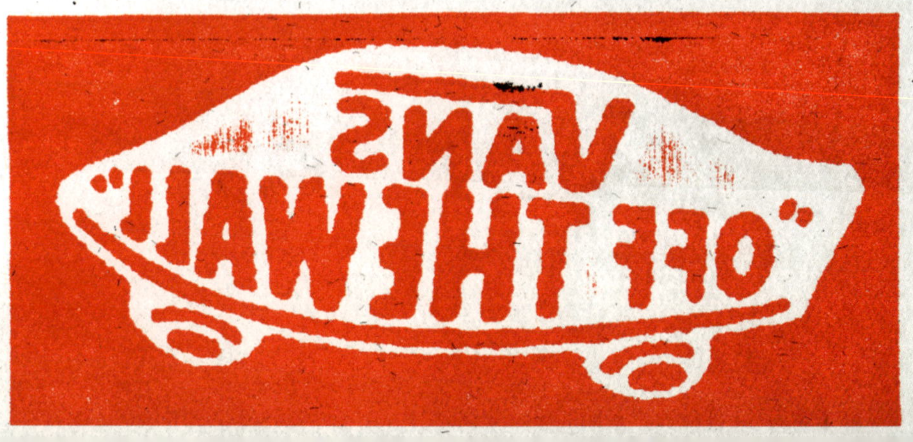
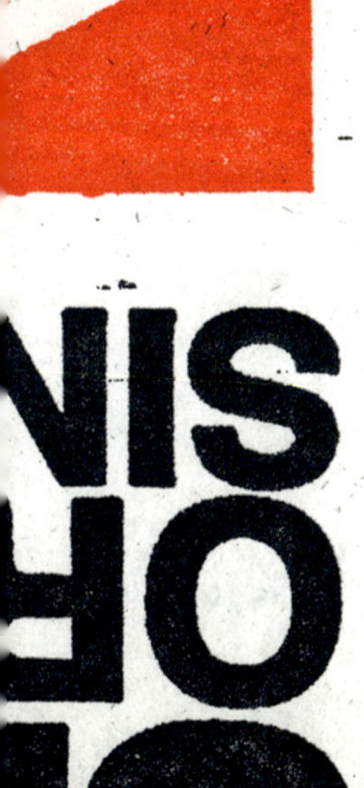

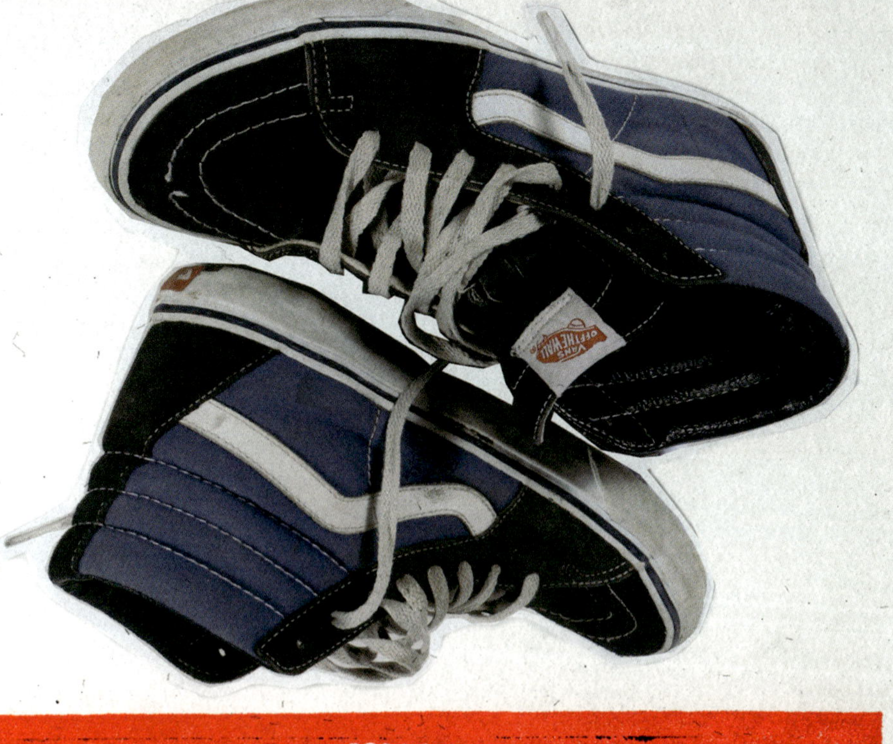
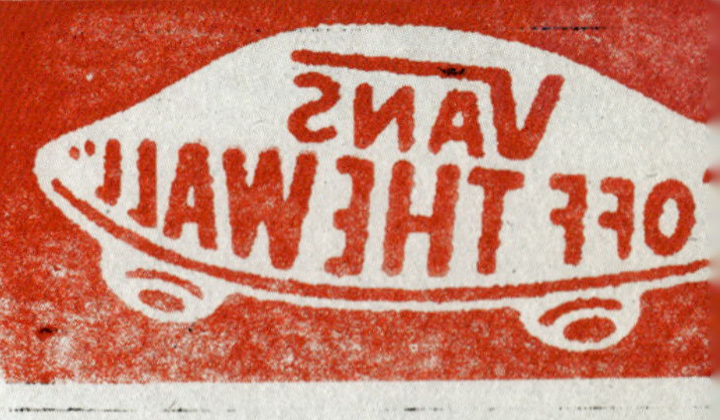
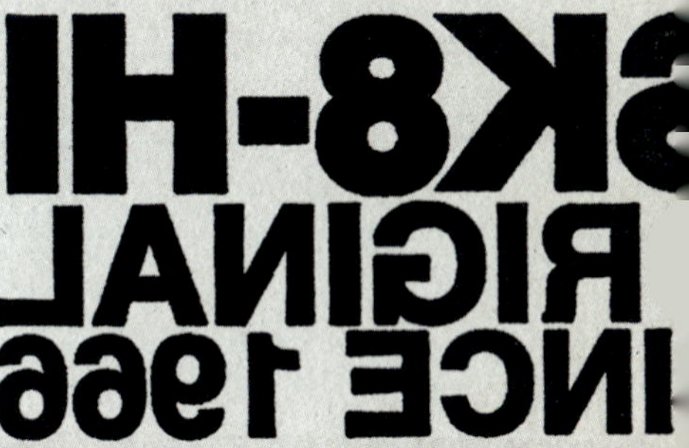
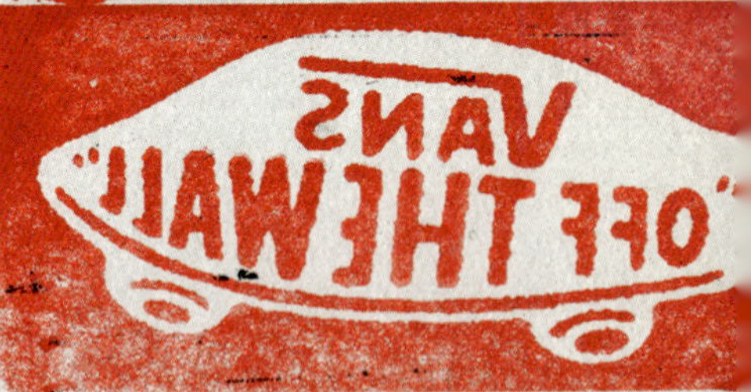
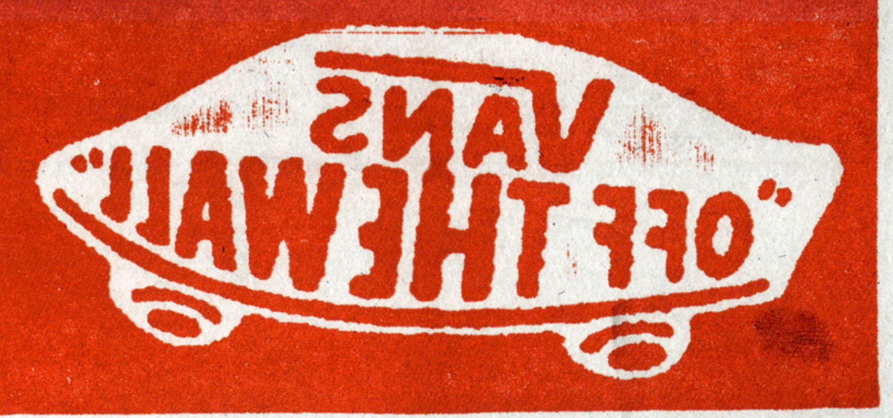
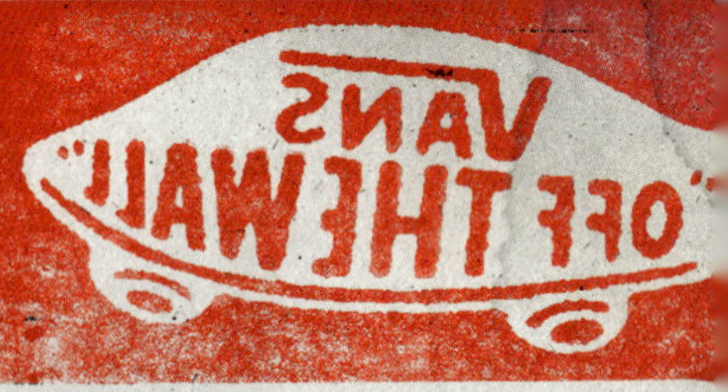

ORIGINAL SINCE 1966
SK8-HI
THIS IS THE SK8-HI, ORIGINAL SINCE 1966.   WWW.VANS.COM

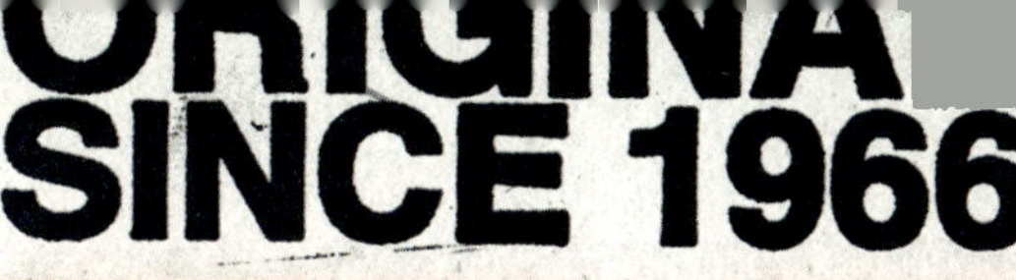
ORIGINA
SINCE 1966

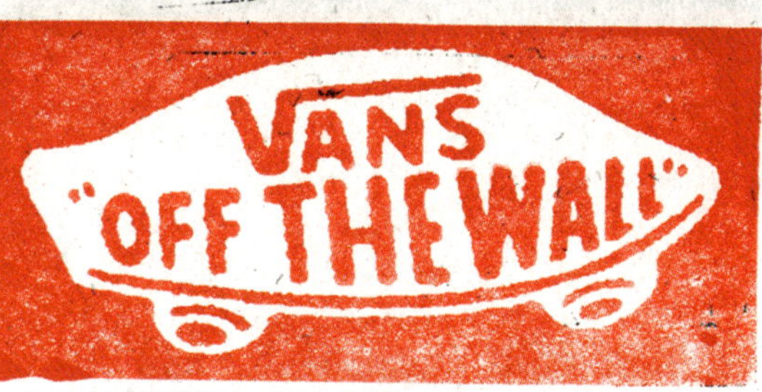
VANS
"OFF THE WALL"

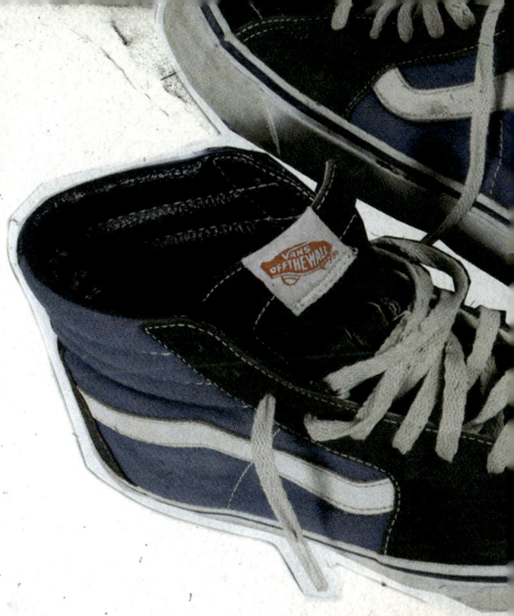

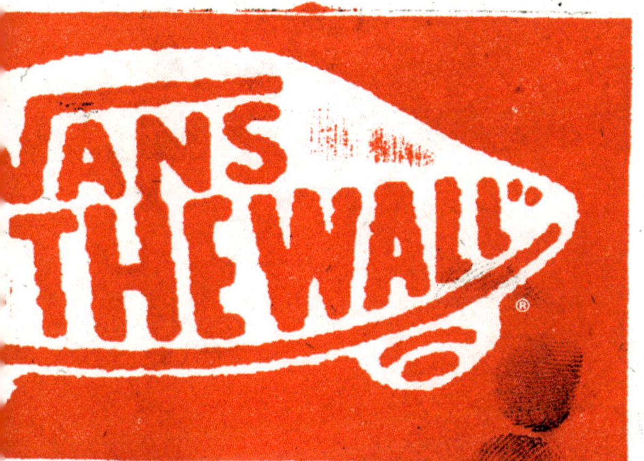
VANS
THE WALL"

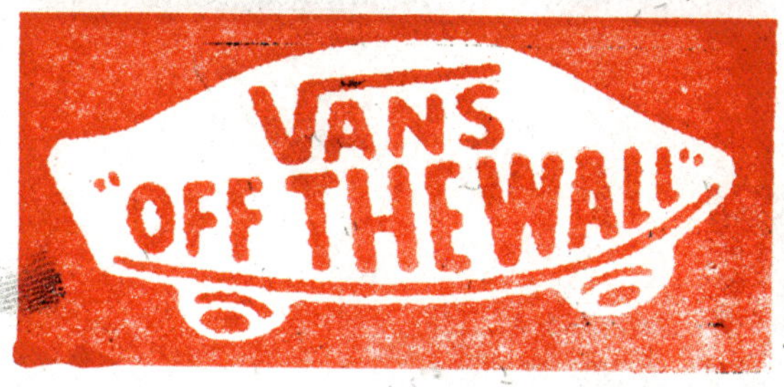
SK8-HI
ORIGINAL
SINCE 1966

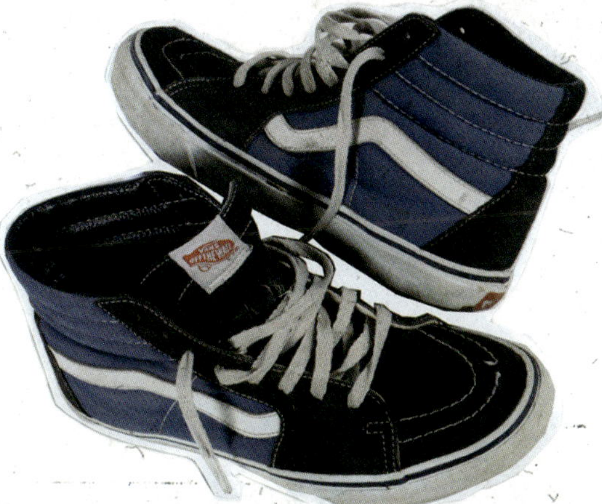
VANS
"OFF THE WALL"

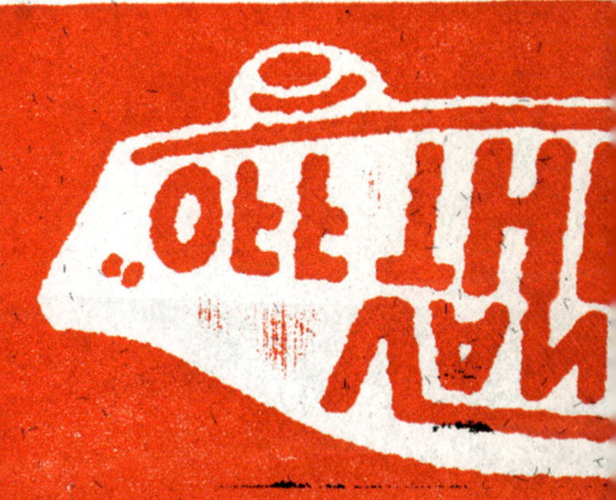

8-HI
GINAL
E 1966

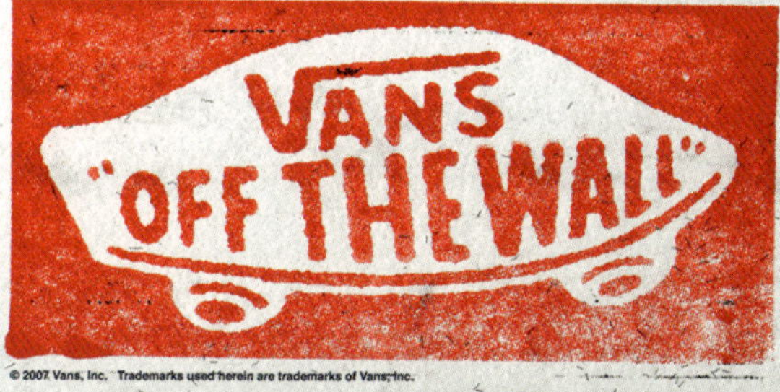
SK8-HI
ORIGINAL
SINCE 1966

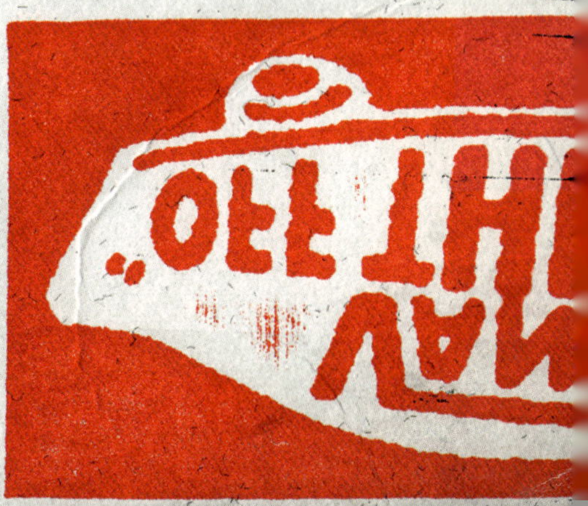

VANS
THE WALL"

VANS
"OFF THE WALL"

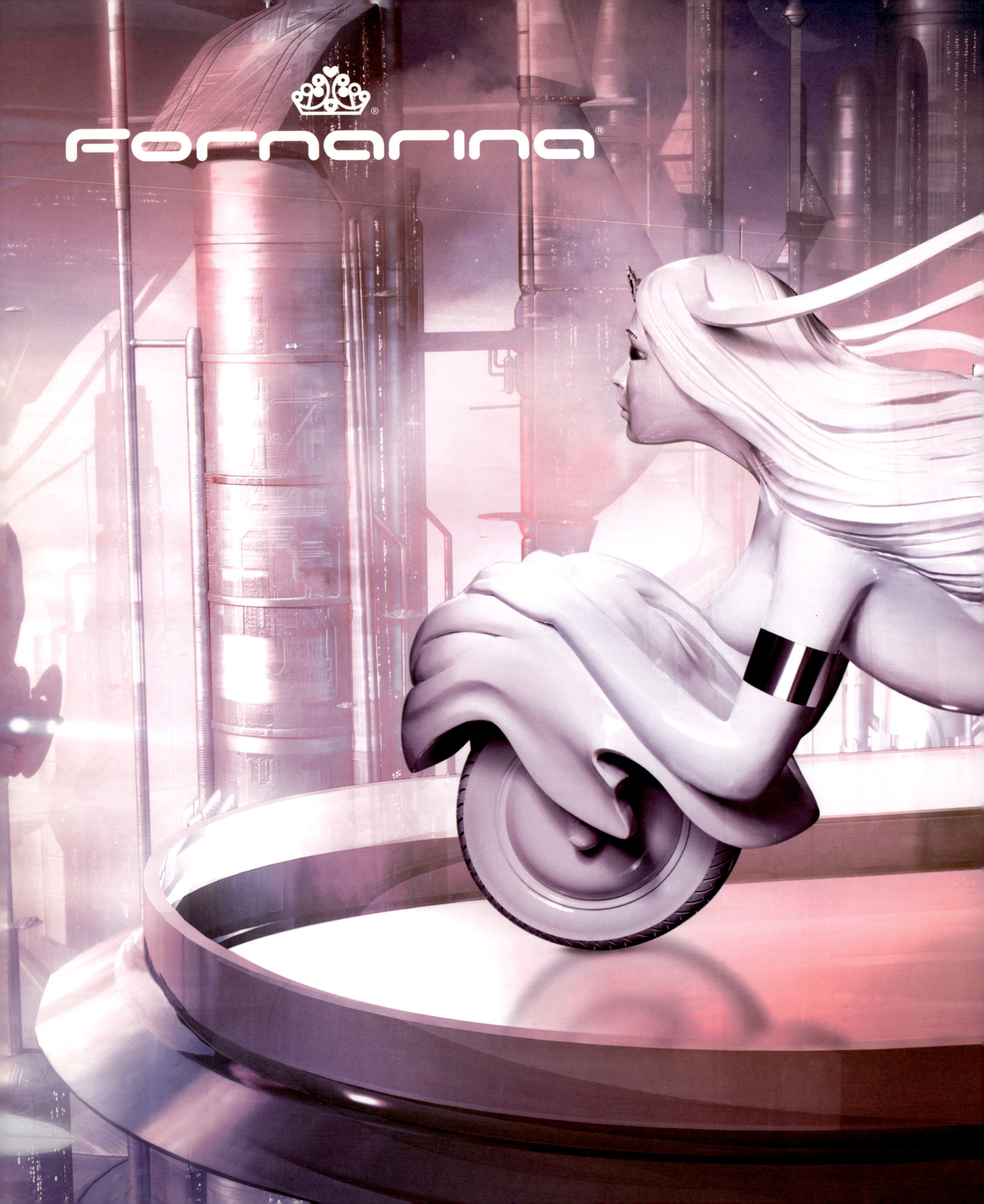

fornarina®

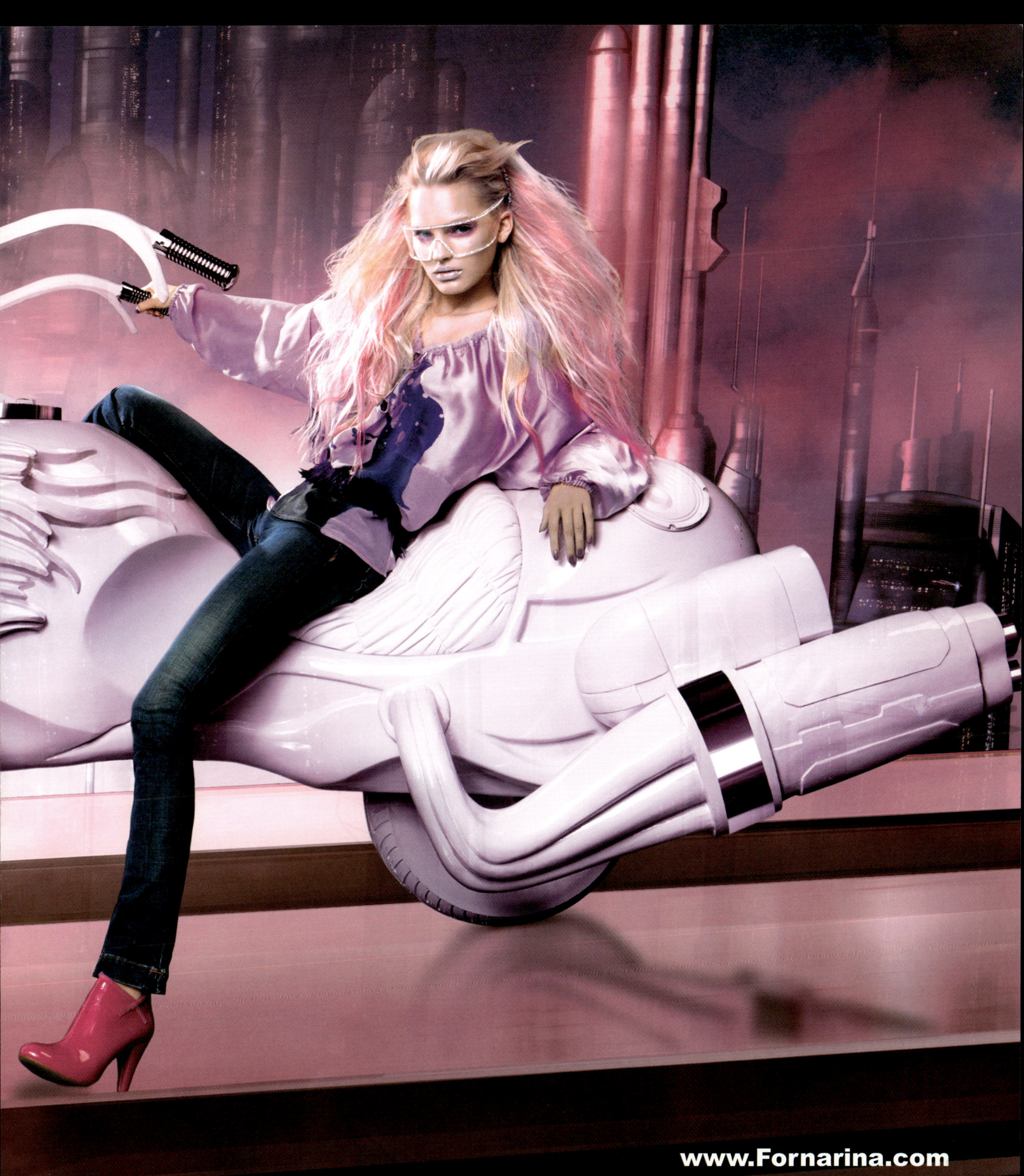
www.Fornarina.com
Please visit for store locations.

ROCK N' RULE

Behold the

King & Queen

by Royal Elastics

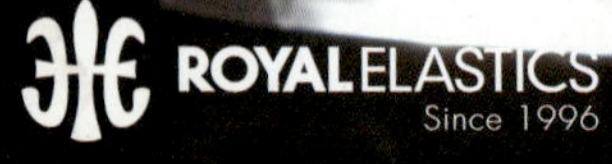

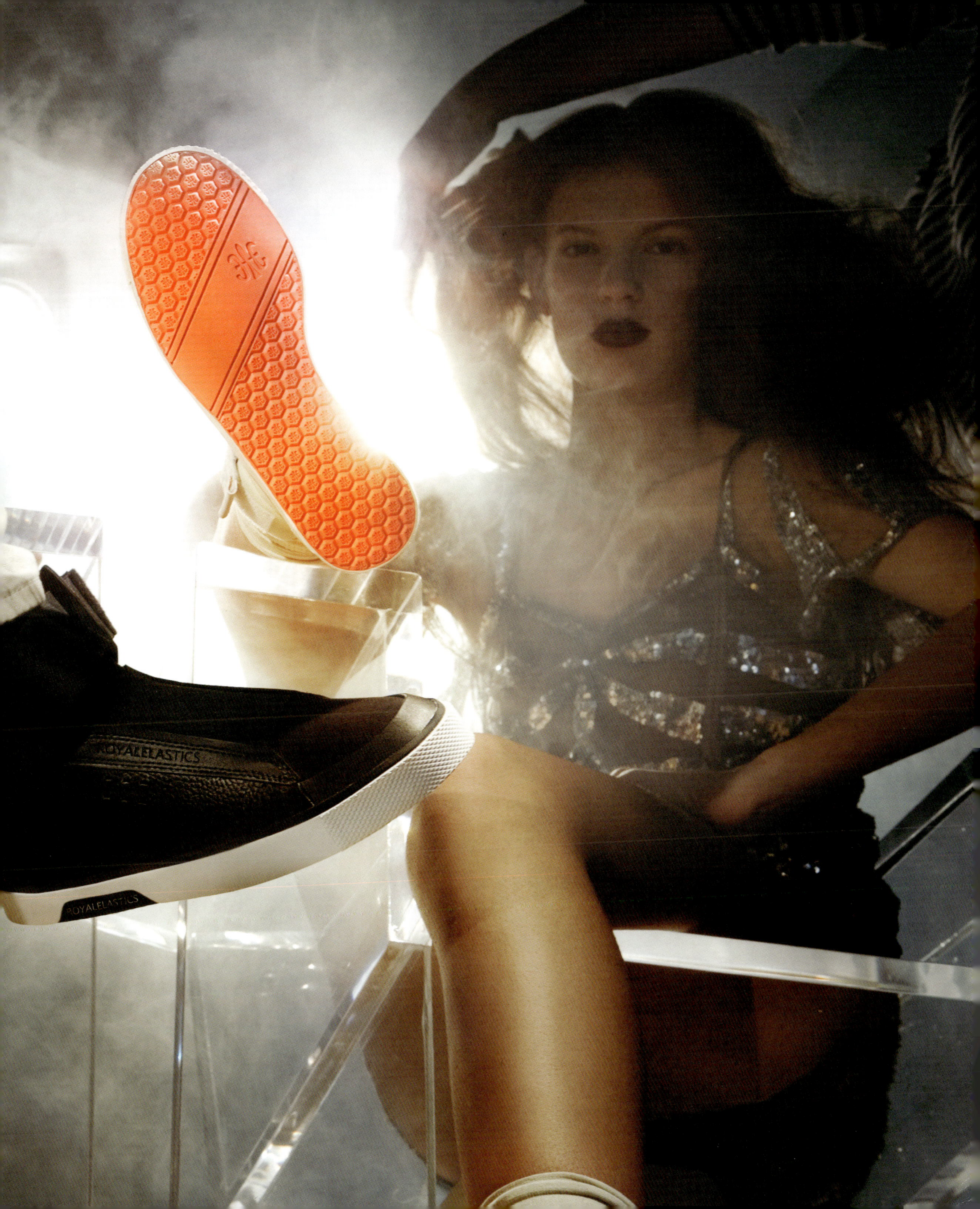

ROYALELASTICS
ROYALELASTICS

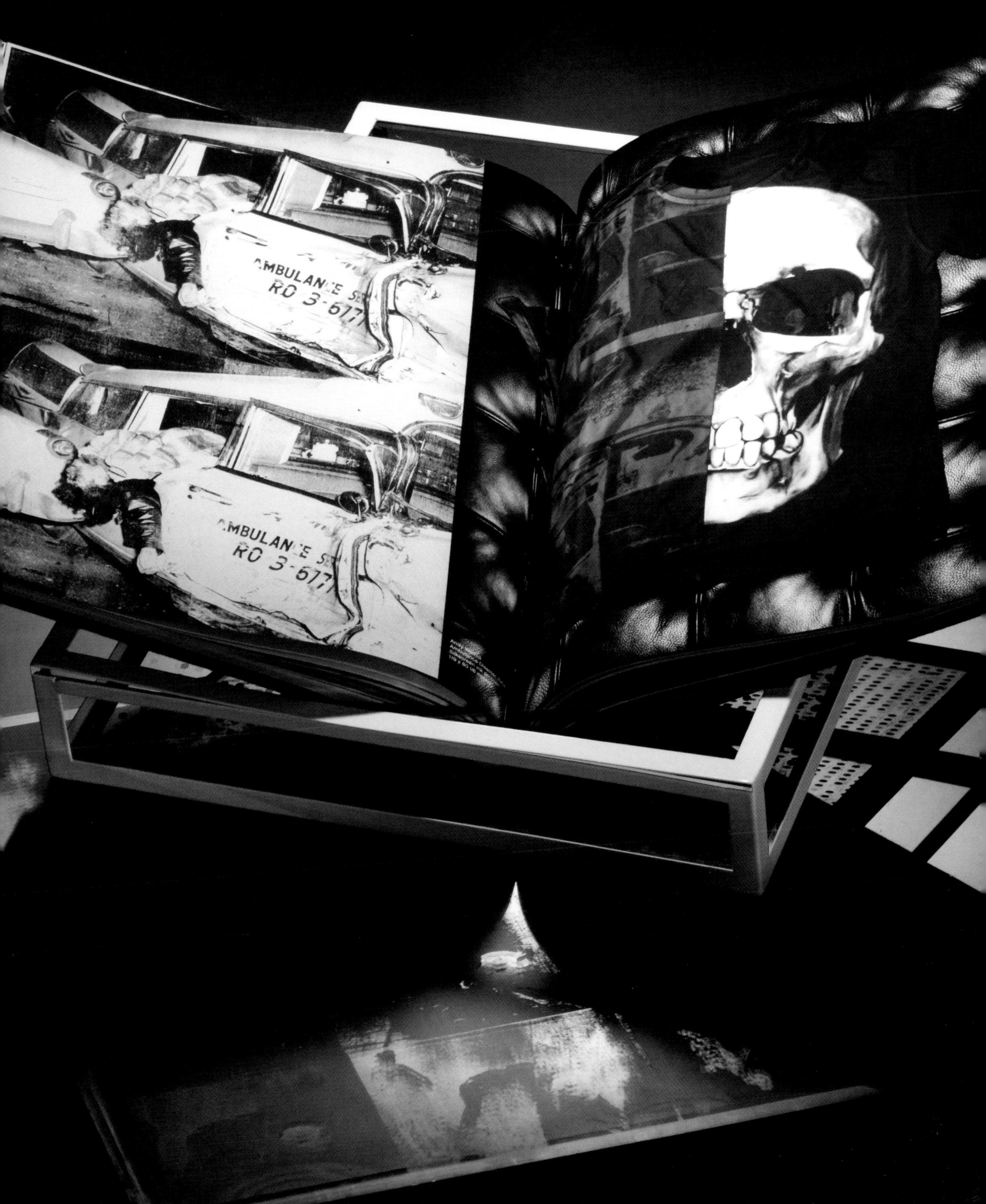
AMBULANCE S
RO 3-577
AMBULANCE S
RO 3-577

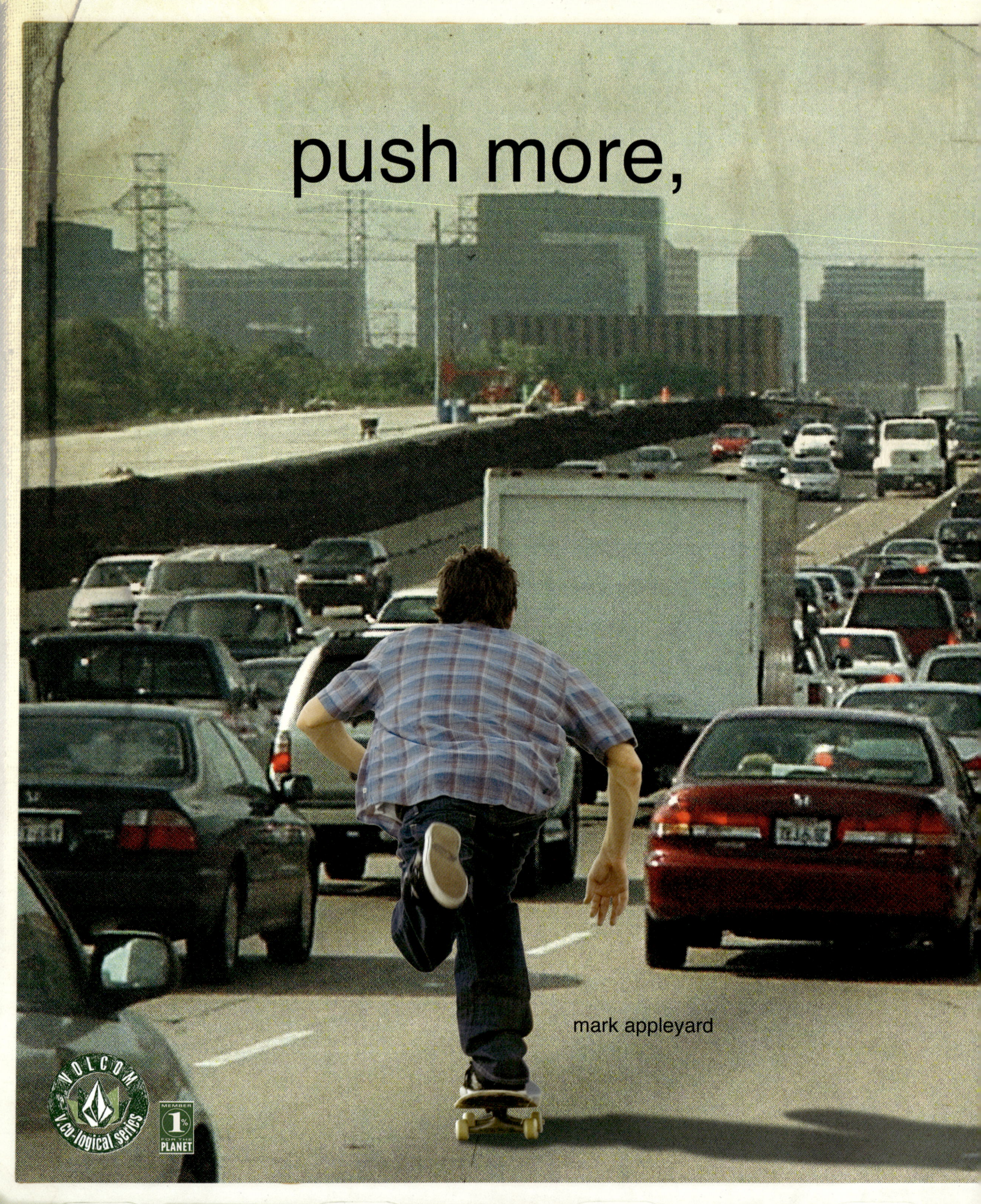

push more,
mark appleyard
VOLCOM
v-co-logical series
MEMBER
1%
FOR THE
PLANET

drive less.

Almost one third of the carbon dioxide produced in the United States comes from our cars, trucks and airplanes. There are many simple, practical things you can do to reduce the amount of carbon dioxide you produce while on the move.

One of which is:
Reduce the number of miles you drive by skateboarding wherever possible.
-Avoiding just 10 miles of driving every week would eliminate about 500 pounds of carbon dioxide emissions a year!

SWINDLE

Founders
Amanda Fairey, Shepard Fairey
and Roger Gastman

Director of Operations
Sonja Teri

Creative Directors
Shepard Fairey and Cleon Peterson
of Studio Number-One

Editor-in-Chief
Roger Gastman

Fashion Director
Claw Money

Art Director
Anthony Smyrski
www.smyrskicreative.com

Managing Editor
Anne Keehn

Deputy Editor
Zio

Production
Leon Catfish

Associate Editor
Ian DeLaurentis

Editor-at-Large
Caleb Neelon

Contributing Editor
Clint Catalyst

Comics Editor
Joel Speasmaker

Special Projects Coordinator
Wendy Worth

Copy Editor
Cathy Lee

Advertising Director
Sonja Teri
tel: 323.669.8819
sonja@swindlemagazine.com

Advertising and Marketing
Stefanie Bodie

Circulation Director
Debbie Dexter / ddmagster@yahoo.com

Staff Photographers
Adam Amengual, Aaron Cobbett, Aaron
Farley, Piper Ferguson, Nikolaus Jung, Dan
Monick, Adam Wallacavage, Jeremy and
Claire Weiss

Staff Artists
Damien Correll, Jason Filipow, Matthew
Goldman, Tim Gough, Kristian Henson,
Justin Thomas Kay, Andrew Jeffrey Wright,
Florencio Zavala

Staff Writers
Simon Creasey, Laura Fumiko Keehn, Yuko
Kitazawa, Camille Lowry, Heather Murphy,
Molly Simms

Contributing Photographers
Benny B., Carlos Batts, Angelika Buettner,
Maile Cannon, Cheryl Dunn, Chad Griffith,
Maurizio Lazard, Rebecca Miller, Elizabeth
Perrin, Trevor Snapp

Contributing Artists
Zach Gibson, Alex Lukas, Casey Ryder,
Theresa Vandling

Contributing Writers
G. Bruno, Michael R. Blaha, Maile Cannon,
Chris Richards, Imran Siddiquee, Trevor
Snapp, Sarah Tomlinson, William L. Wacker

Stylists
Charles Davis, Katharine Erwin

Media Assistants
Sun Hashmi, Kristina Karyakina-Dashul,
Allie Marsiello, Greg Moncada, Hannah
Winslow

Front Cover
Photo by Aaron Cobbett
Vintage jacket by Ozbek
Leggings by Norma Kamali
Gloves by LaCrasia
Watch by Adidas
Chains by Subversive

Back Cover
Dragged, by Cheryl Dunn

Title Page and Endleaf
Florencio Zavala

Newsstand Distribution
Disticor Magazine Distribution Services
Attn: Dave Kasza
tel: 905.619.6565
fax: 905.619.2903
dkasza@disticor.com

Book Distribution
Gingko Press
5768 Paradise Dr., Suite J
Corte Madera, CA 94925
tel: 415.924.9615

ISBN: 978-0-9791621-7-6
ISBN: 0-9791621-7-3

Swindle Magazine
3111 Los Feliz Blvd., Suite 100
Los Angeles, CA 90039
USA
tel: 323.669.8819
www.swindlemagazine.com

Studio Number One
3780 Wilshire Blvd., Suite 210
Los Angeles, CA 90010
USA
tel: 213.383.9299
www.studionumber-one.com

The views expressed in SWINDLE reflect the
views of the contributors, and are not necessarily
shared by the magazine's staff or publishers.

Publisher
New Traditionalists Industries

Creative Services
Joycie Dunga, Stephanie Schonauer

Publicity
Henry Eshelman / heshelman@platformgrp.com
Hilary Carver / hcarver@platformgrp.com

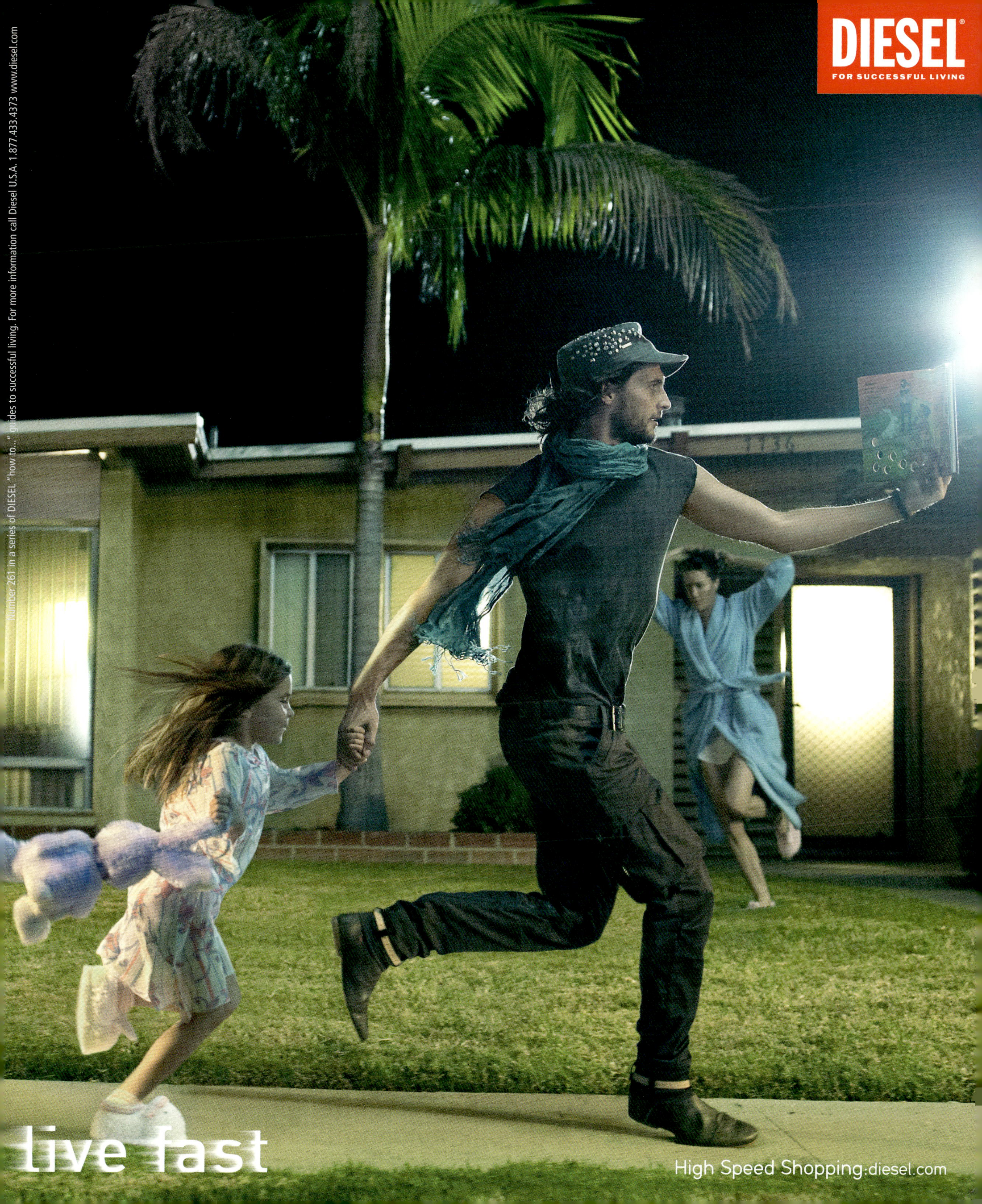

DIESEL
FOR SUCCESSFUL LIVING
Number 261 in a series of DIESEL "how to..." guides to successful living. For more information call Diesel U.S.A. 1.877.433.4373 www.diesel.com
live fast
High Speed Shopping.diesel.com

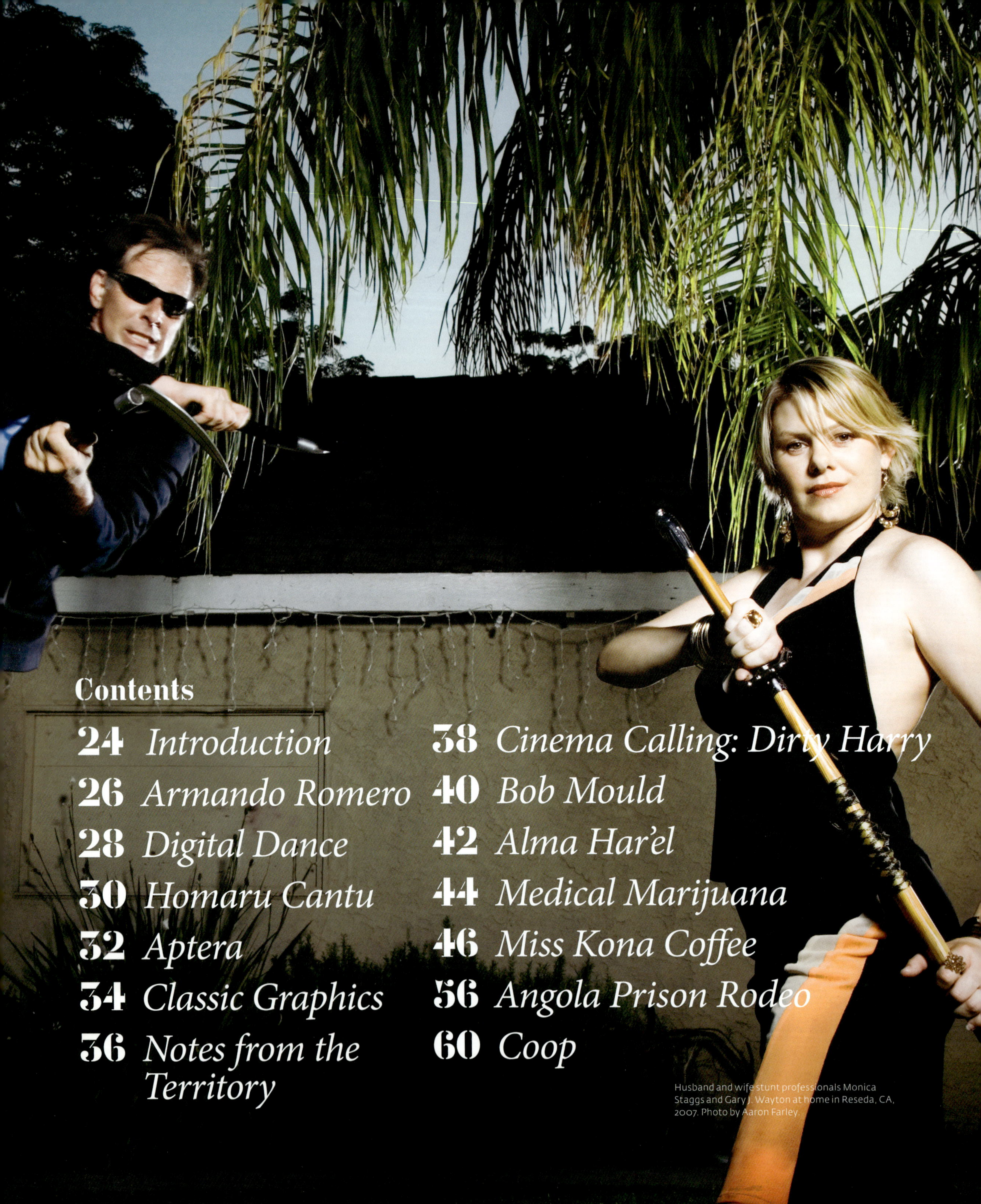

Contents

Husband and wife stunt professionals Monica Staggs and Gary J. Wayton at home in Reseda, CA, 2007. Photo by Aaron Farley.

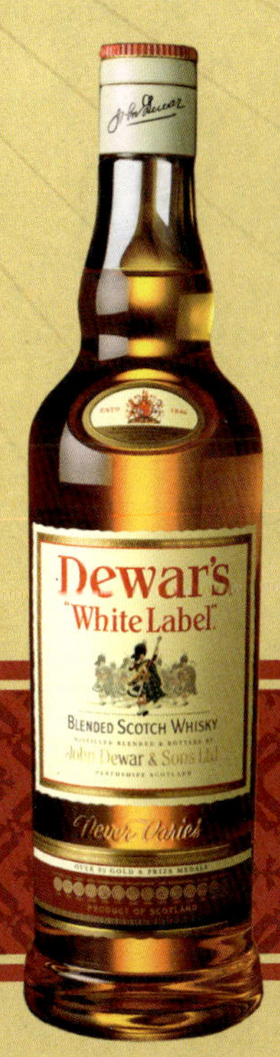

TOMMY DEWAR SAYS...
WHAT WE CALL CONFIDENCE IN OURSELVES
WE CALL CONCEIT IN OTHERS
Dewar's
"White Label"
Dewar's
White Label
BLENDED SCOTCH WHISKY
John Dewar & Sons Ltd.
DEWAR'S ON THE ROCKS: Fill a rock glass with ice. Pour in DEWAR'S WHITE LABEL. Enjoy the flavors of a masterfully Blended Scotch Whisky.
dewarism.com

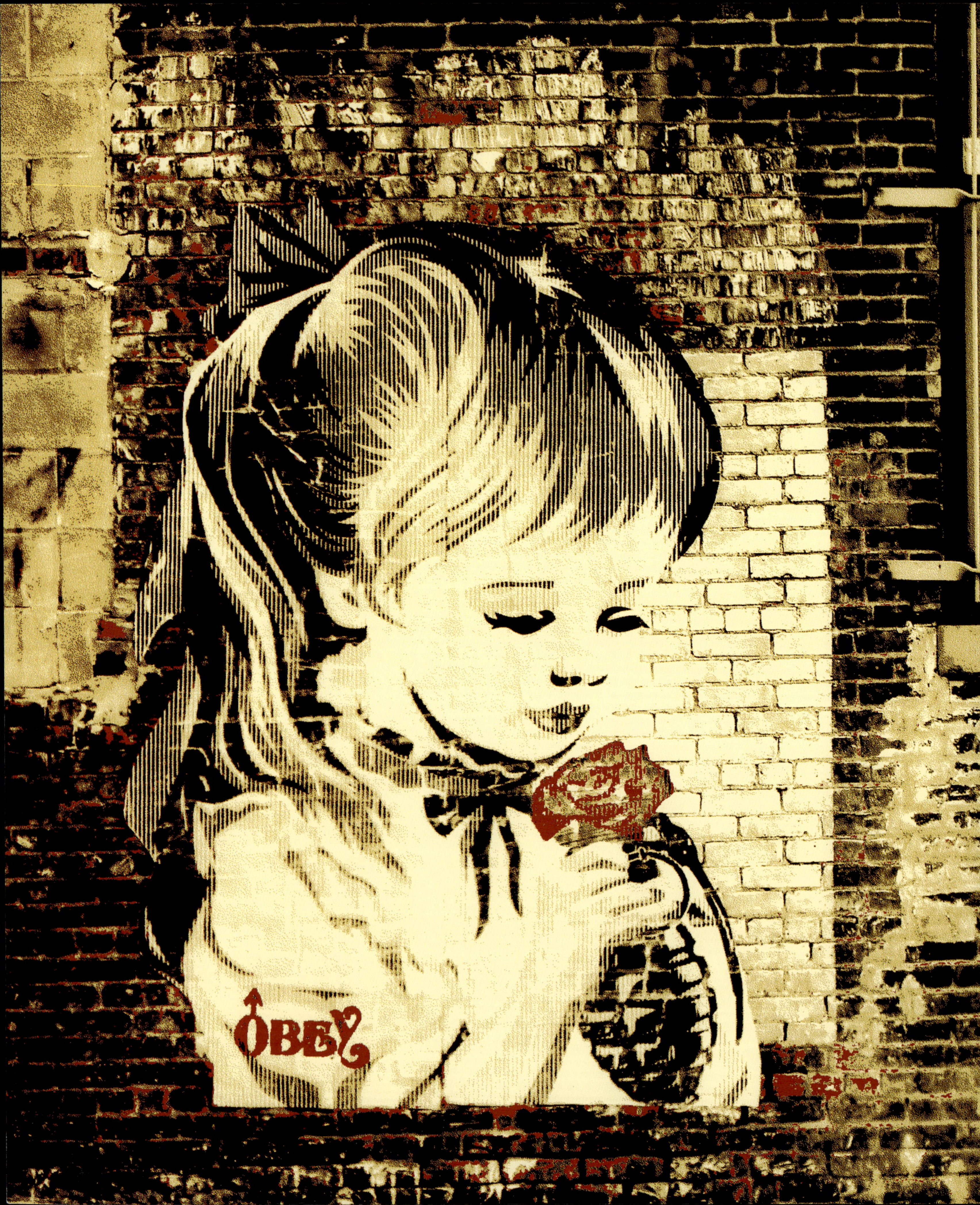

OBEY

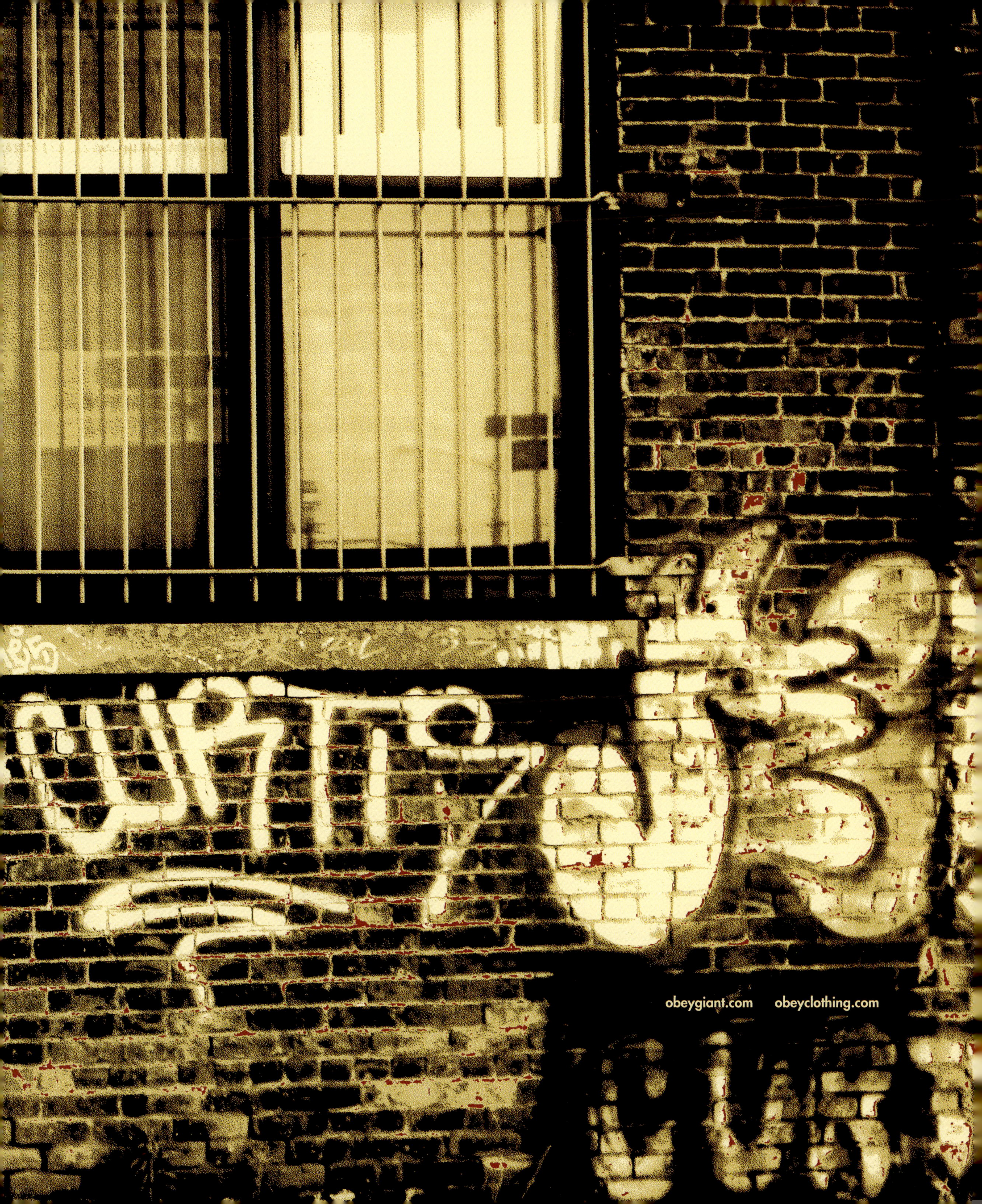

obeygiant.com   obeyclothing.com

Contents

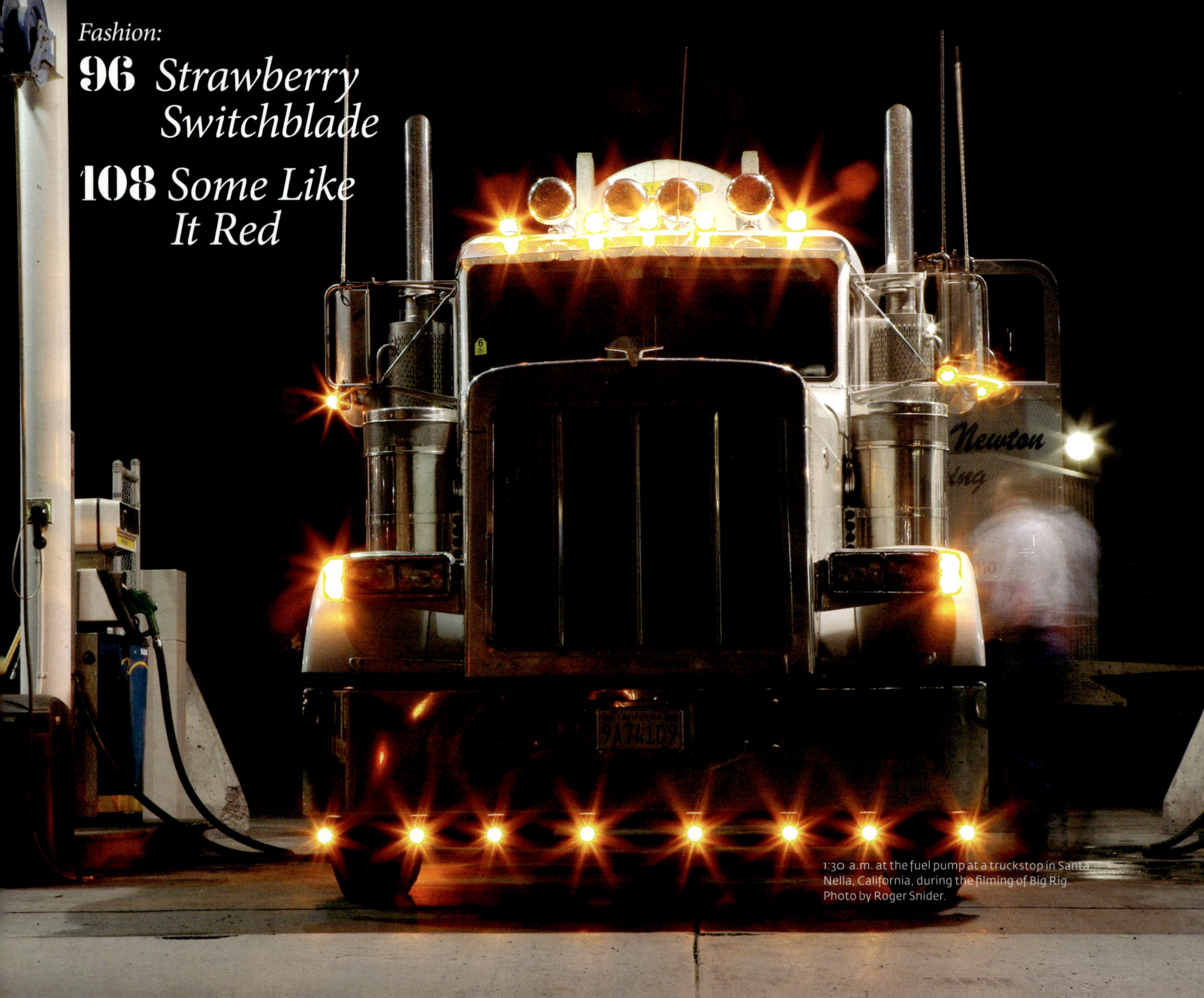

1:30 a.m. at the fuel pump at a truckstop in Santa Nella, California, during the filming of Big Rig. Photo by Roger Snider.

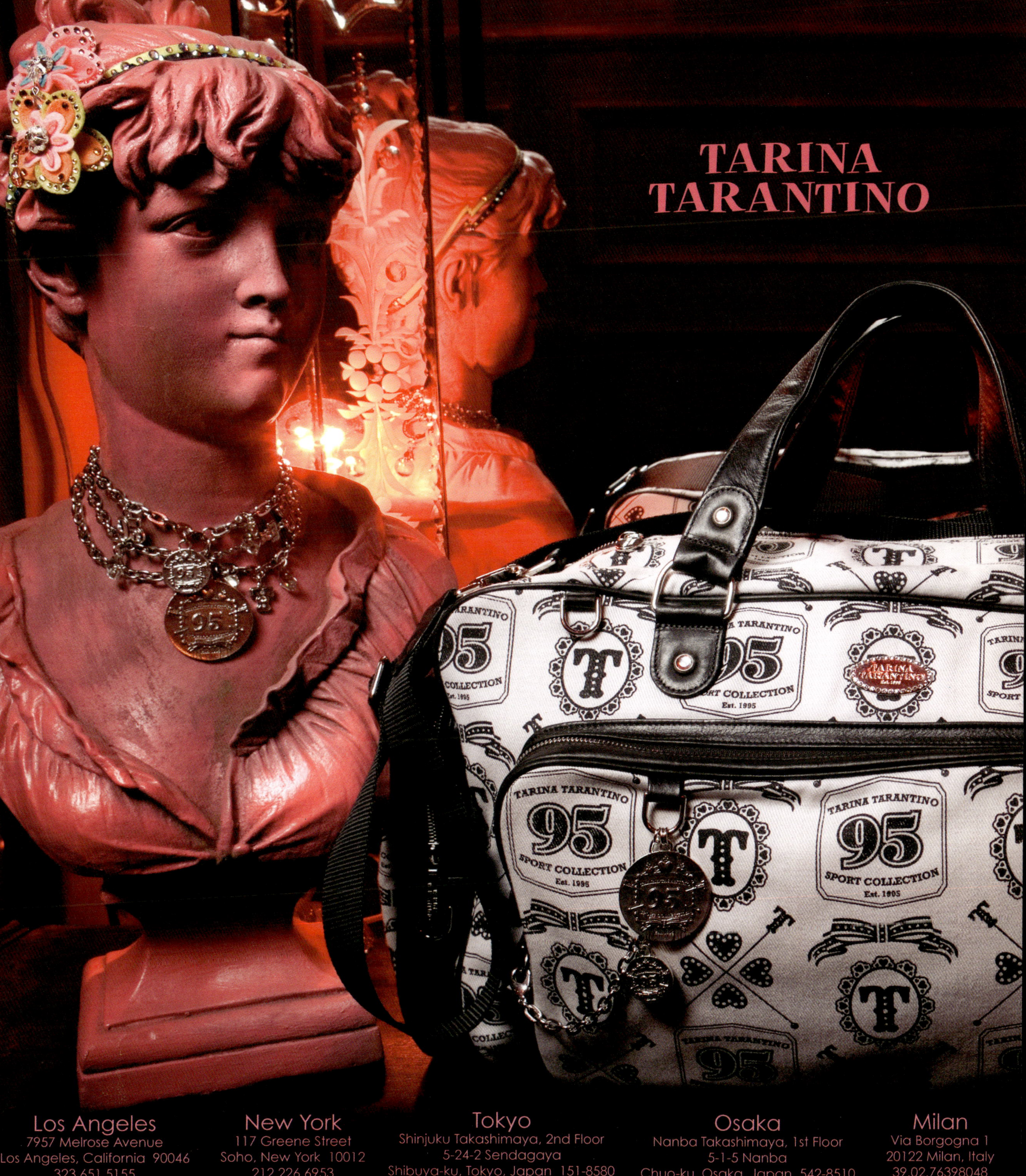
TARINA TARANTINO
Los Angeles
7957 Melrose Avenue
Los Angeles, California 90046
323.651.5155
New York
117 Greene Street
Soho, New York 10012
212.226.6953
Tokyo
Shinjuku Takashimaya, 2nd Floor
5-24-2 Sendagaya
Shibuya-ku, Tokyo, Japan 151-8580
03.5361.2017
Osaka
Nanba Takashimaya, 1st Floor
5-1-5 Nanba
Chuo-ku, Osaka, Japan 542-8510
06.6632.9306
Milan
Via Borgogna 1
20122 Milan, Italy
39.02.76398048

Contributors '15

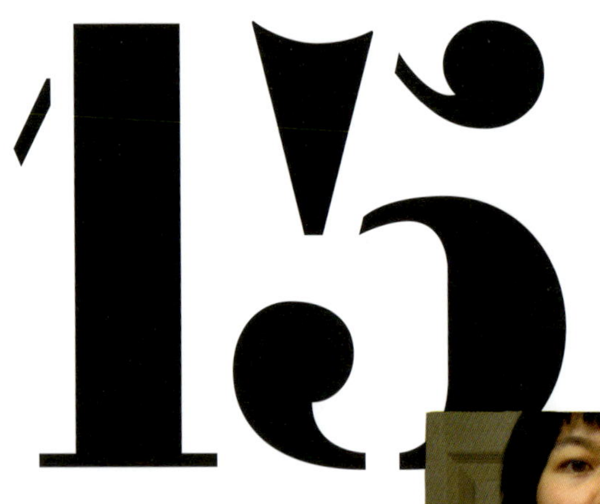

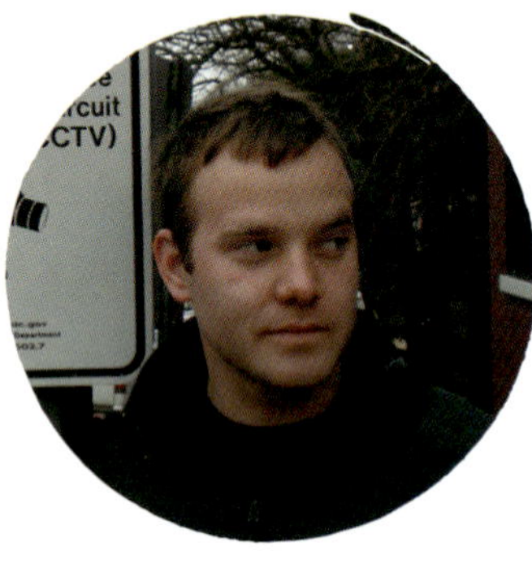

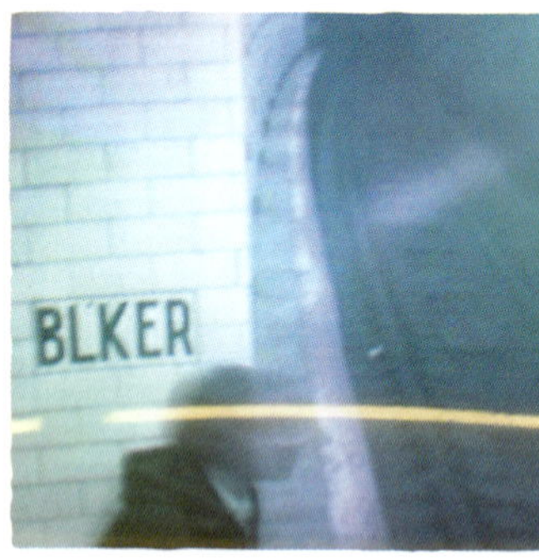

Chris Richards

spent his teenage years jogging around the block, rocking Hüsker Dü tapes on his Walkman. How fitting that, 10 years later, he interviewed former Hüskerman Bob Mould in a café adjoined to one of Washington D.C.'s most popular gyms. When Richards isn't minding his fitness, he's writing about music for the *Washington Post* and *The Fader*.

James Gaddy

is associate editor of *Print* magazine. His articles have appeared in *I.D.*, *Culture+Travel*, *Details*, *Nylon* and *The New York Times*. He is a founding member of deliciousghost.com and makes brief appearances on the security cameras at the Bleeker Street subway stop.

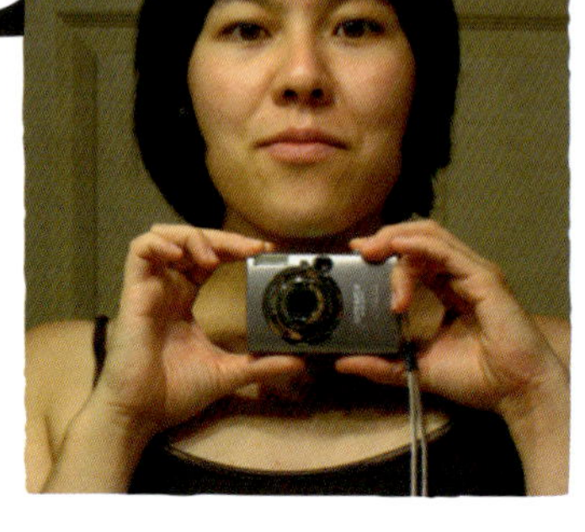

Maile Cannon

is a California-born, Hawaii-raised, Boston-educated writer cum photographer. She has just returned to the United States after living and working in Beijing for three and a half years. When not indulging graphemic pursuits, Maile teaches Mandarin to middle schoolers. Comments, complaints and offers of employment are welcome at mailecannon@gmail.com.

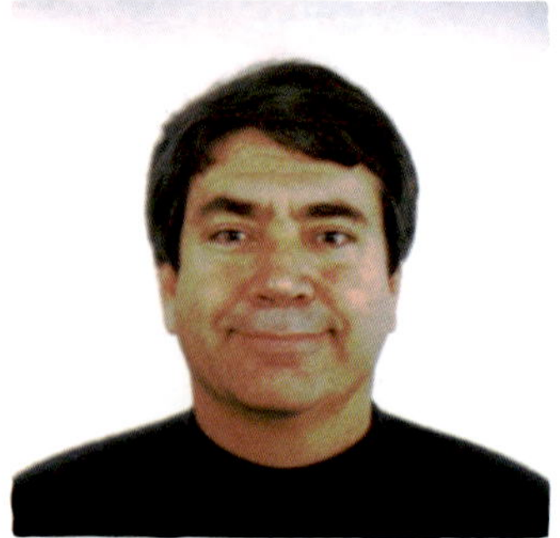

Michael R. Blaha

is an entertainment attorney and award winning film and stage producer. He has produced 16 shows at the Edinburgh Festival Fringe since he first attended the Festival in 2001. Mike is also on the Board of Directors of the Academy for New Musical Theatre and Filmmakers Alliance.

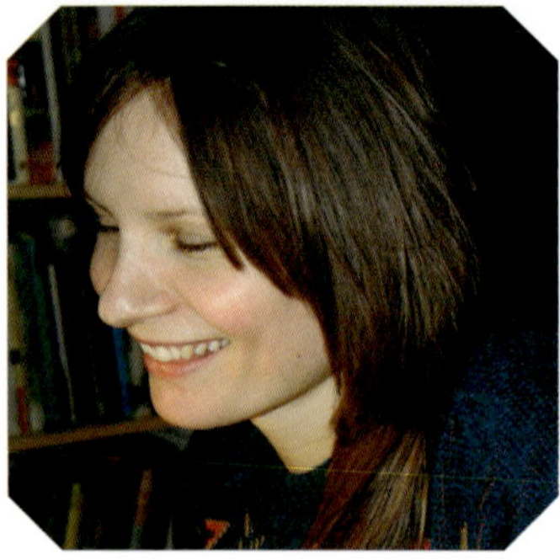

Therese Vandling

is a London-based graphic designer/ illustrator who recently graduated from the Royal College of Art. She is currently busy freelancing and promoting herself, but she still finds time to do a few screen-prints and organize exhibitions with her friends on the side. Her background is in typography but her work also involves conceptual thinking, printmaking, drawing, color and collage. www.vandling.co.uk

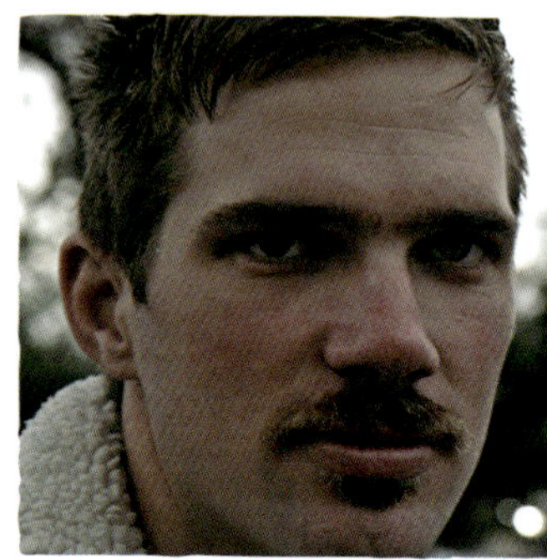

Trevor Snapp

is a photographer and journalist based in Mexico city. More of his work can be seen at www.trevorsnapp.com.

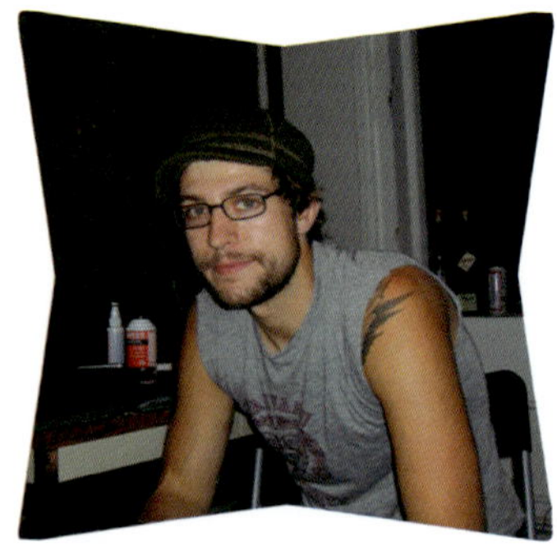

William L. Wacker

is driving, writing, photographing and painting up and down the West Coast from Portland to L.A. and back and forth again while finishing his Master of Education online. He's lived in many cities and countries and kind of likes the idea of living in a cabin as a teacher/ writer… for now. Keep an eye open for his exhibits.

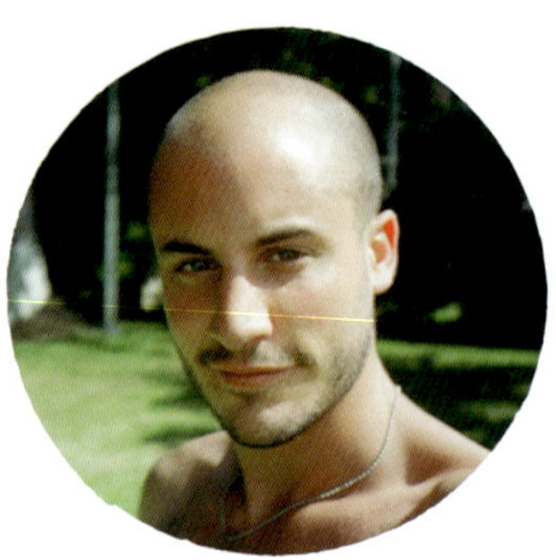

Mauricio Garcia Lazard

is an avid traveler, likes green hues and is a fan of all things sweet. He studied cinematography and photography in L.A. where he lived for seven years. Now residing in Mexico City, he has shot for *Vogue Mexico, Flaunt* and SWINDLE, among other editorials. www.mauphoto.com

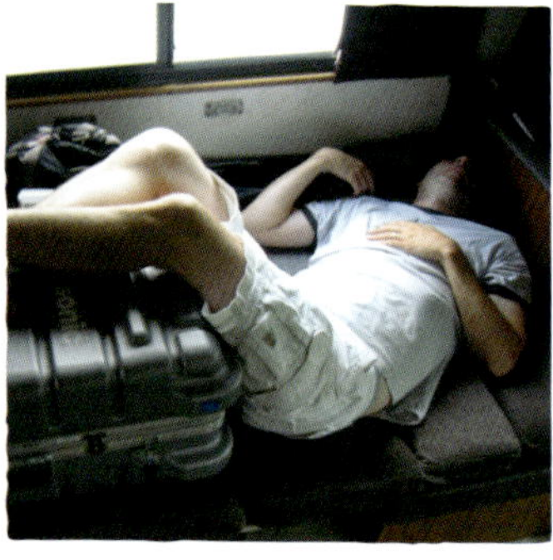

Doug Pray

is an L.A.-based filmmaker known for his feature documentaries about American subcultures. He directed *Scratch*, about hip-hop DJs; *Hype!*, about the early '90s Seattle music scene; and *Infamy*, about graffiti writers. His two newest films are *Surfwise*, about the amazing Paskowitz family, and *Big Rig*, a film about truck drivers, which he writes about in this issue. www.bigrigmovie.com

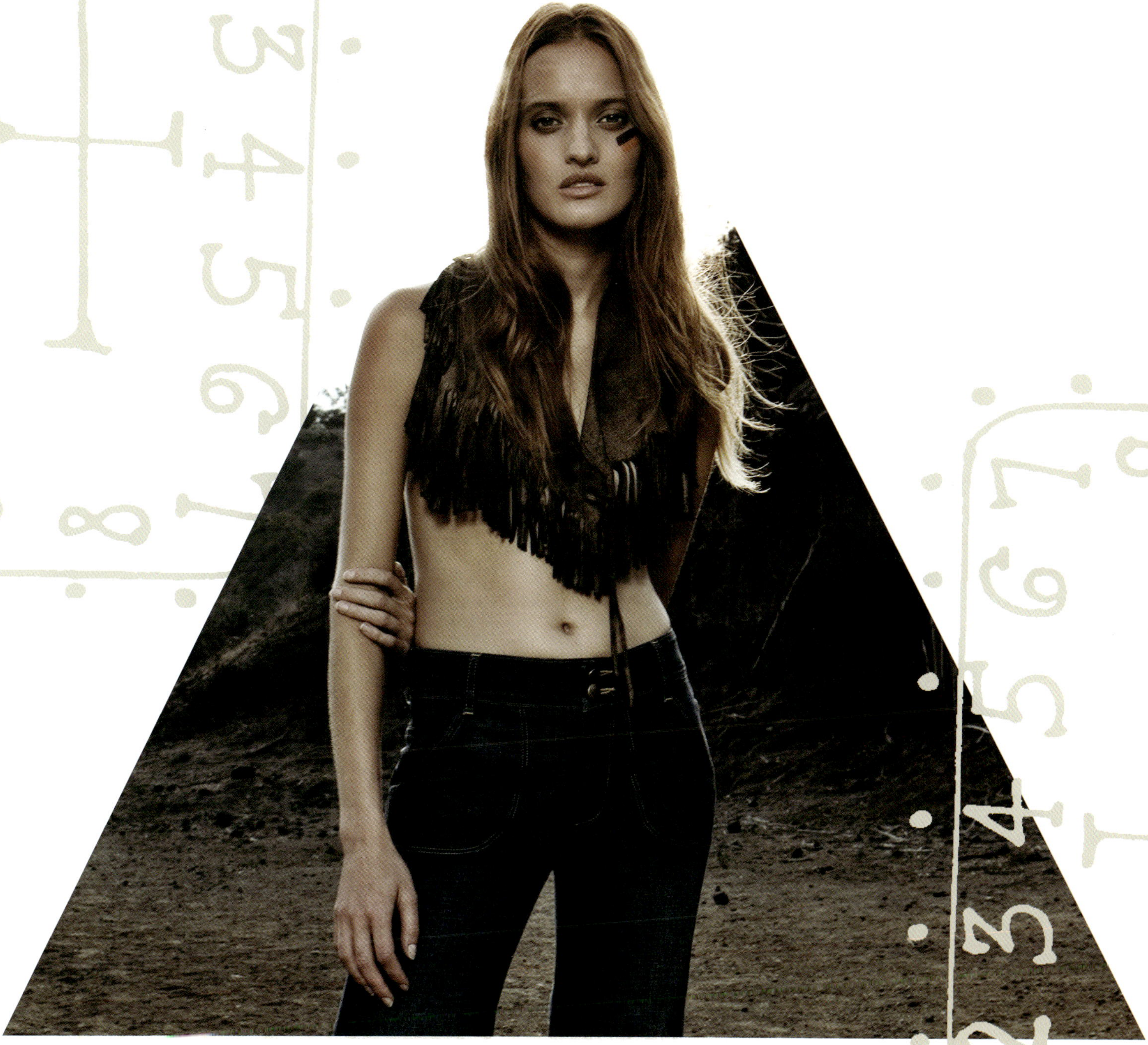

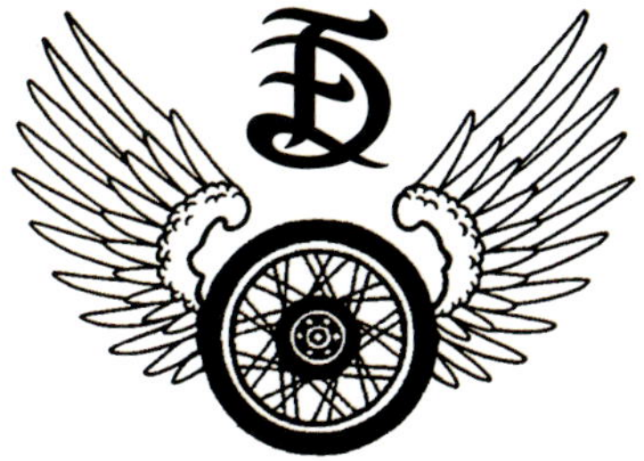
DISTINCTIVE STITCHED

Introduction

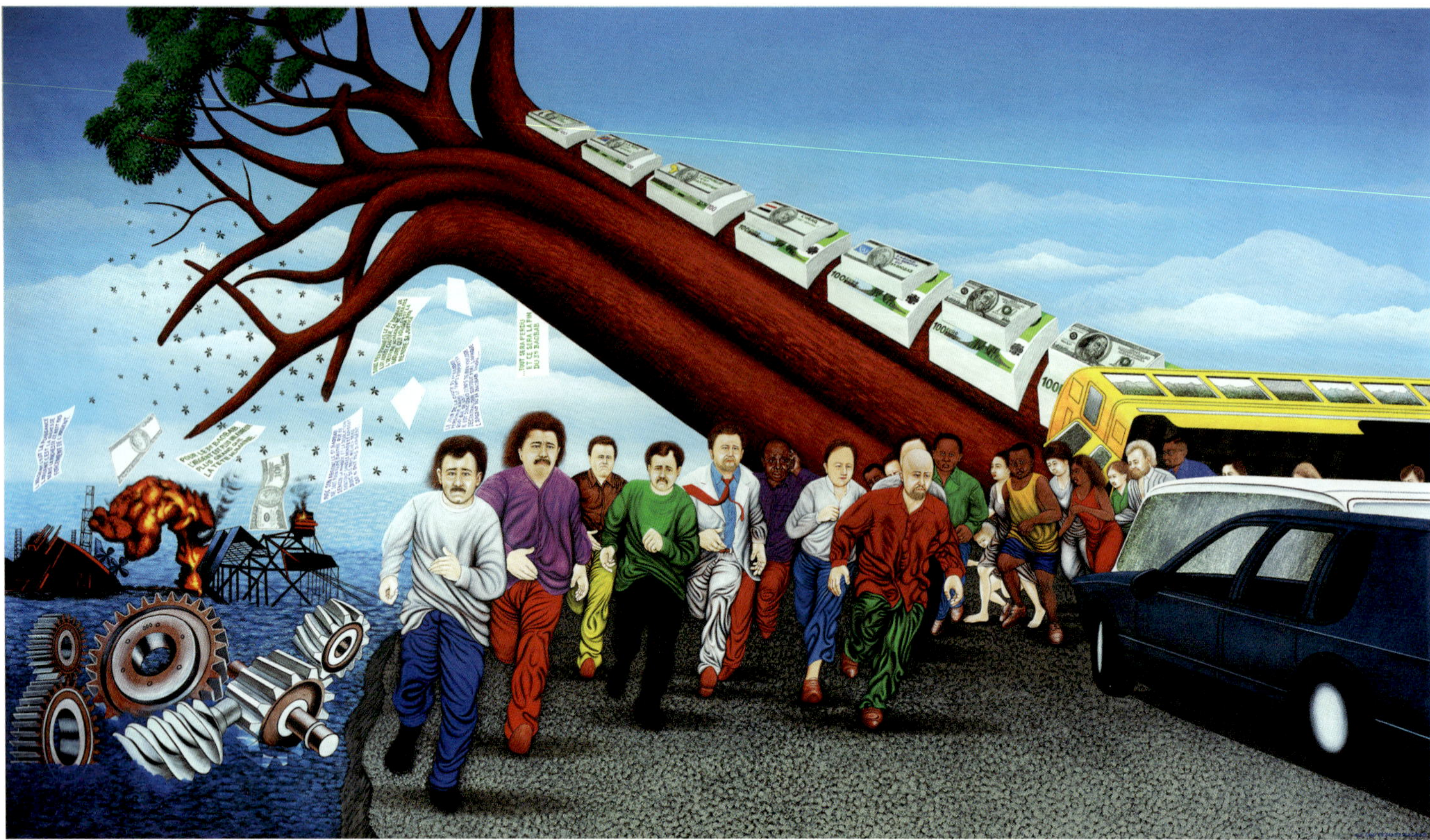

La Chute du 3è baobab
2006
Acrylic and glitter on canvas
300 x 496,6 cm
© Chéri Samba
Courtesy CAAC-
The Pigozzi Collection, Geneva

**"Froth at the top, dregs at the bottom, but the middle excellent."
—Voltaire**

We present to you, dear readers, our first issue of 2008, a magazine chock full of… unsung heroes. The political pendulum is swinging from right to left as, for the first time in U.S. history, an African American and a woman compete to become president; the Golden Globes awards show—that hitherto perennial annual institution of celebrity—was cancelled amidst writers' strikes; and global warming is getting more credence as sales of hybrid cars go through the roof and gas prices skyrocket.

The times they are a-changing. And the power dynamics of our society are shifting. So, we at SWINDLE want to evolve, too. Issue 15 marks the unveiling of our newly redesigned layout. We've made the text more engaging, we've standardized the fonts, and added two regular columns: James Gaddy delves in the visual and cultural history of iconic imagery in *Classic Graphics*, and Henry Rollins gives us *Dispatches from the Territory*. In his introductory piece, Rollins recaps the political sentiments of the last seven years—a sort of "best of" rant against the Bush years, as we gear up for a pivotal presidential election.

And now for our unsung heroes: we've got a feature on stunt doubles, who risk their lives in anonymity to make movie stars look badass; we've got Doug Pray's first-person account of making his latest feature, *Big Rig*, about the truckers who haul all the food, machinery and products that keep the American economy ticking; we present the Democratic Republic of the Congo's "School of Popular Painting," an elite group of artists who showcase the thriving urban culture of their country's capital, Kinshasa—a part of African society rarely presented in Western media; and we look at the choreographers of the mega-hit video game, Dance Dance Revolution, who labor in the Konami offices in Southern California, creating step sequences for players all over the world.

The ruling elite rise and fall with the ebb and flow of culture. Ideals, celebrities and power mongers can be on top one day, but discredited the next. As the zeitgeist constantly morphs, it is important to look at the people in the middle who earn their place from consistent work—not from exhibitionism or power plays. Because their unseen hands lay the foundation from which the glittery ephemera of popular culture is launched.

**"Time makes heroes but dissolves celebrities."
—Daniel J. Boorstin**

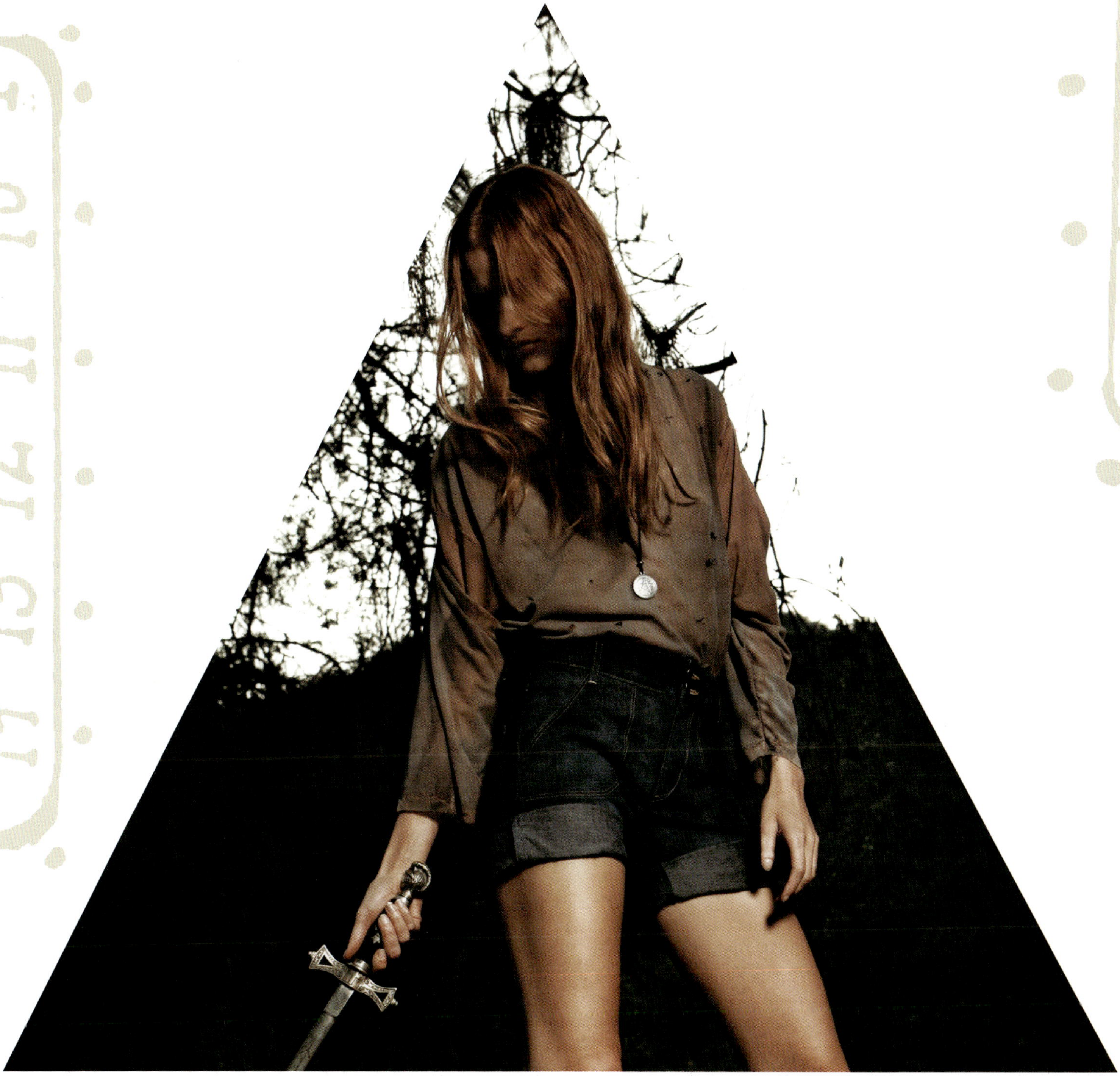

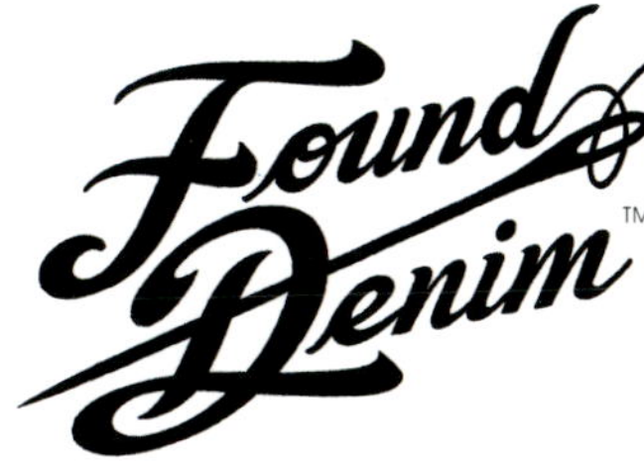

AVAILABLE AT SUGARCUBE IN PHILADELPHIA
CHECK FOUNDDENIM.COM FOR STOCKISTS

High–Low Brow

BY ANNE KEEHN
PHOTO BY MAURICIO GARCIA LAZARD

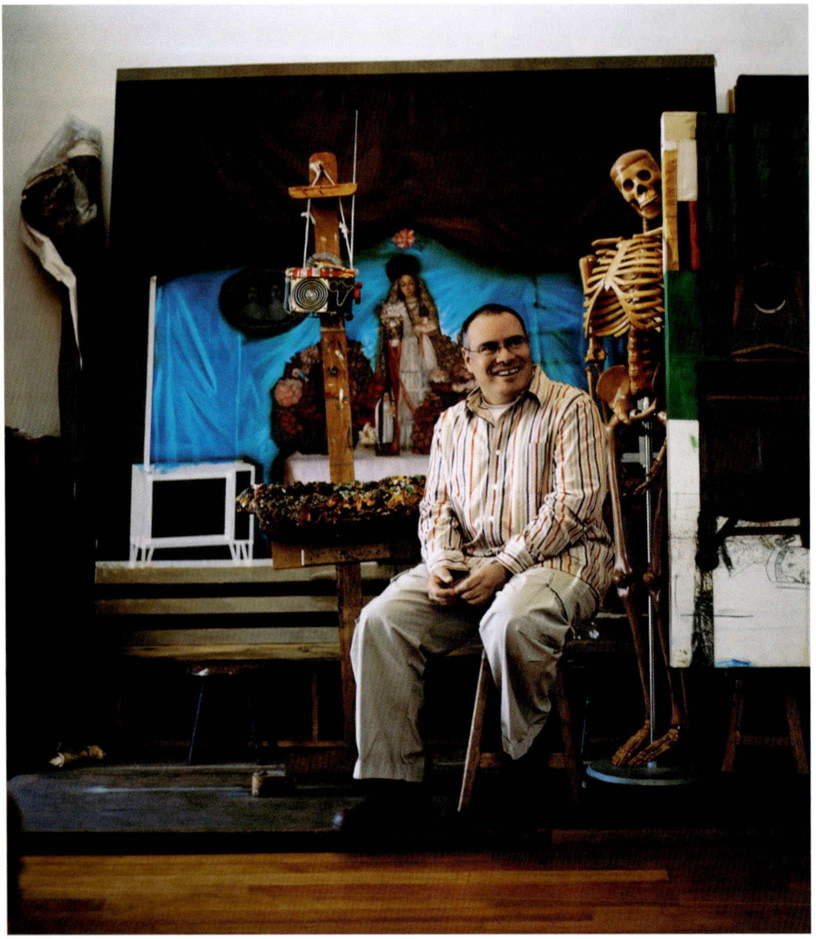

THE ART OF ARMANDO ROMERO

In the Coyoacan neighborhood on the south side of Mexico City, a few blocks away from the so-called Blue House where Frida Kahlo lived with Diego Rivera, and the home where Leon Trotsky lived—and was assassinated—in exile, the artist Armando Romero keeps his studio. It is a welcoming mix of Scandinavian minimalism and cozy log cabin clutter: clean, wooden surfaces blend into bookshelves filled with vintage toys and books. A papier-mâché caricature of him, wearing a T-shirt emblazoned with Dexter from the Cartoon Network's *Dexter's Laboratory* hangs from the door. He says his girlfriend made it for him.

Romero works here, every day, religiously. He learned this discipline as a student at the prestigious National School of Painting, Sculpture and Graphics, Mexico City, otherwise known as "La Esmeralda." He studied seven days a week. He received a classical education, staying up late to work with models and going for month-long trips into nature to paint landscapes. Amidst this rigorous training, Romero learned how to exalt the masters—and also to deface them.

He is an avid collector of *Star Wars* memorabilia and science fiction-themed vintage toys, like Japan's iconic post A-bomb cartoon character, Atom Boy, or the robot from *Lost In Space*. These objects "really get to me," he says, through a translator. "They touch me." Comic books and the ever-changing graffiti on the walls of his home city have always been sources of inspiration on a par with Vermeer and Caravaggio.

So, he incorporated this kaleidoscopic range of influences into his artwork. "Non-traditional imagery was prohibited in art school," he says. So he rebelled. Teachers would tell him to do one thing, and he would do the opposite. He says he wanted to mix high and low imagery together, "like the bar in *Star Wars*."

Romero lived for a time in New York City as an exchange student, and studied in Paris, but he never learned to speak another language. Instead, he became adept at reading the visual language of cities around the world. And his analysis is blunt: "In Mexico and the U.S., graffiti doesn't have a message, it is about who wrote it. In France, the content is more important than the writer," he says. "Culturally, L.A. is richer than New York. It is more of a cross roads of the world. San Francisco is pretty but artificial."

His artwork parodies the masters, skillfully copying a painting by, say, Rembrandt—for instance, *The Anatomy Lesson of Mr. Tulip*, which features a group of medical students and an instructor huddled around a cadaver. Romero replaces the cadaver with Frankenstein's monster, and "defaces" his own work with paintings of stickers and chalk marks. He even slashes on the canvas and frame. The result is a piece that looks like it was hung on the street, amassing the visual reflection of the city. "Mexico is very segregated," he says. "There is a clear hierarchy. Every social class has a different cultural, visual language. I like to grab from all of it."

www.tasendegallery.com

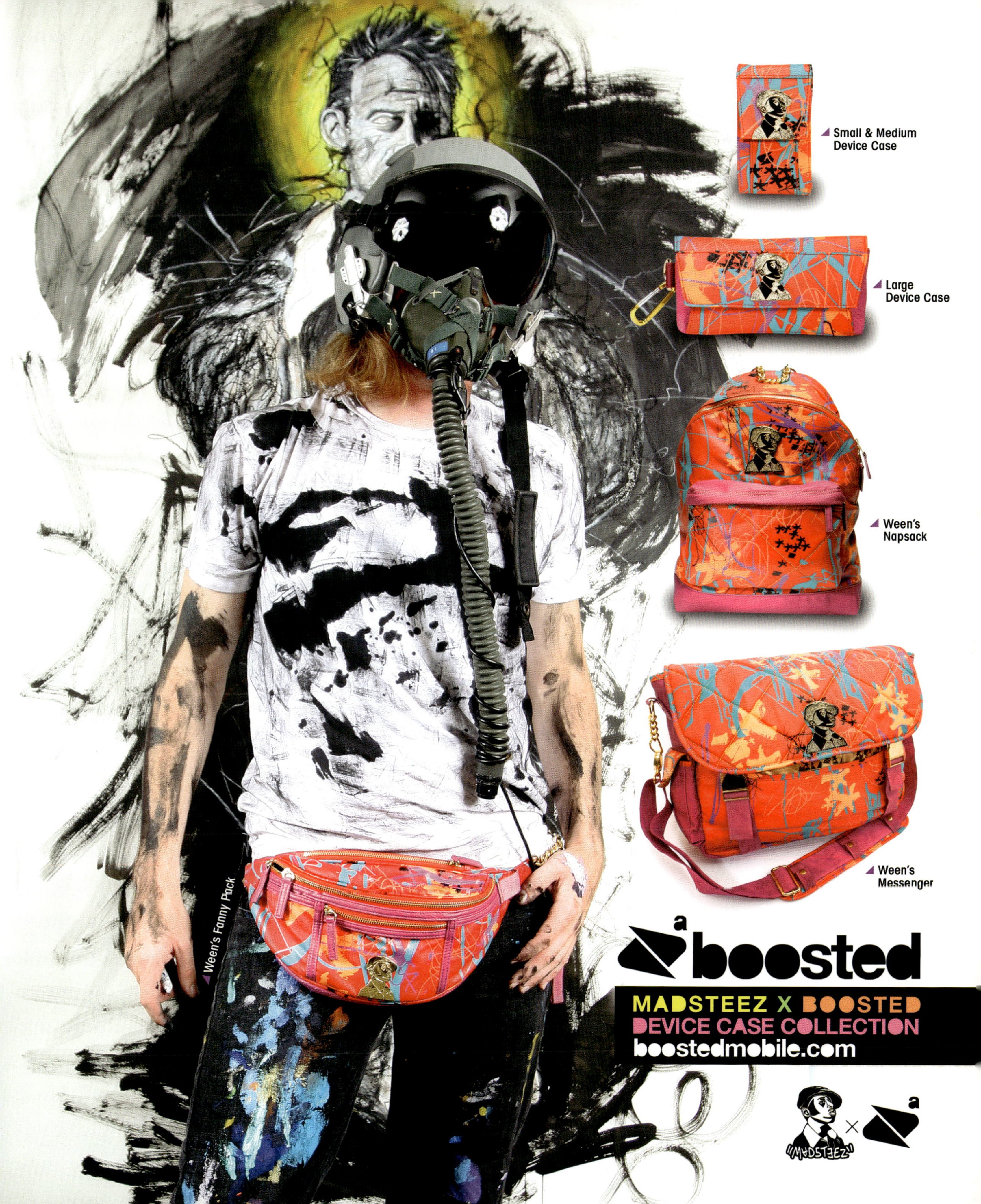

Small & Medium
Device Case
Large
Device Case
Ween's Napsack
Ween's Messenger
Ween's Fanny Pack
a
boosted
MADSTEEZ X BOOSTED
DEVICE CASE COLLECTION
boostedmobile.com
MADSTEEZ

Digital Dance:

THE CHOREOGRAPHERS OF DANCE DANCE REVOLUTION

BY ANNE KEEHN
PORTRAIT BY NIKOLAUS JUNG

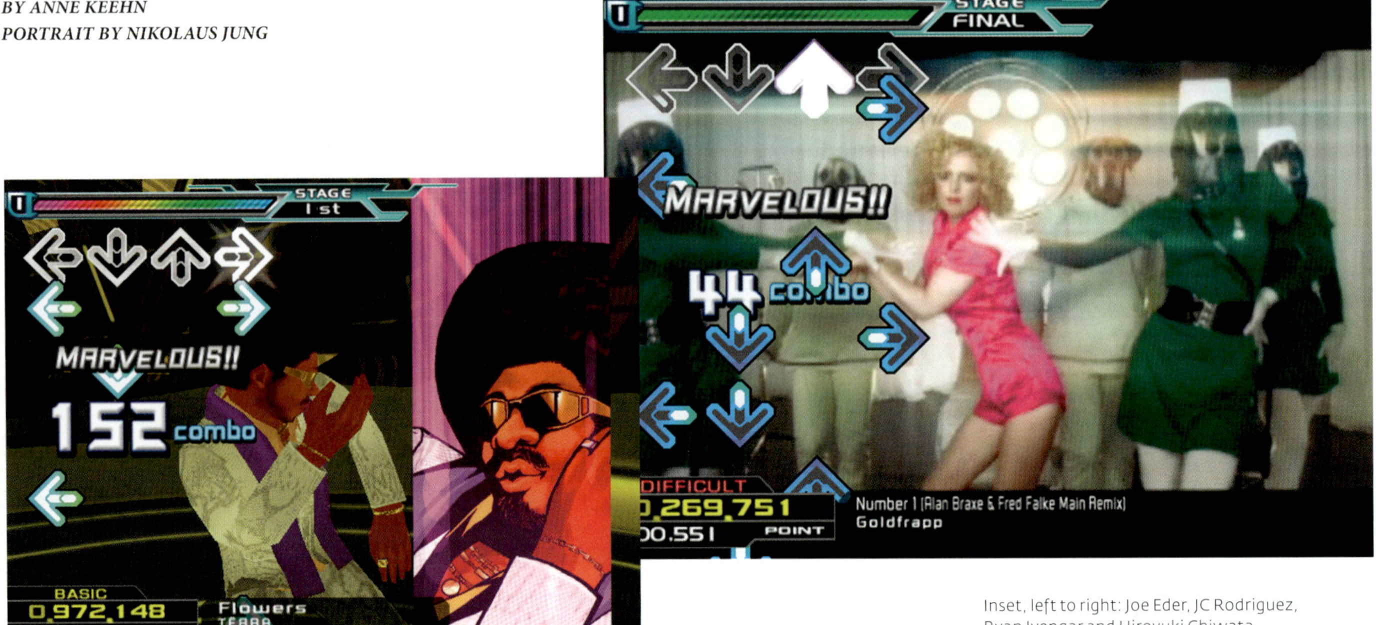

Inset, left to right: Joe Eder, JC Rodriguez, Ryan Iyengar and Hiroyuki Chiwata.

In the Metal Gear Solid-themed boardroom at the L.A. offices of the Konami video game company, game producer Hiroyuki Chiwata jumps up and down on the Dance Dance Revolution (DDR) step pads, his eyes fixed on a TV monitor. His feet tap the sensors on the pad in time with the arrows on the screen, as Franz Ferdinand's "Take Me Out" blasts from the speakers—and he misses a few cues. "I am a producer, not a step creator," he says. He turns to the other people in the boardroom—JC Rodriguez, one of the step creators who designs the dance steps for DDR, Michael F. Shelling, the Konami PR Director, and me—and asks, "Who's next?"

Rodriguez, a classically trained percussionist and former middle school and high school music teacher, takes his place on the dance pads. He discovered DDR at Disneyland's Tomorrowland, during a high school band trip. "It was a little awkward" at first, he says. But he soon became obsessed. "It's really deep. On the basic level, the steps are always left, right, left, right," he says, swaying from side to side to demonstrate. "We've tried to make a computer program that could create dance steps—but you need that human touch. You need to feel the flow of the song." He begins dancing on the pads to "So Fine" by The Freestylers. "The first thing you think about [when designing dance steps] is the player, and how they feel. Every song has got that sweet spot that just gets you. You try to make the steps feel that."

DDR is versatile. It is one of the few games—Konami's Guitar Hero and DrumMania are others—that thrive in the arcade as well as in home entertainment systems. With the advent of home video game consoles, arcades have become increasingly archaic. But DDR focuses on performance, and features song playlists exclusive to the arcades. Shelling says, "The arcade is still symbolic and iconic for DDR."

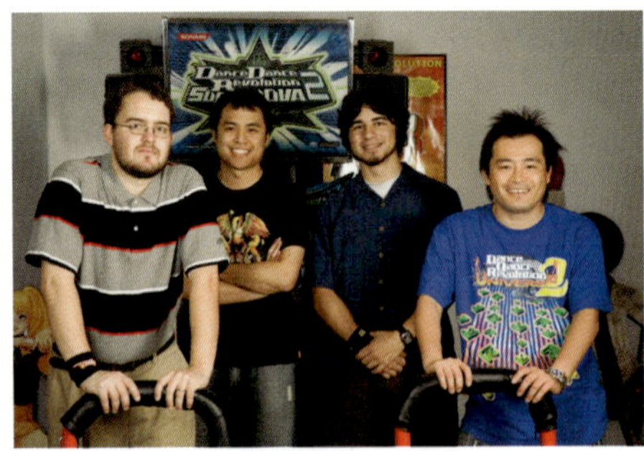

Since its introduction into Japanese arcades in 1998—and its tremendous crossover success in the West and worldwide—the game has become an intrinsic part of a generation of players' lifestyles. As of 2006, over seven million DDR games have sold internationally. Schools across the U.S. are employing the game in P.E. class—according to an article in *The New York Times*, 1,500 schools will incorporate the game into their P.E. curriculum by the end of the decade. (Rodriguez says that he lost 35 pounds by playing DDR.)

There are two other step creators at the Southern California Konami offices: Joe Eder and Ryan Iyengar. Both were chosen in an audition process in 2007, when Rodriguez—who was on staff in the Redwood City offices—was relocated down south to build a new step team. Job postings were put on Benami-interest websites, like Benamistyle.com. (Benami is the division of Konami video games that are beat and action oriented.) The job description called for a "strong musical background," and at least three years of experience playing DDR.

Eder, a bespectacled, sandy-haired young man, is a graduate of Cal Poly San Luis Obispo, where he went at least once a week to the nearest arcade—a 35-minute drive away—to play DDR, and organized a DDR appreciation club on campus. Iyengar is an undergraduate at Cal State Fullerton. He discovered DDR in 2004, when he was in high school. "I went to the arcade and brought my towel, sweat suit," he says. "I'd just go and sweat and dance."

When the three step creators jump on the DDR pads, they become transfixed—their eyes freeze on the screen, their feet speed across the pads below them. Shelling says, "The kids who grew up playing video games are now the parents of kids who play video games." For these second-generation gamers, making a living creating step sequences is a dream come true.

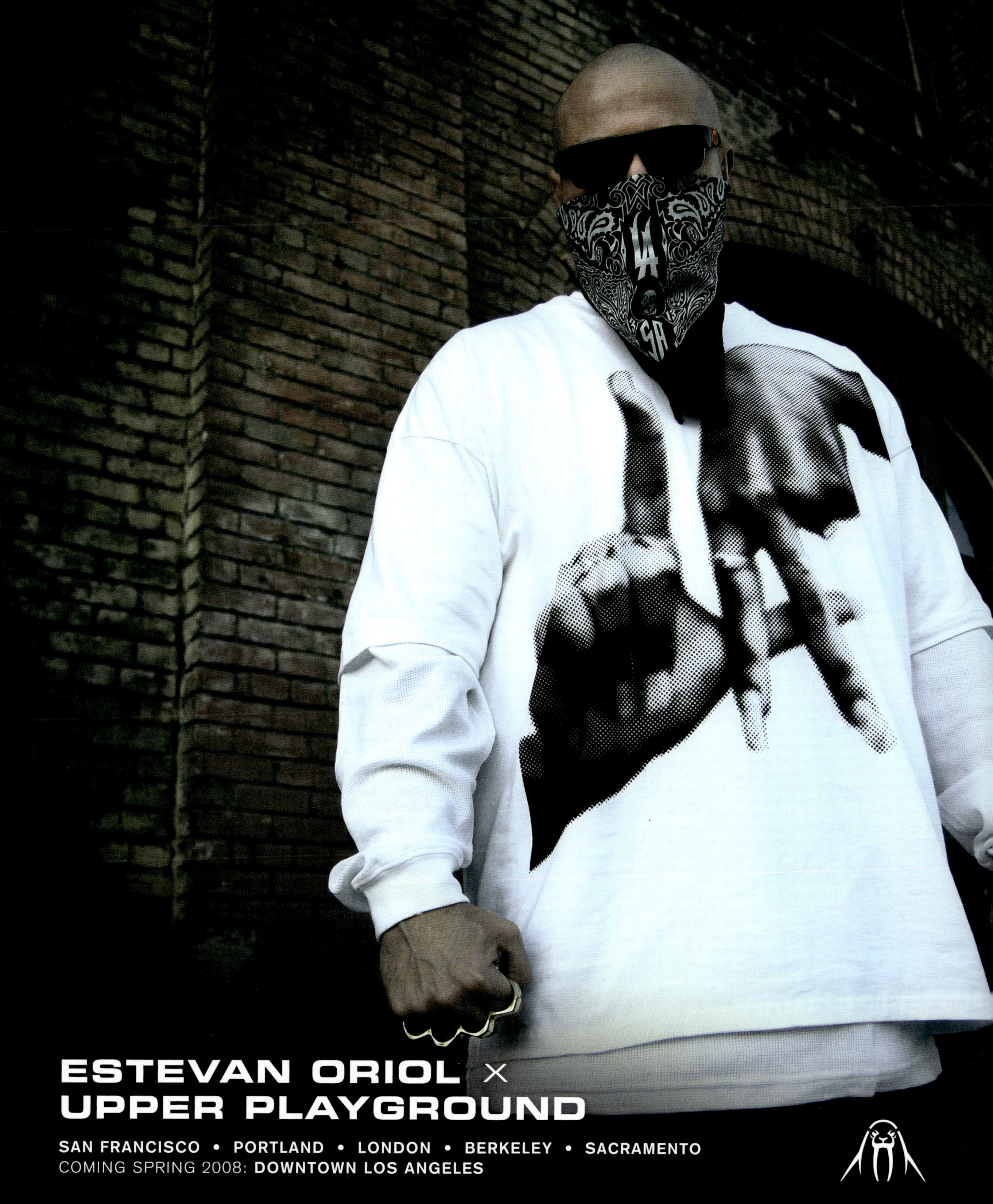

ESTEVAN ORIOL ×
UPPER PLAYGROUND
SAN FRANCISCO • PORTLAND • LONDON • BERKELEY • SACRAMENTO
COMING SPRING 2008: DOWNTOWN LOS ANGELES

Chef Special Sauce:

HOMARO CANTU COOKS UP SPACE-AGE FOOD AND A SCHEME TO SAVE THE PLANET

BY YUKO KITAZAWA
PHOTO BY BENNY B.
ILLUSTRATION BY ZACH GIBSON

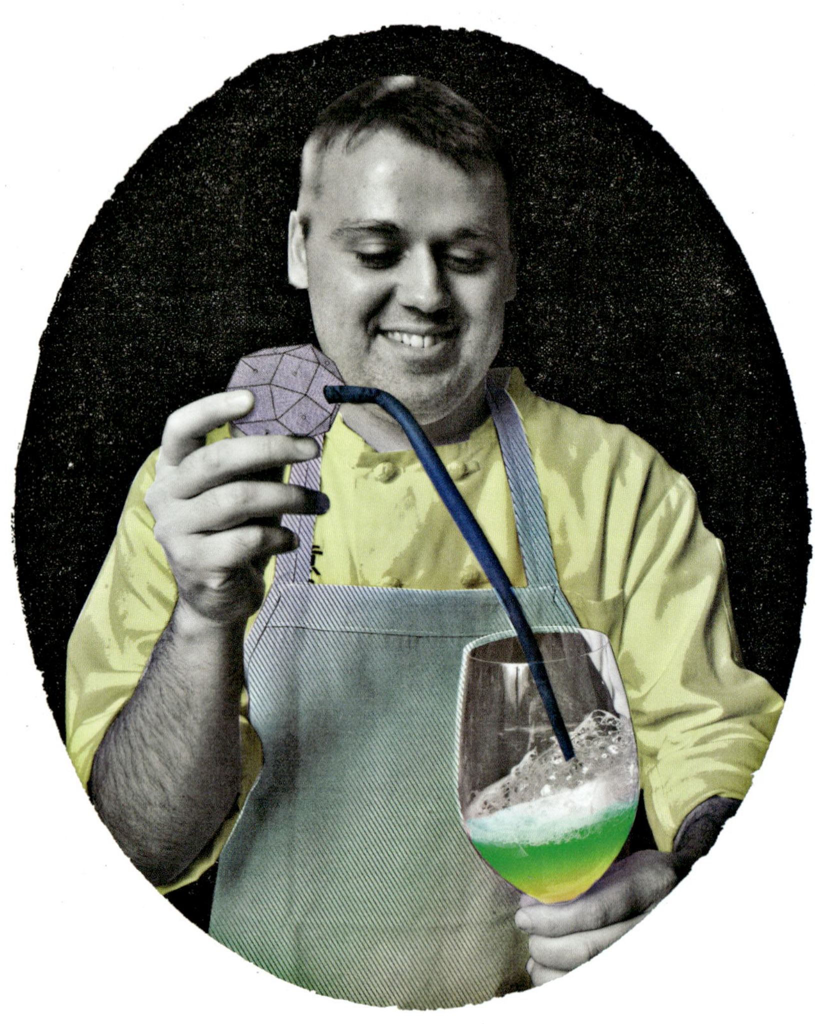

"AVOID EXPOSURE: Laser radiation is emitted from this aperture" is a sign you might expect to see in a hospital surgery unit, not a gourmet kitchen. But when the kitchen belongs to Homaro Cantu, a relentless innovator in the world of postmodern cuisine, anything is possible.

At Moto Restaurant in Chicago, Cantu uses the powerful Class IV laser to zap concentrated essence out of a vanilla bean. It is then fused into wine for extra flavor. While a conventional chef might revere a cast iron skillet for most of his cooking needs, Cantu can't live without liquid nitrogen, which transforms goat cheese into flaky "snow," and peas and carrots into perfect spheres that melt in your mouth.

Diners at his restaurant are inducted into his sensory wonderland with an edible menu printed with organic vegetable ink. Served with a side of cucumber dip, it is one of numerous patent-pending inventions he developed in collaboration with deepLABS, a Chicago-based team of designers and engineers.

As whimsical as his creations are, some critics and bloggers have shrugged them off as novelty, not four-star gourmet fare (though at $70 minimum for a tasting course, one is justified in expecting spectacular and delicious food).

According to Cantu, such an observation misses the point. He has bigger ambitions than to simply please the palate. He is concerned about the way we are ripping through our planet's limited food resources, and hopes that his inventions will provide new ways to grow, cook and preserve food while keeping our reserves in check.

"I think that we lie to ourselves when we believe sustainable agriculture is sustainable," he says. "It's not. Every farm on planet Earth relies on one element to grow food and that's called phosphate. At the current rate of extraction, phosphate will be extinct or completely used up in 60 to 80 years." The only real solution seems to be to do away with traditional means of producing food and rely on high-tech engineering. For instance, Cantu is working with NASA to create a "3D food printer" that will somehow print nutrient-rich food with an indefinite shelf life.

To the cynics who dismiss his wacky food as a gimmick, he says, "There's a much larger problem to worry about than gimmicky food. We have energy prices going up and that's going to affect our food supply. For the most part we think outside the box not because we want to, but because we have to."

www.motorestaurant.com

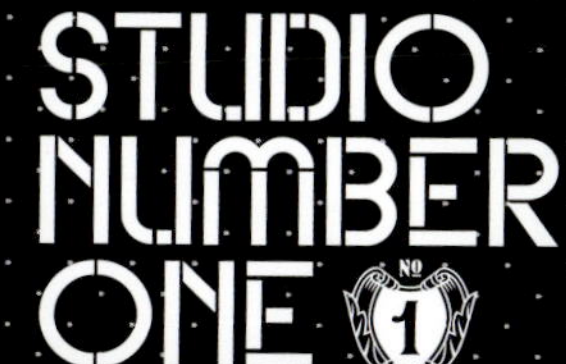

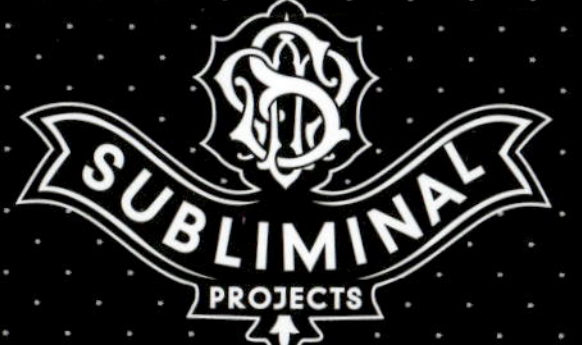

NEW LOCATION

1331 W. SUNSET BLVD
LOS ANGELES, CA
90026

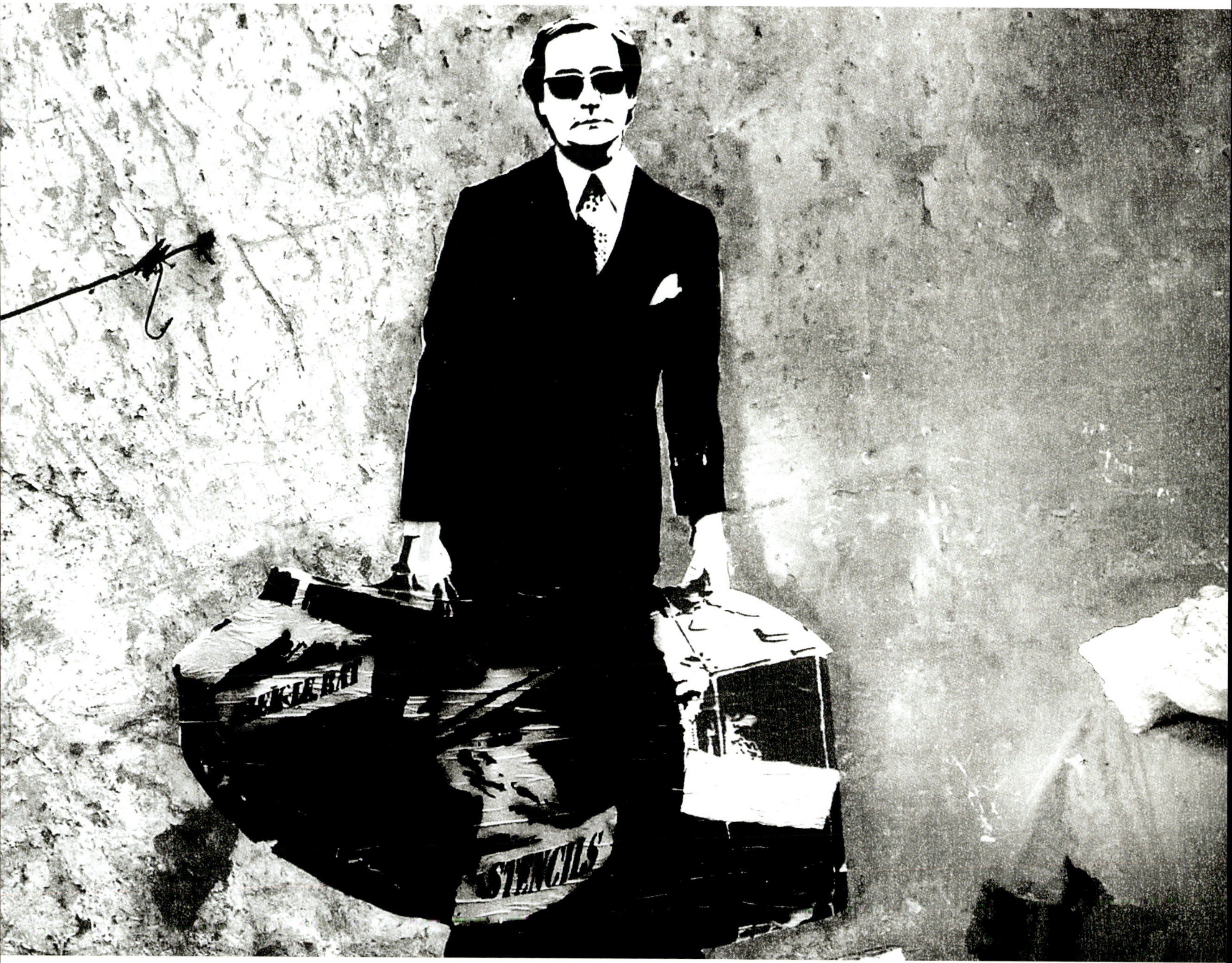

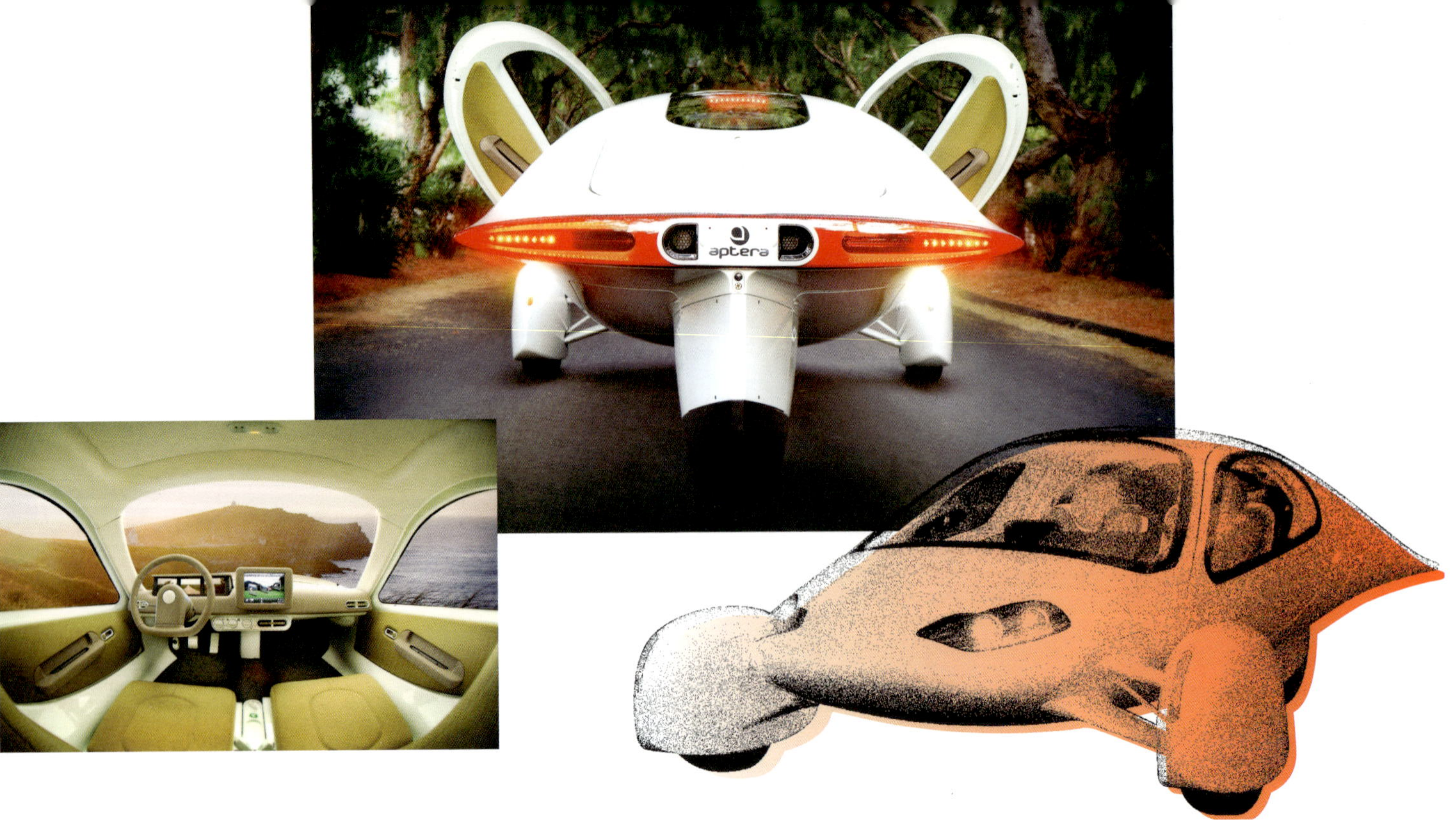

APTERA: THE ECO-FRIENDLY CAR OF THE FUTURE?

BY CAMILLE LOWRY
PHOTOS COURTESY OF APTERA

Five years ago, Steve Fambro was suffering through a hellish commute to his electrical engineering job at a biotech firm. He watched as motorcycles passed by and dreamed of a safe vehicle that would allow him to zip down the carpool lane. In 2006 he founded Aptera Motors, Inc., formerly known as Accelerated Composites.

In November of 2007 Aptera Motors unveiled the Aptera Typ-1, a vehicle that signals an exciting turn in car design, using aerodynamics and composite technology to produce a radically efficient mode of transportation.

This two-seat, three-wheel vehicle features a sleek, futuristic style reminiscent of *The Jetsons*. Due to the Aptera's design it's officially classified by the DMV as a motorcycle, qualifying it for the carpool lane, even with one passenger. The Aptera handles like a small sports car, its speed topping at 85 mph. The model accelerates from 0-60 mph in less than 10 seconds, has a tank capacity of five gallons, and runs up to 230 mpg on trips of 120 miles with a fully charged battery. Otherwise, the vehicle runs approximately 120 mpg.

Early on, addressing the issue of drag—the resistance to forward motion caused by air friction—was a motivating challenge for Fambro. He realized that in most cars, "half of the electrical energy was just going to push the air out of the way." Fambro hired Jason Hill, the designer of the Smart Car, and asked him to collaborate with an aerodynamicist. Fambro recalls, "I gave him a shape to start with, and said, 'You can do anything you want except you can't increase the drag.' We let the aerodynamics frame the style." The collaboration produced unique details such as recessed windshield wipers and rearview cameras instead of mirrors.

Safety was also paramount to the design. "I realized you could make it 1,000 miles to the gallon, but if it wasn't safe people wouldn't buy it," Fambro says. The Aptera's safety measures include rollover protection and airbag-in seatbelt technology. The website reads: "We decided not just to meet many of the specs for passenger vehicles, which are set above and beyond the requirements for motorcycles, but we chose to exceed them whenever possible."

The arrival of the fuel-efficient Aptera is timely, considering that President Bush recently signed a bill requiring passenger vehicles to gain an efficiency of 35 mpg by the year 2020, which according to *The New York Times* is "the first significant increase in mileage standards since 1975."

The target audience of this electro-gas hybrid is a class of consumers who have compassion for the environment and purchase products based upon their values. To meet their priorities the designers used sustainable, recycled material to reduce the ecological footprint, and mounted rooftop solar panels.

The website states that the Aptera Typ-1 will begin production in late 2008. The company is currently taking reservations for the vehicle, which has a purchase price of $26,900 for the all-electric model named, and $29,900 for the plug in hybrid.

www.aptera.com

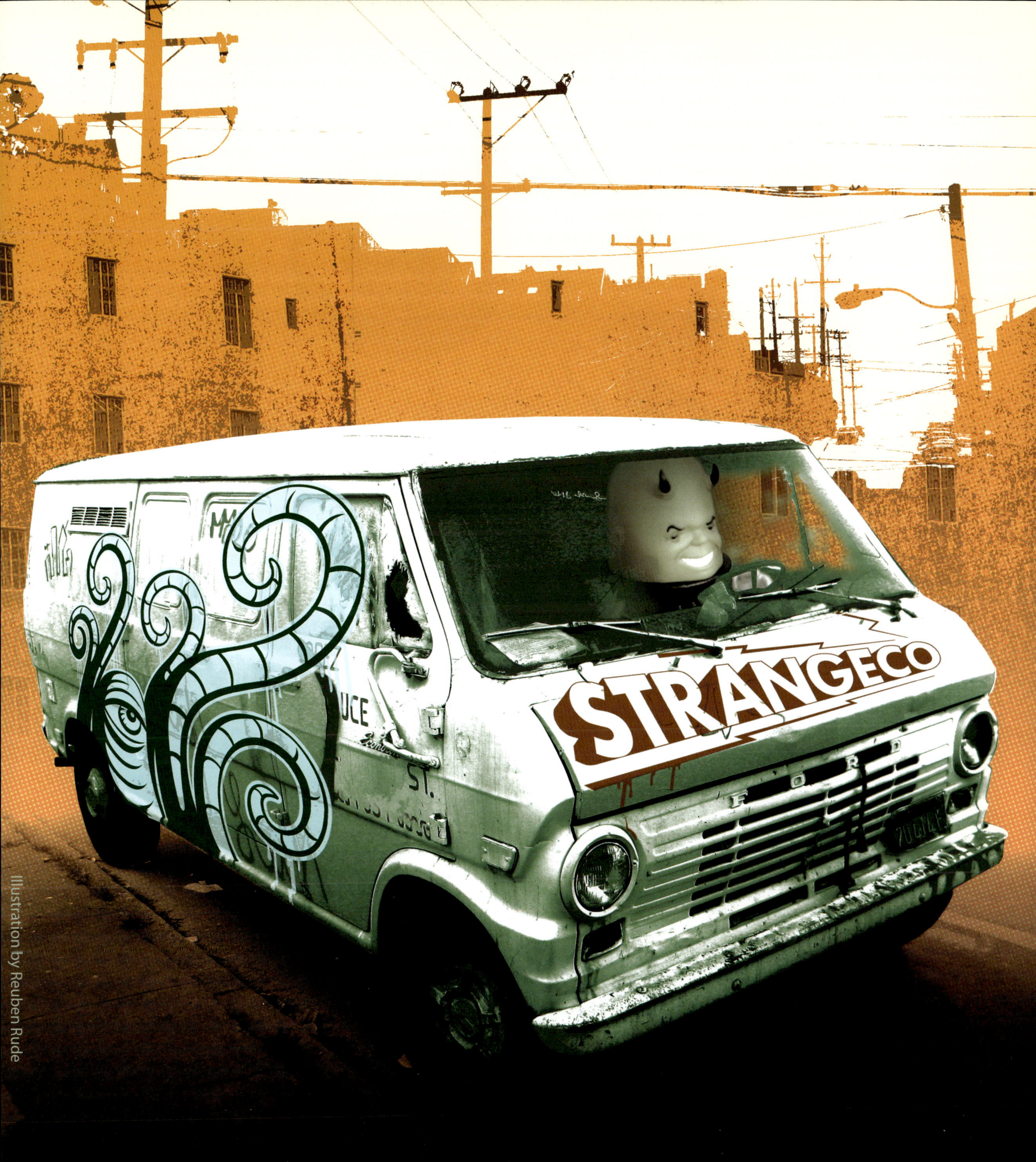

PURVEYORS OF THE PECULIAR!

www.strangeco.com

Classic Graphics: Television

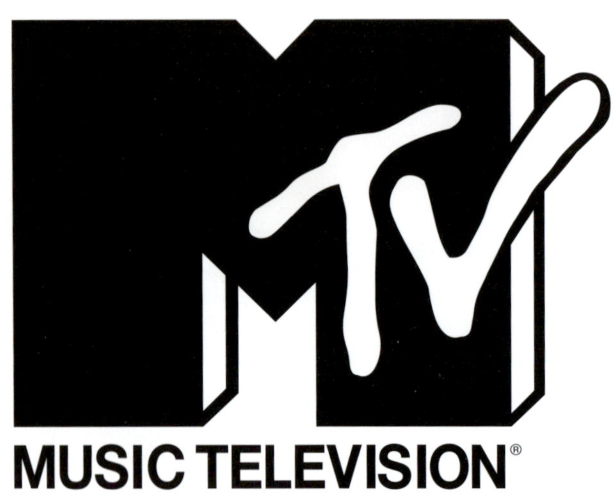

BY JAMES GADDY

The idea of a "classic" graphic is a bit of an oxymoron. Graphics, by their very nature, are of the moment; they change with the times. Strangely enough, one of the most enduring "classics" arose in the most ephemeral media possible: television.

In 1951, long before the phrase "Kill Your Television" became a buzzword, CBS realized that a company in the business of broadcasting images needed a powerful one for itself. The "Eye" logo was an instant hit. It has remained virtually unchanged since its designer, William Golden, oversaw its creation after being inspired by Shaker art—specifically the hand-painted eyes on barns that were supposed to represent the all-seeing eye of God. With the artist Kurt Weihs, who re-drew the eye in a more proportional, abstracted version of the Shaker eyes, Golden turned the eye into a camera's lens for "looking at the world"—an appropriate motif for the medium. Designers don't all agree that Golden was responsible, suggesting that his talented CBS colleague Georg Olden deserves at least partial credit, but this claim has never been proven. The logo worked across all the company's media but was built to be used in motion graphics and animation.

Five years later, during the birth of color television, CBS' rival broadcaster NBC applied its own appropriate symbol for television's possibility: the peacock. The channel's director of design, John J. Graham—who, incidentally, hired Andy Warhol for some of his first commercial work in the '50s—created the peacock's body in black and white after initially rejecting his original idea, a butterfly. The bird's 11 "feathers," in color, fanned out in a 12-second animation, revealing to audiences that, yes indeed, they were watching a color television. And yes,

it was on NBC. Unlike the CBS Eye, the peacock would go through endless permutations and adjustments, sometimes taking on a kaleidoscopic approach, sometimes disappearing altogether for years at a time, until the design studio Chermayeff & Geismar (who also created the PBS "Everyman" logo) redrew the peacock in 1986, cutting off five of its feathers and abstracting the body as a silhouette where the colors meet.

By that point, the major networks were competing with the rise of cable, which was led by the bratty hit channel MTV. In May 1980, Fred Seibert, who would become the channel's first creative director (and later went on to create the Nick at Nite concept), hired Manhattan Design to come up with a logo that would "burn into the viewer's minds—literally 'brand' the network." The fat, weightier M, held its ground with smaller, more handwritten "tv" to form an irreverent contrast, but Seibert's real ingenuity lay in his commissions for the endless incarnations of the logo for an endless stream of station IDs, defying decades of network logic. For the channel's first spot, Seibert tweaked public-domain footage of the astronauts on the moon, who plant a flag bearing the MTV logo on the lunar surface. The no-rules attitude proved the very point of a classic graphic: you can change it a million times and it will still be timeless.

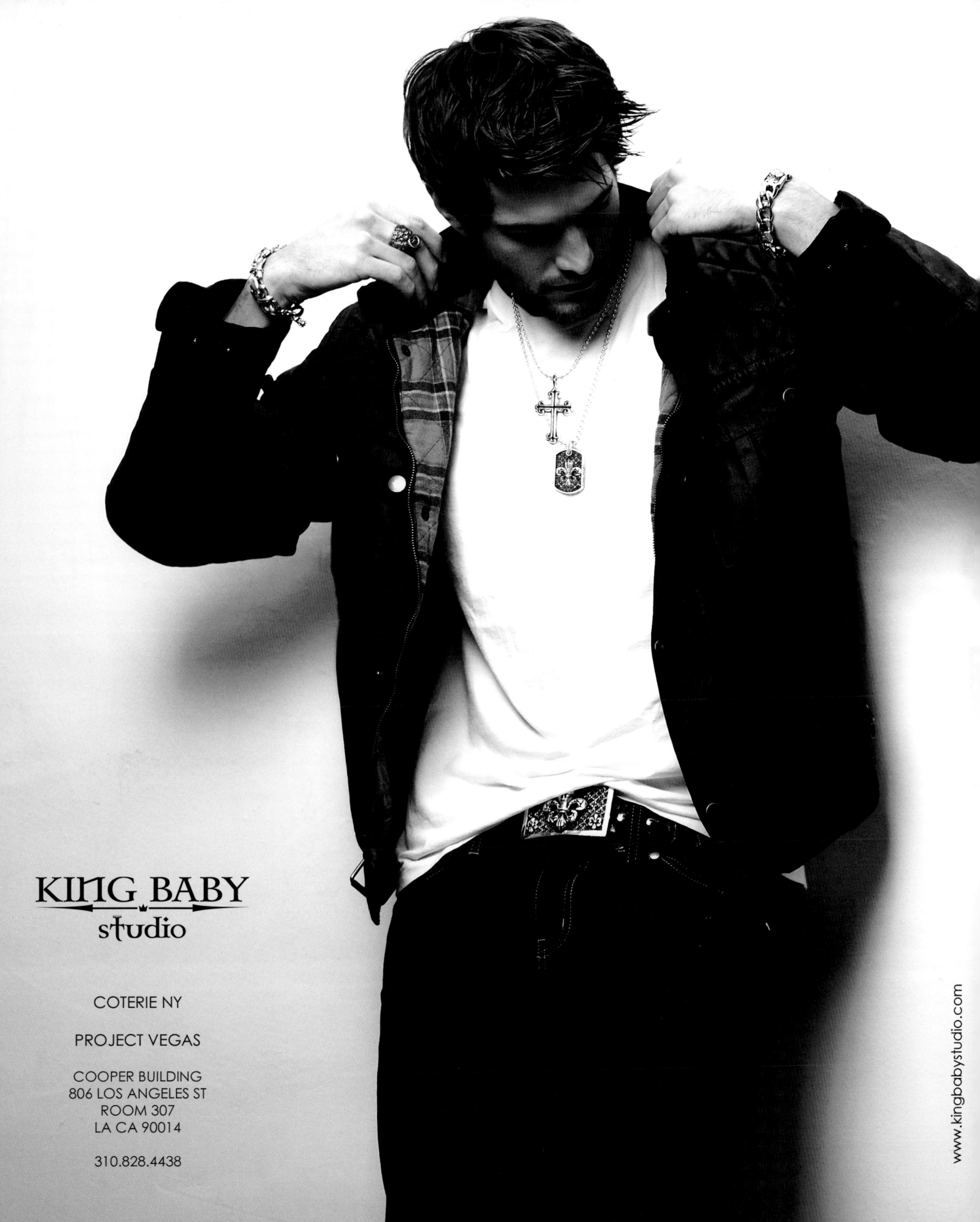

KING BABY
studio

COTERIE NY

PROJECT VEGAS

COOPER BUILDING
806 LOS ANGELES ST
ROOM 307
LA CA 90014

310.828.4438

www.kingbabystudio.com

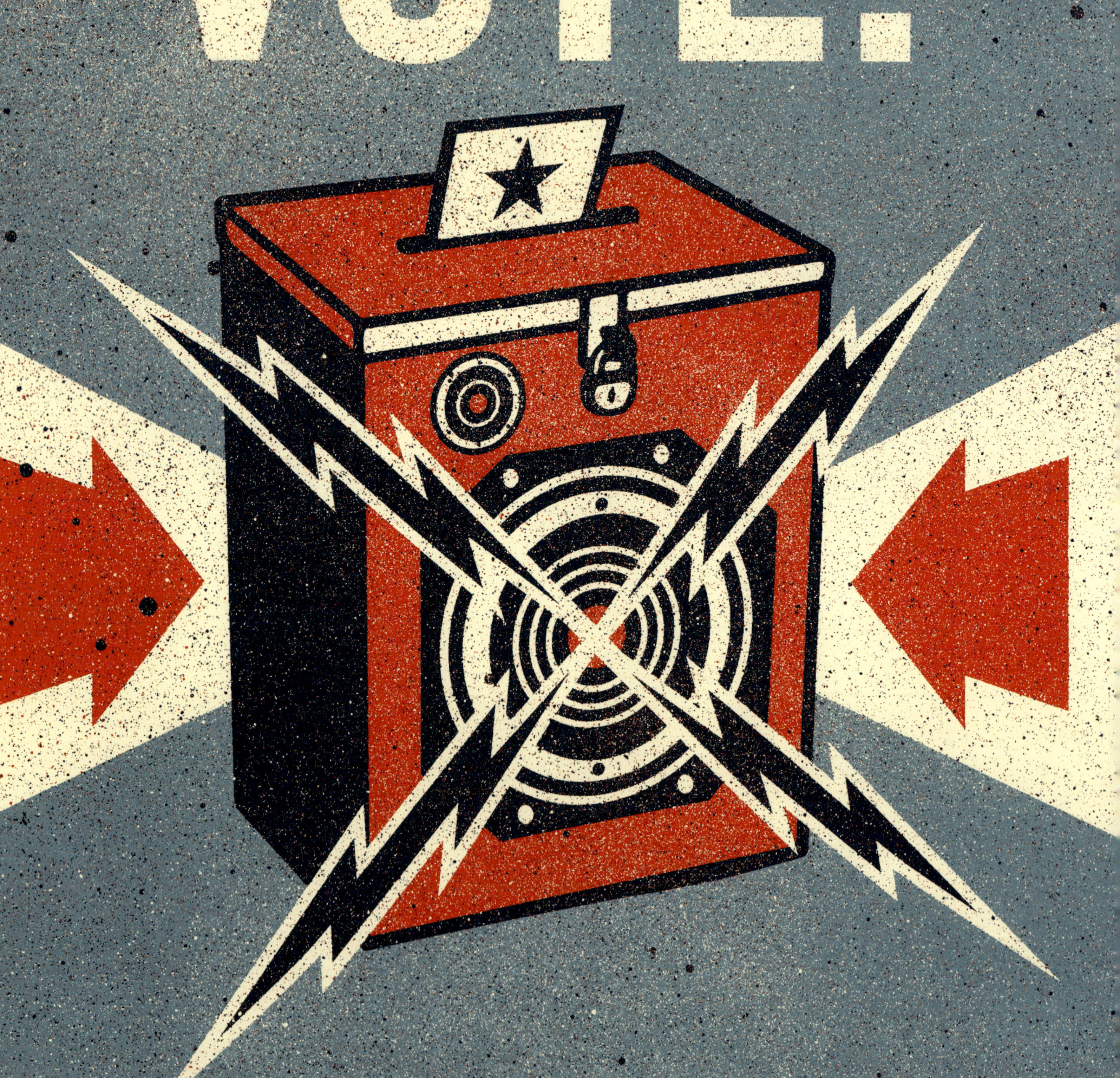
VOTE!

HENRY ROLLINS:
Notes From the Territory

TOPIC LINE: OUT, OUT, DAMNED RADICALS!

GEORGE WALKER BUSH AND HIS FILTHY FLOCK OF AMERICAN FLAG LAPEL PIN WEARING MANIACS WILL BE REMEMBERED BY HISTORY AS THE MOST RADICAL GANG EVER TO TAKE CHARGE OF AMERICA. THINK OF THE DIFFERENCE BETWEEN HOW IT WAS BEFORE THEY CAME TO TOWN AND HOW IT IS NOW. HERE'S A MERE FRACTION OF WHAT THEY GOT AWAY WITH ON YOUR WATCH, YOUR DIME, IN FULL VIEW. RADICAL!!!

Everything is for sale.
Like the Bushman once said before he let a chuckle escape, "Money trumps peace sometimes." You're damn right it does, especially when you can make a fortune destroying a place and then make another in its seemingly never finished "reconstruction," which in the case of Iraq and New Orleans is the code word for Operation Spend A Lot Don't Do A Fucking Thing. These radicals are so busy greasing the palms of their no bid contract buddies they don't see that the grease-in-hand is actually blood-on-hand. Backwards is the new way forward. Disaster is the new opportunity and critical thinking is the abused wife gently weeping in the corner of the American consciousness. *Booyah!!!*

It's a Christian nation, stupid.
You're just living in it. Christ is on the move and the purse strings are flapping in the pre-Rapture breeze as millions of dollars nearly catch fire as they fly into the coffers of faith-based organizations to impose their very negative abstinence-only sex education and abstinence-until-marriage initiatives. Go to 4Parents.gov right now and decide which fucks with you more, getting your intelligence insulted or that you paid for this nonsense. Stop touching yourself and pray, you horny heathens! *Hey now!!!*

Are you my pal?
Then you're in! Loyalty over qualification is one of the hallmarks of the most radical gang in American history. How else would ex-Utah governor bird flu boy, that Tamiflu taskmaster Michael "Methyl Tertiary Butyl Ether Boy" Leavitt end up heading up the Environmental Protection Agency for four years and then gently splashdown as Secretary of the U.S. Department of Health and Human Services four years later? *Chaka Khan!!!*

If you've got nothing to hide . . .
These radical bastards will know for sure. The Patriot Act and other acts are firmly in place to make sure those black helicopters are perpetually circling in your mind as you log on the Internet or speak on the phone. This gang don't need no stinkin' warrants because as long as terrorists walk the earth . . . never sleeping . . . always plotting . . . the Whitehouse Wild Bunch needs to know what you jack off to. *Hammer time!!!*

Everything is possible when the rule of law doesn't apply to you.
Ten years ago, you would have not believed that America would torture and imprison people without charging them or allowing them access to legal council. Years ago, had someone proposed the Abu Ghraib environment for extracting information, you would have said, conduct of that nature was reserved for totalitarian dictators drunk on power that went unchecked. Then you would have gone into your whole rap about "America would never lower itself to such extreme methods, we're the good guys, we gave the world The Ramones and P-Funk! We could never justify . . ." But now, things have changed. *In your face!!!*

Die hardest.
The ultimate triumph of this fear-fueled paranoia posse is that they were able to get millions of Americans to come along for the southward spiral into foreclosure, out-of-control credit debt, evaporating employment and endless rotations through the little town KBR put on the map, Iraq while simultaneously delivering an incredibly ignorant, intolerant and xenophobic message as its foreign policy. Fox News reported, millions lapped from the troth while every major news outlet fell in line and buckled. Hearing this gulag collective of financially unstable cultists defend the Bush mob is akin to hearing that Stalin liked dogs and therefore wasn't so bad after all. *Now I know why tigers eat their young!!!*

It will get better.
When you realize that the only thing standing in the way of the death of Democracy and freedom as you know it is you. It's been an interesting seven years, but it's time to kick this poison from our bloodstream before it's too late. To be succinct: I can't wait for the most radical gang in American history to go back to their gated communities and never come back. Don't get me wrong, it's been a damn good time ridiculing this over-privileged slacker president and his pack of liars but we have to get going. *Vote!!!*

Henry is always in motion. Catch up with him at HenryRollins.com

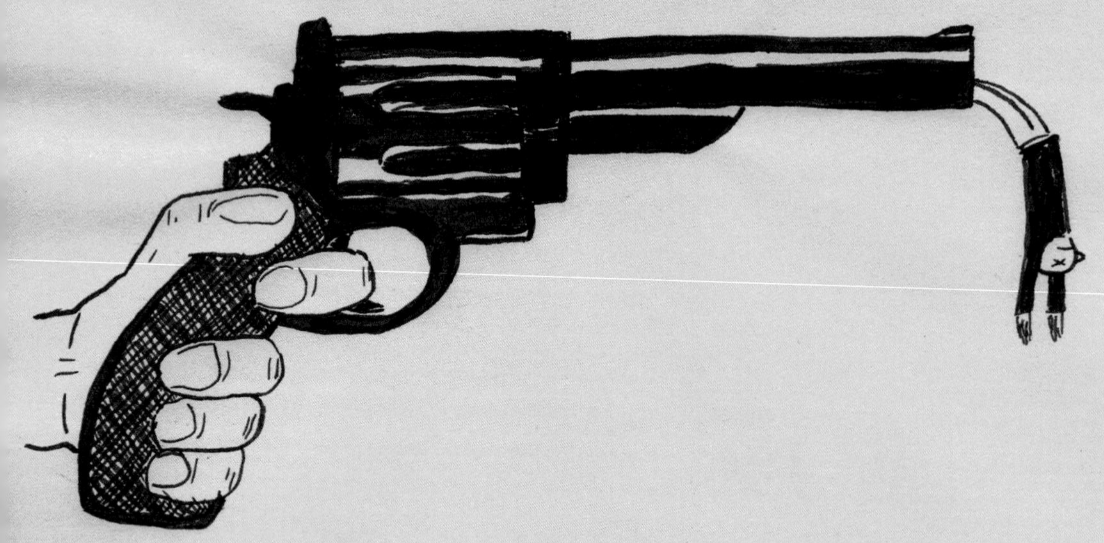

Dirty Harry

BY IAN DELAURENTIS
ILLUSTRATION BY ANDREW JEFFREY WRIGHT

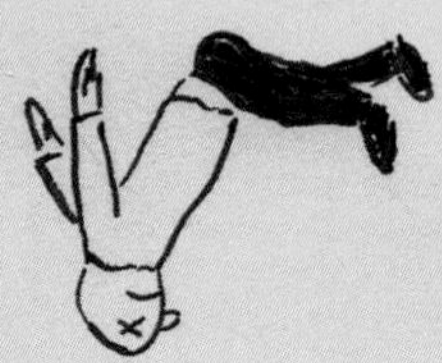

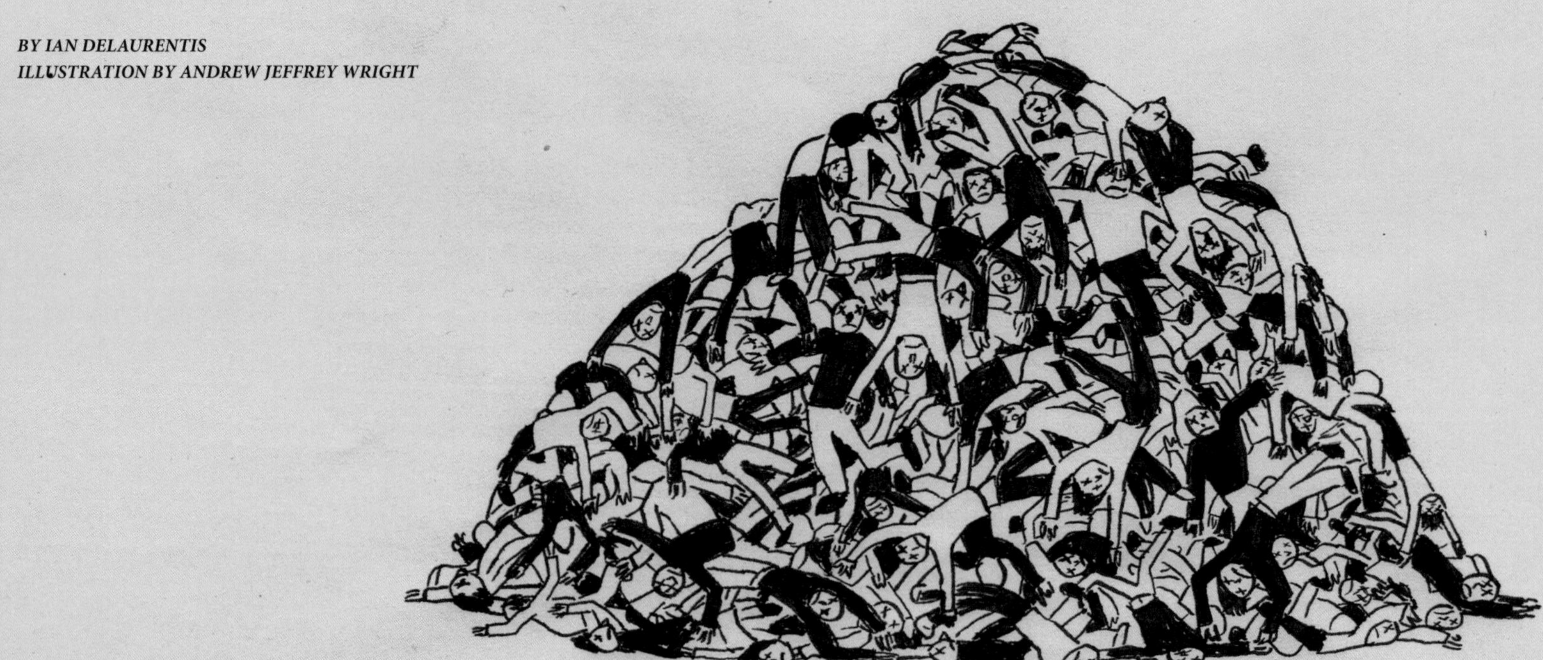

CINEMA CALLING DIRTY HARRY

You underestimate Dirty Harry. I know you do. Somehow the sands of time and the short attention spans of today's movie-going audience have conspired to push the godfather of tough-guy cops to the brink of obscurity. Clint Eastwood's portrayal of Inspector "Dirty Harry" Callahan set the definitive standard for hardboiled cops who work outside the system. Nicknamed for his habit of taking on the dirtiest cases and solving them by any means necessary, Dirty Harry combined the ruthlessness of vigilantism with the invigorating justice of the law to create a unique series of films.

The original *Dirty Harry* debuted in 1971 and centered on Harry's pursuit of a serial killer named Scorpio. It's a sinister affair filled with torture, brutal violence, surprisingly un-P.C. language and a legitimately scary villain that brought about four sequels. Surprised to hear there were that many movies? You shouldn't be. Consider what Dirty Harry says at the end of the movie before he executes Scorpio: "I know what you're thinking: 'Did he fire six shots or only five?' Well, to tell you the truth, in all this excitement I kind of lost track myself. But being as this is a .44 Magnum, the most powerful handgun in the world, and would blow your head clean off, you've got to ask yourself a question: 'Do I feel lucky?' Well, do ya, punk?" That quote is still used today, but people might not be too sure where it comes from. You'd be smart to remember it's from *Dirty Harry* and that these sequels are also pretty badass:

Clint Eastwood Is Dirty Harry In:
MAGNUM FORCE
This Time Harry Says: *"A man's got to know his limitations."*
Body Count: 30

The first sequel looks at the difference between a cop who has to break the rules for justice and a cop who breaks the rules for justice, which isn't very much. It seems there are some new cops on the force who are into killing crooks that have managed to elude the law. They drive motorcycles, carry .357 magnums and talk smack about how they used to be Army Special Forces. In short, they are total dicks. Dirty Harry opens the movie waiting to be put back on homicide detail after being suspended for killing the villain at the end of the last movie, when he crosses paths with this "Magnum Force." Harry feels that these guys are crossing the line with their brand of vigilante justice, even though it's remarkably similar to his brand of vigilante justice. This clash of philosophies basically amounts to the difference between moderate and rightwing republicans until the Magnum Force guys offer Harry membership in their crew. He declines, and then gets super pissed when they try and kill him by planting a bomb in his mailbox. A bomb in Dirty Harry's mailbox? That's straight nonsense. You gotta shoot this guy before he goes all "Do you feel lucky punk?" on your ass. Stupid rookies.

Clint Eastwood Is Dirty Harry In:
THE ENFORCER
This Time Harry Says: *"I'm standing on the street corner, and Mrs. Grey there comes up and proposi-tions me. She says if I come home with her, for $5 she'll put on an exhibition with a Shetland pony…"*
Body Count: 13

The Enforcer was billed as being the "dirtiest" Harry of them all, but it's actually pretty tame compared to the other films in the series. Yeah, Harry totally shoots and beats up a bunch of perps but his heart doesn't seem to be in it. The plot is pretty out there, touching on subjects such as militant groups based on the Symbionese Liberation Army, the Black Panthers, the role of policewomen working in the field, the porn industry and the treatment of veterans. The dialogue is way politically incorrect and the sex humor is kinda out of place. To make things worse the villains take the mayor of San Francisco hostage on Alcatraz and want a ransom of a whopping $2 million, which doesn't really hold up very well when re-watching the movie in this day and age. On the other hand, the bad guys do have an arsenal of rocket launchers, so they get bonus points for style. What *The Enforcer* adds to the *Dirty Harry* cannon is the extra evidence that being Callahan's partner is about as safe as being the drummer in Spinal Tap. Not one, but two of his partners get killed off in this movie. When you add that to the bodies piled up in the other movies you start to get the sense that having a desk job might not be such a bad thing after all.

Clint Eastwood Is Dirty Harry In:
SUDDEN IMPACT
This Time Harry Says: *"Go ahead, make my day."*
Body Count: 18

Considering that it was made in 1983, the plot to *Sudden Impact* reads a whole heck of a lot like the grindhouse movies that were made decades earlier. We see an older Dirty Harry being constantly reprimanded for ignoring the law to shoot and harass suspects as he sees fit. It's funny that his superiors act all outraged that he broke the law and killed three people and then they tell him to take some time off. Re-watching these films really gives you the sense that you could do anything back then and get away with it. Meanwhile, the victim of a sexual assault is tracking her attackers down and extracting revenge by shooting them in the genitals and then the head. She soon crosses paths with Harry and then things get confusing with a bunch of bonus bad guys who provide cannon fodder. In the end Harry helps the female victim kill her assailants and blame the murders she committed on them. *Sudden Impact* is a dark movie that's a little uncomfortable to watch in some spots, but still one of the better films in the series.

Clint Eastwood Is Dirty Harry In:
THE DEAD POOL
This Time Harry Says: *"You're out of bullets. And you know what that means… you're shit outta luck."*
Body Count: 14

1988's *The Dead Pool* certainly isn't the strongest exclamation point to Dirty Harry's movie career. It's not as gritty as the other movies and it's not even as good as the imitation *Dirty Harry* movies that were prevalent by this time. That's not to say it's terrible though. Callahan still has a knack for dialogue and violence, and there is a fair amount of action. There is a curious sequence where Harry is chased all over the city by a remote-controlled car carrying a bomb. He's driving a real car during the chase so you'll either think this scene is awesome or the stupidest thing you've ever laid eyes on. Either way, it's good fun. But let's be honest: There are only two real reasons why *The Dead Pool* is worth a damn: Guns N' Roses and Jim Carrey. That's right—in one of his first roles, Carrey plays soon-to-be-murdered rock star Johnny Squares. Squares fronts a band featuring the members of Guns N' Roses and they lip sync "Welcome To The Jungle" together. In another scene, Slash shoots a harpoon off a boat while Axl stands around in a red bandanna. This is all so amazing that you'll partially forget that instead of standing around Dirty Harry should be pistol-whipping a guy for loitering.

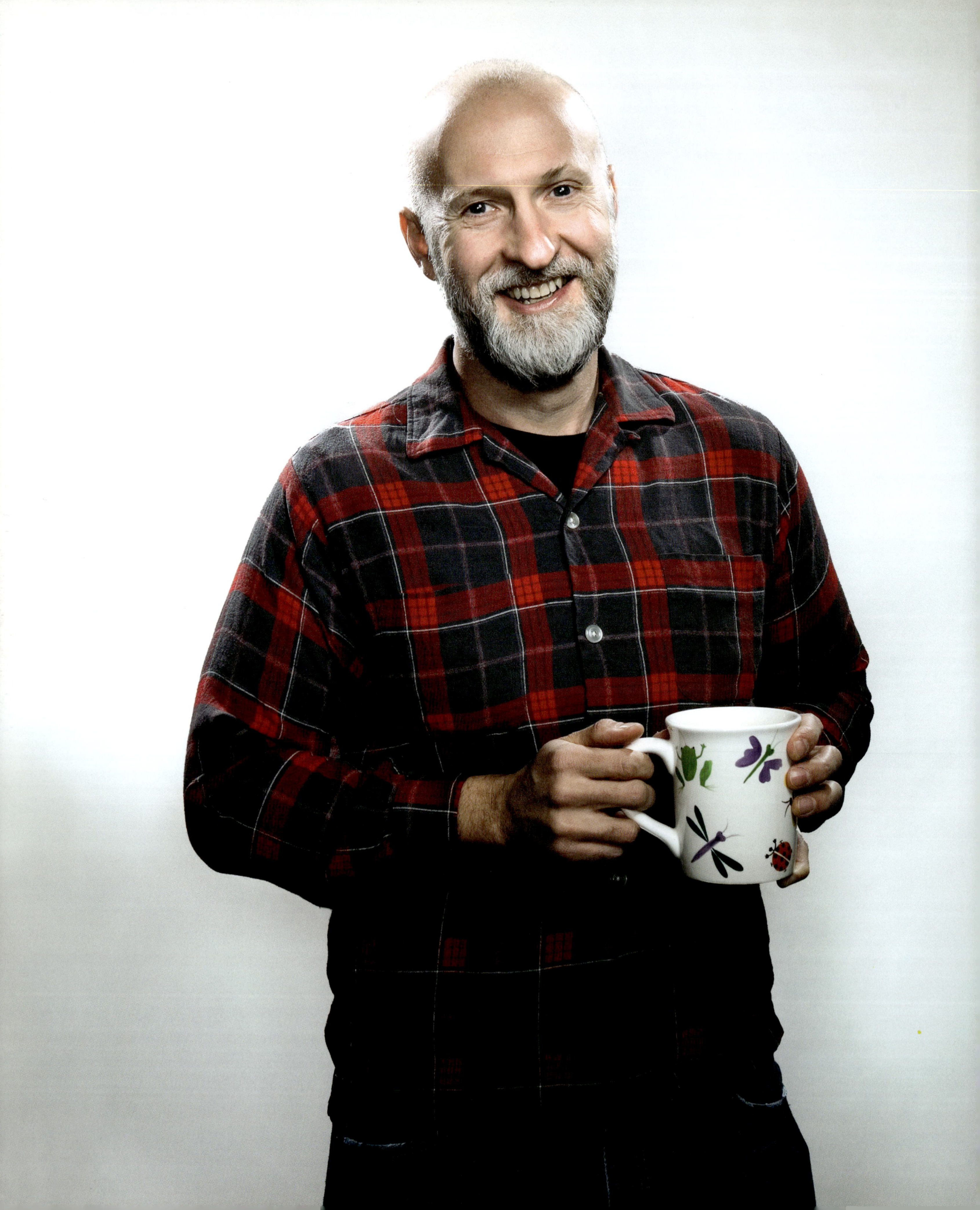

MEET BOB MOULD AGAIN

Hardcore punk icon turned alterna-rock god turned electronic music maestro turned pro-wrestling consultant turned *advice columnist*?

BY CHRIS RICHARDS
PHOTO BY CHAD GRIFFITH
ILLUSTRATION BY TIM GOUGH

The latest title on the Mould's resume comes courtesy of the *Washington City Paper*—D.C.'s free alternative weekly that recently printed fresh counsel from Mould every Thursday. (Before he penned his farewell "Ask Bob" column in December, fans have asked the Hüsker Dü-alum for moving advice, how to buy a guitar and to confirm the veracity of the 1969 NASA moon-landing.)

"It's fun," shrugs Mould, who's lived in Washington since 2002. And all in a day's work for an artist known to wear numerous hats atop a head still brimming with fresh ideas decades after Hüsker Dü burned a thermonuclear fissure into America's rock consciousness. With the Hüskers, his '90s troupe Sugar and numerous solo albums, Mould's emotive song-craft and colossal sonic sensibilities have influenced everyone from My Bloody Valentine to Daft Punk.

His latest solo effort, *District Line,* may not offer mind-melting guitar textures but it certainly matches confessional lyrics with superlative melodies—the same kind that gave Hüsker Dü's visceral thrashing such depth. And while Mould stands by his early work, he seems more proud of the underground network Hüsker Dü helped forge. "How do you connect with like-minded people having to use mail and telephone and not having *Pitchfork* directing traffic?" He wonders at the accomplishment.

Yet after a tumultuous eight-year run that delivered hardcore masterstrokes *Zen Arcade* and *New Day Rising*, the band imploded, leaving Mould to strike out on his own. "After Hüsker Dü wrapped up in January of '88, I had just moved up to a farm in northern Minnesota," he recounts. "I sat up there for a year and a half re-learning the vocabulary of music and wanting to make something that didn't sound like what I had done prior." He bought a new guitar, (the same one he still plays everyday), and began penning the songs to his 1989 solo-debut *Workbook*. Along with Hüsker Dü's *Zen Arcade* and Sugar's *Copper Blue*, Mould says it's "one of the three records I'm most proud of."

But the solitude didn't last long. By '89 Mould had relocated to New York and quickly found himself in the sweet company of future Sugar band mates Malcolm Travis and David Barbe. "When the three of us got together and started playing I realized, 'These aren't session guys,'" Mould says. "Let's make it a band."

The trio hit the ground running with *Copper Blue*, an album that paired Mould's soulful warble with distortion-spangled guitar riffs. "We did a van tour in July of '92," he says, recounting the band's rocket-ship ascent. "And from there we went to 'NME Album of The Year' to playing for 70,000 people in Belgium."

It certainly wasn't dumb luck. 1992 was the hey-day of alternative rock, a time where MTV was transforming petulant 20-somethings into pop icons almost overnight—quite the contrast to Hüsker Dü's persistent slog a decade before. "Hüsker Dü was a battle," Mould says. "The '80s were a battle—a battle against the times, against Reagan, against corporate music. Then being on the road with the Sonics, Nirvana and the Pumpkins and seeing it all blow up, it was like,

'Wow! Punk rock won!'"

But Sugar's rapid climb still took a heavy toll on the band and Barbe's family obligations and Mould's tour fatigue led them to disband in 1995. The songwriter returned to New York to work on something new: his personal life. "I wanted to put the touring-rock-musician-persona away," he says. "I didn't have any time to be an integrated gay man in New York City. I wanted to be at home with friendships and a life that didn't involve getting in a van."

Musically, the story picks back up in 2002 with Mould boasting a left-turn electronic album, *Modulate,* and a new Washington D.C. zip code. Along with his friend Richard Morel, Mould began DJing at the Blowoff, a popular D.C. dance-night. When asked why he started hosting the event, Mould laughs, "I wanted to make friends!" Now, almost five years later, the Blowoff packs D.C.'s 9:30 club on an almost monthly basis. "I would have never thought I would have done that," Mould says of his success on the ones and twos. "This is the electronic music I spent the '80s trying to destroy! That and the wrestling gig are the two greatest sidebars to everything that I've done."

"The '80s were a battle—a battle against the times, against Reagan, against corporate music."

Wait—wrestling gig!?

"I've been a life-long fan," Mould says of professional wrestling. "I watched it as a kid, read the magazines, went to the matches." Having made some friends in the industry, Mould was hired as a paid consultant to the WCW (World Championship Wrestling) in 1999. He describes a seven-month tenure spent choreographing wrestling matches as "a roller coaster of great moments and terrible moments. It was like the HBO show *Oz.* When the catering comes out, where you sit decides your political fate. It was such a harder job than music."

And it's not the only place on cable television where you've experienced Mould's work. He's also the guy who penned the theme music to Comedy Central's wildly popular *The Daily Show.* In Washington, a city brimming with politico types, you'd think this feather in his cap would have folks nominating Mould for mayor. Instead, Mould prefers to stick to his neighborhood—a truth that resonates throughout the songs from *District Line.*

"These days, I have a very small life. It rarely goes north of U Street, south of P Street, east of 9th or west of 18th," he explains, using his hand to trace the neighborhood grid on the tabletop. "It's a really simple place inside of a more complicated, spiritually ugly place. And the tragedies that happen here are the simplest of human stories. I stay in this box and have a very simple life inside this box. And that's what this record is about."

THE TIMES WE HAD

BY IMRAN SIDDIQUEE
PHOTO BY PIPER FERGUSON

The video for indie darling Beirut's "Elephant Gun," a tune that perfectly captures singer Zach Condon's acute sense of wanderlust, begins with an ornate compass giving way to confetti and empty wine bottles. From there it expands into a lavish study of temptation, distance—both emotional and physical—and home. It's not only one of the best music videos of 2007, but also represents the meeting of two inspired minds: Condon and Israeli-born video artist Alma Har'el.

Har'el began her career in photography, working on album art for diverse Israeli acts like Yoli Sobol and Tal Gordon. After spending some time with *National Geographic*, as a director and correspondent, she began documenting live concerts and festivals around the globe—which eventually led to her work in music videos. Har'el created clips for some of the top talents in her homeland—from Balkan Beat Box to hip-hop artist Mooky. In addition to directing two critically acclaimed videos for Beirut, she recently relocated to Los Angeles and signed with Partizan, an international company that represents preeminent video directors like Olivier and Michel Gondry.

The young director is also an avid collector of Super 8 home videos and a fan of performance art. Like Condon does with his music—combining Eastern European sounds with American folk—Har'el seamlessly fuses past and present styles of visual expression into her videos.

Here, Har'el talks to SWINDLE about her connection with Beirut, her vision as a director, and *Death in Love*, a film she recently co-produced.

What originally drew you to Beirut? Were you already a fan of their music?

I was getting frustrated with the music I was getting offers for, and was looking to do a music video for a musician that tries to break the mold of rock, pop and all the rest of it, and hopefully has some Eastern European influences, as well. In the past five years I've been listening to music from [that] part of the world and found it painfully beautiful. It makes me think of my grandparents who were from Poland and about the loneliness that hides inside us when we're happy, drunk or in love. It's a wonderful round feeling that expands the rooms of your heart. Because of all of those things I was an instant fan of Beirut.

I feel like a longing for the past is apparent in much of your work. How would you describe this feeling?

It's like missing something you never knew… Missing the past is like having a fantasy. The past is gone and when it was the present I'm convinced it didn't feel like I imagine it did. It's like listening to Bob Dylan and missing him although you never met him or looking at a tombstone and hoping the person that died knew some happiness. It is a feeling of longing for more attention to detail and having more romance in your step.

How did you start directing music videos?

My first music videos were made for Israeli musicians, I moved here to L.A. from Tel Aviv about two years ago.

My last music video before I moved here was for a hip-hop artist from Tel Aviv that goes by the name of Mooky— it was a horror music video about a time in the future when only the dead can bear children.

I also worked for more than a year with a great band called The Balkan Beat Box. We had a show that was like a little traveling circus of music, video art and dance, and after I stopped performing with them they turned it into this really wild dancehall show.

I actually just saw [The Balkan Beat Box] warming up Beirut in Central Park and it was a very special evening for me. They mix Hebrew with English and Arabic; it really is something you rarely hear.

You have also worked in TV and photography. What is it about capturing images that interests you? Do you find moving pictures more compelling than still photography?

I love them all and I think the only reason I ended up doing more music videos is my personality. There is something about the execution of a dream-like concept that I enjoy more. The journey you take from your imagination, to include all the crew and the people you work with, and then later the viewer, is a very collaborative process that makes me feel more understood as a person. I also love movement and dance.

How do you think music videos will develop in the future?

That all depends on the way the music industry will deal with the fact that it took them too long to come to terms with digital downloads. They were trying to sue people instead of coming up with a solution that would satisfy the users. The vacuum created a generation that wants its music for free and until the music industry finds a way to make free music profitable it seems music videos will be the last thing on people's minds.

I love the low-cost solutions that lead to creativity in the music video world and the effect YouTube [has] had on a lot of directors.

You were recently involved in the production of a feature film. Is this a direction you would like to take your career in?

The film is called *Death in Love* and it's written and directed by Boaz Yakin who is my husband. It's an intense drama about the way our parents' secrets and past shape our emotional and sexual lives.

I co-produced the film and directed the second unit. It was the most intense learning experience. I loved diving into it. Music videos are like a brief, beautiful romance and film is like love, it suggests more challenging moments and hard times but the reward is deeper and it really becomes part of your life. I really hope to direct my own film one day.

Who do you look up to as an artist?

I love so many things and hate choosing. I look up to a lot of filmmakers but other arts inspire me more than filmmaking. One of the things I love most is to see a filmmaker capturing another art form on film. I love mime and physical theatre and I love music, of course, and dance and books. I also get a lot of ideas from looking at nature.

I love artists and filmmakers that are adventurous with their symbolism and are brave in sharing their inner dialogue. I enjoy art that balances a need for fantasy with blinding realism and vice versa. It's in that thin line between the real and the fantastic or the old and the new that I wish to exist in and find a way to express myself.

www.almaharel.com

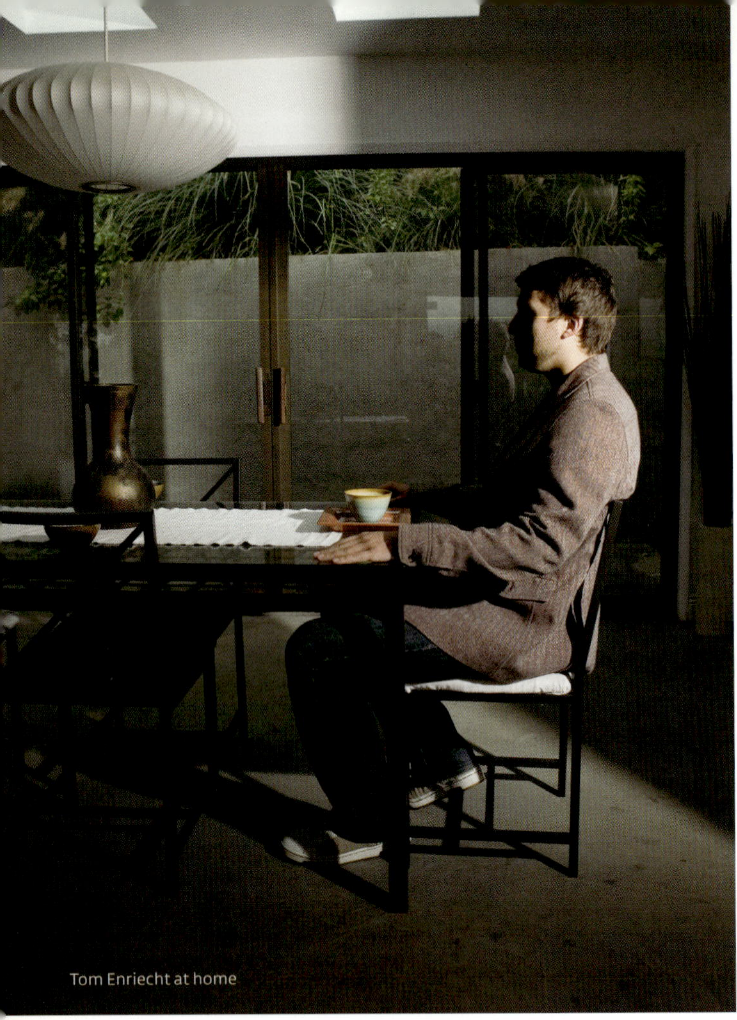
Tom Enriecht at home

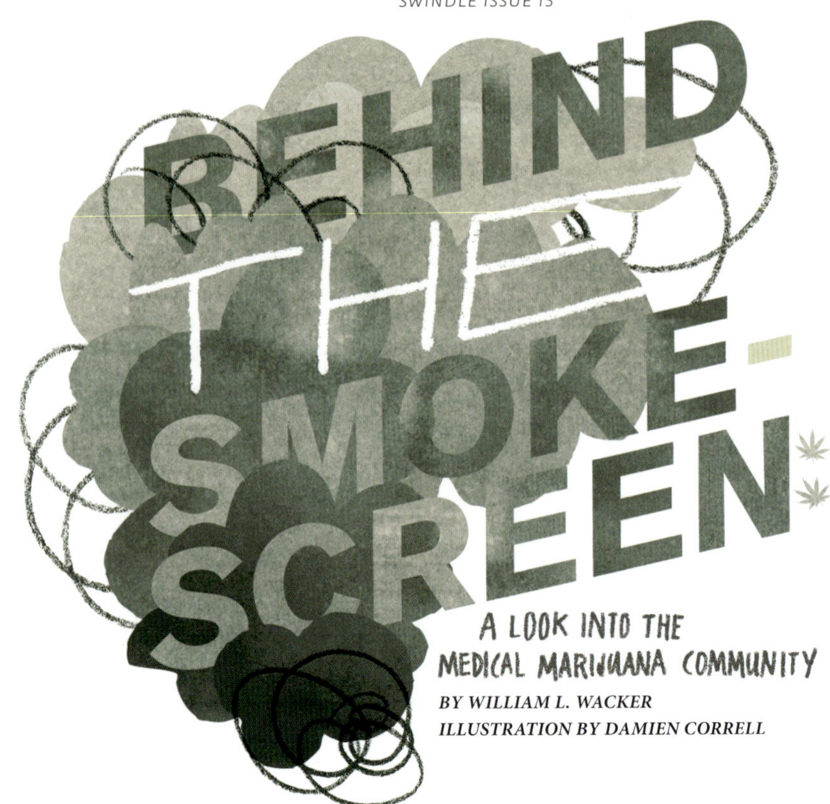

BEHIND THE SMOKE-SCREEN*

A LOOK INTO THE MEDICAL MARIJUANA COMMUNITY

BY WILLIAM L. WACKER
ILLUSTRATION BY DAMIEN CORRELL

IT TAKES LITTLE TO PUSH TOM ENRIECHT * INTO TALKING EXCITEDLY, IF CAUTIOUSLY, ABOUT HIS WORK WITHIN THE MEDICAL MARIJUANA (MMJ) COMMUNITY. WHEN HE BEGAN WORKING AT AN L.A. CANNABIS DISPENSARY ROUGHLY THREE YEARS AGO, HE KNEW NOTHING ABOUT MMJ. NOW, TOM IS A CONSULTANT FOR THE INDUSTRY. HE IS NOT A MEDICAL MARIJUANA PATIENT, NOR DOES HE USE RECREATIONALLY. HOWEVER, HE UTILIZES WHAT HE DESCRIBES AS HIS "NUMEROUS PATIENT EXPERIENCES" TO REFINE AN MMJ DISTRIBUTION SYSTEM THAT "BENEFITS THE [DISPENSARY] OWNERS AND PATIENTS ALIKE."

Tom says he provides "the most up-to-date information to collective owners, primarily about the details of what is and what is not included in Proposition 215 and Senate Bill 420." He also says that dispensary owners "are all aware of the federal implications of being involved in the industry, however, on the state level, the laws are commonly diluted with half truths and propagated by hearsay."

Proposition 215 (aka The Compassionate Use Act of 1996) legalized the cultivation and possession of medicinal marijuana in California for those with a doctor's recommendation. Senate Bill 420, passed seven years later in 2003, clarified the hazy vagueness of Prop 215. A voluntary ID card system was implemented, for patients permitted to use MMJ, guidelines for co-ops and dispensaries were solidified, caregivers were given permission to possess MMJ, and restrictions were placed on the number of marijuana plants patients could grow.

In recent months, NPR, the *Wall Street Journal* and numerous local papers in Northern California have flourished attention on the influx of organized criminals cashing in on grow houses, and moving into upper-middle class neighborhoods. These stories have fogged the distinction between legal and illegal marijuana operations. Tom says, "It all appears the same in the mainstream media. The layman cannot distinguish MMJ from the mob." Rob Taylor*, an MMJ co-op owner in Northern California agrees: "I don't think the public understands at all."

In the last decade, the MMJ community in California has silently bloomed. The community self-regulates—as Tom says, "Differences… can be disputed via arbitration in the courts, whereas the street market continues to have escalated violence." He says that some areas have formed coalitions of co-ops, instilling a set of rules and guidelines that the community voluntarily adheres to. If one dispensary breaks the rules, notices are placed in other co-ops to deter patients from supporting the offender. "They self-police very efficiently," Tom says.

After the Drug Enforcement Agency (DEA) raided a number of L.A. dispensaries this year, Mike Adams, a consumer health advocate, stated, "These raids are the perfect example of the tyranny of the United States federal government and the influence of pharmaceutical companies which are attempting to outlaw and eradicate all forms of natural herbal medicine. The real threat to our safety is an out-of-control DEA that uses terrorist tactics to eradicate a form of medicine that is not politically accepted by the current administration."

"Imagine this," Tom says. "A collective is surrounded by 20 armed DEA agents with bullet proof vests and M16s. They break down the door… they violently throw everyone on the ground and restrain them with zip ties. From there they separate everyone into groups and the threatening begins." Tom explains that they first single out the owner/manager and threaten a minimum of 20 years imprisonment for distribution. During this questioning of anyone on site, two scenarios start to unfold. The first: "Everyone follows the protocol that they were taught in Americans for Safe Access's legal training. [ASA is a member-based organization that provides information on how citizens can handle brushes with the law.] Some people are taken down to the headquarters and then released within six hours. Everyone then celebrates that the ordeal is over, no charges are pressed against anyone and—even though all product is seized— the collective is open for business the next week. Your tax dollars at work, right?"

In another scenario, the staff of the collective begins to talk to agents out of fear or with hopes of getting released sooner. The DEA pits the staff against each other. Some will "give three to go free" (give three names of suppliers to walk) or—as sometimes happens—an owner or employer can turn informant.

Rob says that he has only heard first hand accounts of MMJ dispensary raids, in which no charges were pressed. However, this does not mean that the incidents were harmless. He recounts the raiding of one shop, owned by a man in his 60s. The man was not charged with any crime but Rob says, "They seized all his bank accounts, they foreclosed on his business, and he soon had to foreclose on his house… They didn't take him to jail, but they basically ended his life."

In 1925 the U.S. government subsidized a study on marijuana in the Panama Canal Zone. This study, later quoted in *The Military Surgeon Volume 73—July-Dec. 1933* concluded that marijuana smoking had no negative effects on soldiers. Later, the 1937 Marihuana Tax Act was implemented by Harry J. Anslinger, the very first commissioner of the Federal Bureau of Narcotics, with strong support from newspaper magnate William Randolph Hearst.

Both Anslinger and Hearst used racial slanders against Mexicans and African-Americans to bolster the ban on Marijuana. Anslinger testified in a 1937 Senate hearing, "There are 100,000 total mari-

juana smokers in the U.S., and most are Negroes, Hispanics, Filipinos and entertainers. Their satanic music, jazz and swing, result from marijuana usage. This marijuana causes White women to seek sexual relations with Negroes, entertainers and any others." Hearst's newspapers ran sensationalist headlines like "Marijuana Makes Fiends of Boys in 30 Days," spouting racial rhetoric and playing up the Mexican threat of crime, violence and drug use. (This is covered in detail by writer Jack Herer in his book *The Emperor Wears No Clothes: The Authoritative Historical Record of Cannabis and the Conspiracy Against Marijuana* [Quick American Archives].) It should also be noted that Hearst had business interests in the timber industry, and the industrialization of hemp would have affected his earnings.

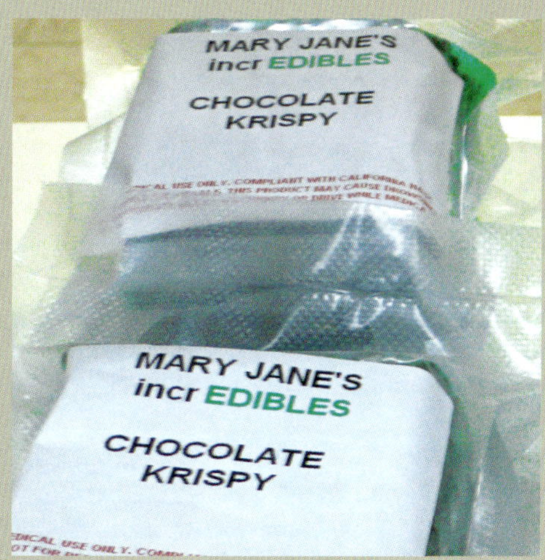

Marijuana laws continued to get stricter, and in 1970, under The Controlled Substances Act, the drug was classified as Schedule 1—where it remains to this day—which means it is considered a highly addictive substance with no accepted medical use in the United States. To put this into perspective, cocaine, methamphetamines and opium are Schedule 2 drugs, which means they can be prescribed under medical supervision. Currently, the U.S. Federal Government has granted only seven patients the use of marijuana for medical reasons. Since 1968, the federal research organization, the National Institute on Drug Abuse (NIDA) has put the University of Mississippi under contract to grow marijuana for scientific research. To this day, the university has a monopoly on federally sanctioned marijuana production.

In 1997, the year after California passed Proposition 215, the U.S. government subsidized a third party study of marijuana's medicinal properties to be conducted by the Institute of Medicine (IOM), a non-partisan organization whose stated mission is to provide "independent, objective, evidence-based advice to policymakers, health

professionals, the private sector, and the public." The IOM's findings stayed on the fence—they stated that marijuana could be effective for patients who "suffer simultaneously from severe pain, nausea, and appetite loss," they reported. But they also reported: "we see little future in smoking marijuana as a medicine."

The DEA controls all testing done on marijuana, although many individuals—notably Lyle Craker, a University of Massachusetts Amherst professor who has garnered support from Senators Edward Kennedy and John Kerry—have gone to the courts for permission to grow and study marijuana. Craker told the *Washington Post*, "Our work is focused on finding medicinal uses of plants, and marijuana is one with clear potential. There's only one government-approved source of marijuana for scientific research in this country, and that just isn't adequate."

Professor Craker filed an application to the DEA for permission to grow marijuana for legal research in June of 2001. In 2007, DEA Administrative Law Judge Mary Ellen Bittner recommended that he be granted this request, saying it "would be in the public interest." In her exhaustive report, Bittner recounted instances in which the NIDA road blocked access to marijuana for scientific studies approved by the FDA, and that "there is currently an inadequate supply of marijuana available for research purposes." DEA Deputy Administrator Michele Leonhart must now accept or reject Bittner's recommendation in order to grant Craker permission to grow marijuana for research— though there is no deadline for this decision. The matter is as yet unconcluded.

Recently, Stephen Dubner's *Freakonomics* blog for *The New York Times* printed thoughts—both for and against the legalization of marijuana—from accomplished government agents, professors and researchers. The panel ended with a rather sobering statement from author Richard Lawrence Miller: "There is no debate, merely theater. Discussing drug policy is like discussing gun control or abortion: facts are irrelevant." Tom corroborates, saying, "Especially over the last few years, there has been overwhelming research published on the benefits of marijuana. Irrefutable evidence shows that there are numerous conditions in which marijuana provides relief more efficiently than traditional pharmaceuticals."

Names have been changed.

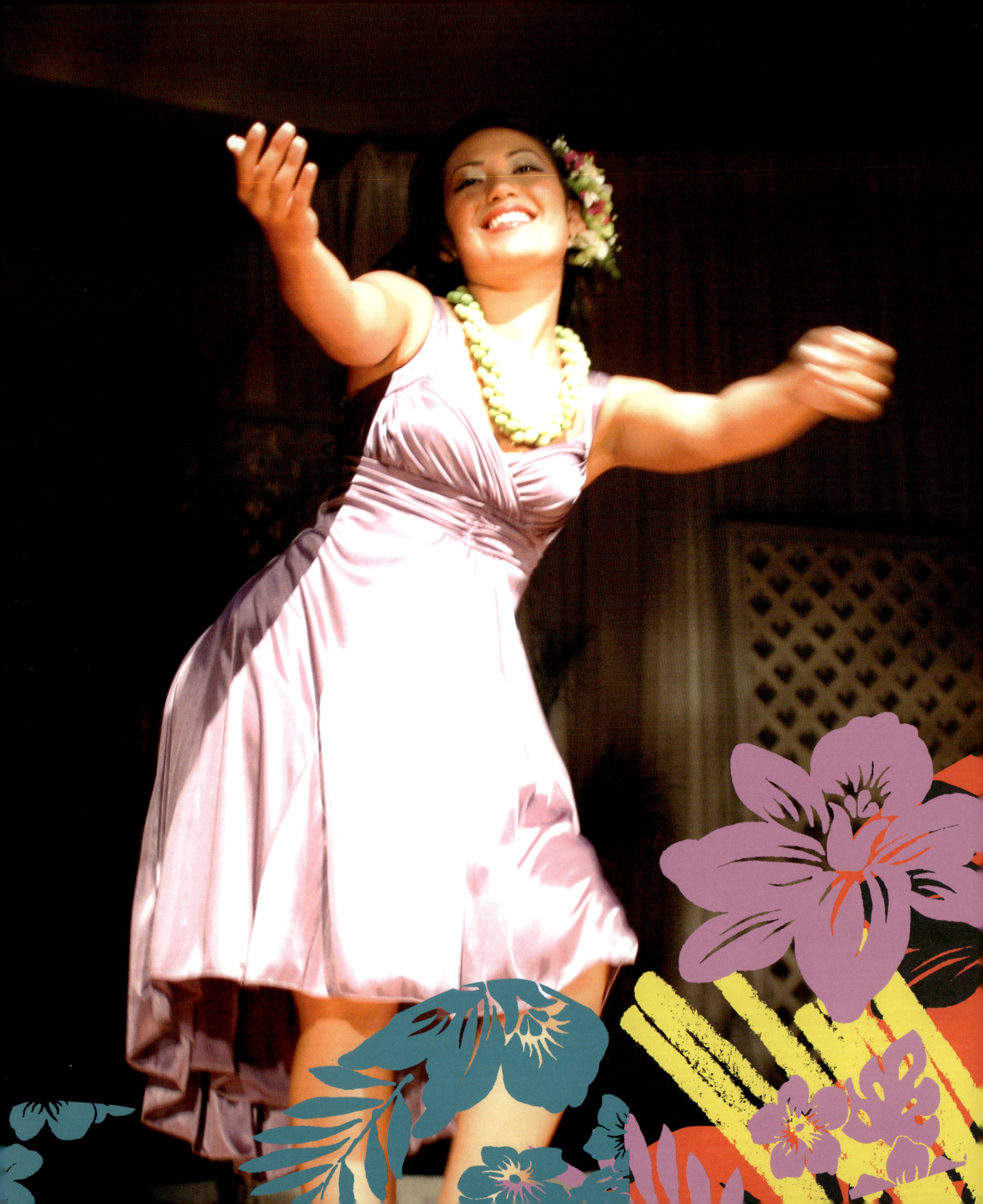

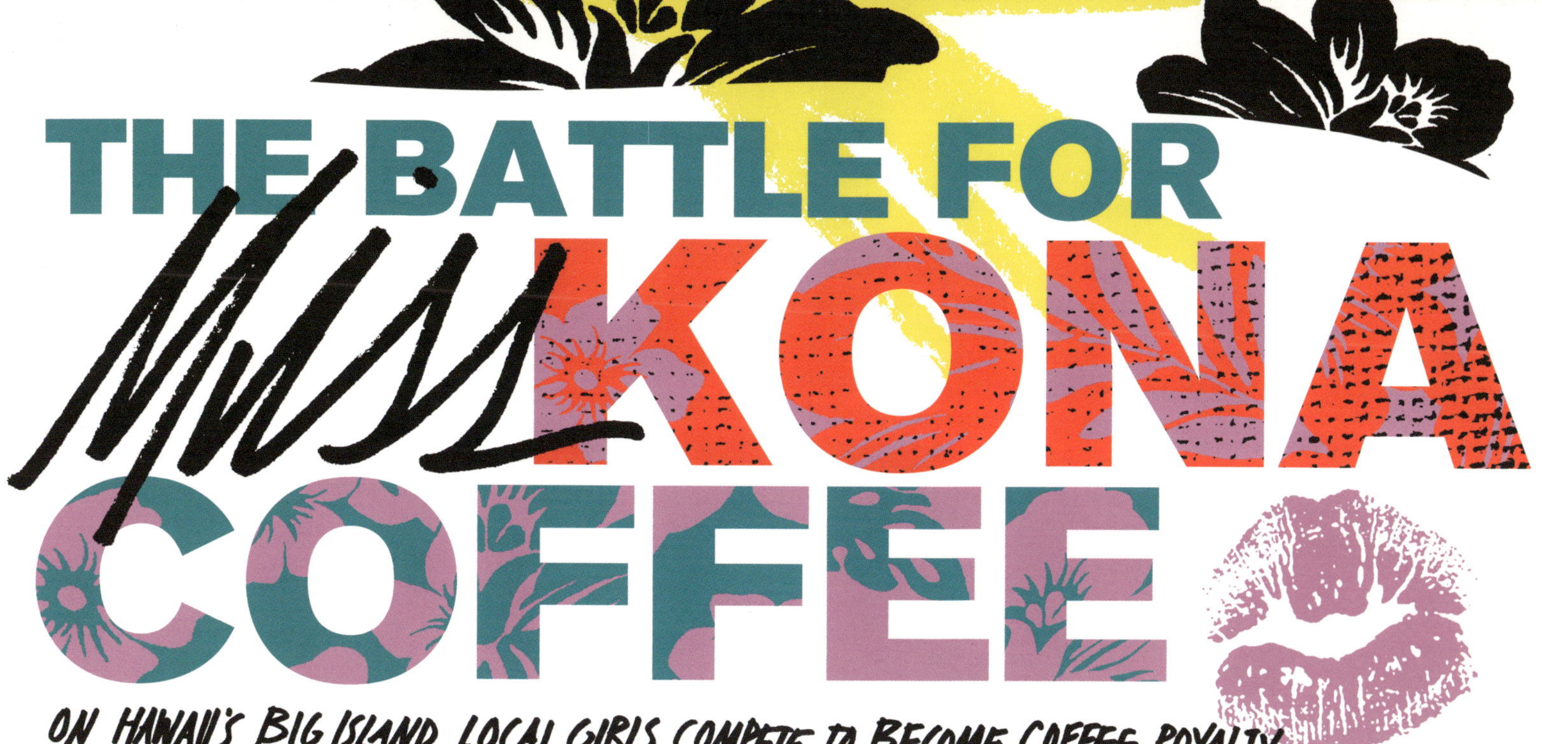

TEXT AND PHOTOS BY MAILE CANNON / ILLUSTRATION BY DAMIEN CORRELL

THE GIRLS SPARKLE. THEIR HAIR IS PULLED, CURLED, SPRAYED, PILED, TEASED, TUCKED, TWISTED AND PINNED. THEIR EYELIDS SHINE WITH COLORFUL EYE SHADOW THICK ENOUGH TO SMEAR ON BREAD. THEIR LIPS ARE SLICK AND FULL. RHINESTONES DANGLE AND FLASH. EVENING GOWNS, FULL OF SATIN, VELVET, RIBBONS, RUFFLES, BEADS AND SEQUINS SWEEP ALONG THE STAGE. ANYTHING THAT MIGHT SLIP TO REVEAL TOO MUCH SKIN HAS BEEN FIRMLY GLUED INTO PLACE.

The girls are all smiles—showing off their brilliant, perfect white teeth. Each girl is the best they have ever been. They are just a dozen belly-sucked-in breaths away from knowing *who* they will be.

To get to Miss America, one must first be "Miss" of their own state. To be the "Miss" of a state, one must first be "Miss" of a smaller region. On the Big Island of Hawaii, the only way to compete for Miss Hawaii—and then get a shot at Miss America—is to first be crowned Miss Kona Coffee.

"Miss Kona Coffee is poised and intelligent," explains Auntie Grace, a Hawaiian grandmother with an impressive shock of salt-and-pepper hair, who has run the pageant on and off since its inception 37 years ago. "She is not only beautiful, but talented and articulate. We are a scholarship pageant, not just a beauty pageant." The queen must also know a thing, or two, about Kona coffee. Part of her job description is to be the Hawaiian spokesmodel for the Ueshima Coffee Company, the pageant's official sponsor. Miss Kona Coffee tours Japan at least once for the company.

The Kona Coffee Pageant is a family affair. Auntie Grace's daughter, Priscilla, once held the title. She still does her part by choreographing the show's dance numbers, which inevitably involve ensembles of local performers, students from the public middle school, and her own children, Zion, 8, and Ruby, 6. Daveyann, Priscilla's sister, organizes hair, costumes and makeup. A third sister, Lori, coaches the girls in elocution.

Every Saturday, the contestants meet in Auntie Grace's home studio for rehearsals. Some drive for two hours to be there, or fly in from Honolulu. The house is perched above a coffee farm. Outside the window, rows of coffee plants roll down broad, green Kona slopes and taper into the sea, that stretches out into a wide, blue horizon.

Rehearsals start five months before the pageant. The girls must learn how to pivot in big, silver heels; dance routines must be mastered; makeup application is practiced, with assistance from the local Mary Kay representative; lessons in coffee production and processing are required; and two intensive mock interviews are conducted, complete with a panel of amateur judges. Attendance is mandatory. Under the tutelage of Auntie Grace, as well as Auntie Kapina and Auntie Tracey, the girls train for the pageant. They must watch CNN, read the newspaper, practice talking in front of a mirror, participate in community service, exercise and cut back on junk food. On average, each contestant spends about $1,000 to prepare for the pageant. Participation is a serious commitment.

"I keep doing this because it's amazing to see the girls change," says Auntie Grace. Between Auntie Grace and Auntie Kapina, tens of thousands in personal funds are spent each year to keep the pageant going. "My husband would kill me if he knew how much it really was," says Auntie Kapina.

"Last year we had a girl from Kohala who didn't even have a phone in her home," says Auntie Grace. The Big Island is still rural, and the pageant can be a life changing experience for its participants. For many, it is the first time they have been asked to seriously think about a world outside of Hawaii.

Feminist worries about the exploitation of women seem to never be an issue for the contestants. Many participants say they feel empowered by the pageant. Money for college, a trip to Japan and a pile of prizes donated by the community, are worthy rewards. The girls have grown up isolated from the rest of the U.S., separated from the mainland by miles of ocean. But the pageant can springboard contestants into bigger and better opportunities beyond the Big Island. Pretty, blonde Marina Terwilliger, who took the crown in 2001, landed a modeling contract in Japan, and then relocated to New York. Ironman triathlete-cum-model Lokelani McMichael held the title in 1999. In 1992, Carolyn Sapp became the first Miss Hawaii ever to be crowned Miss America, and she, too, got her start as Miss Kona Coffee.

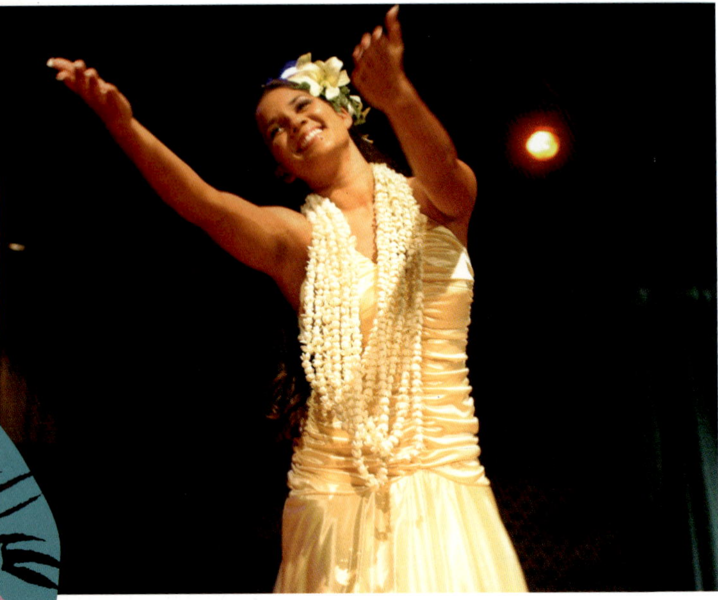

There are eight girls competing for the title of Miss Kona Coffee 2008: Anuhea, who is planning to become a massage therapist; Mary Brittainy, who is named for her mother's favorite country, England; Bianca, who speaks Tagalog at home with her mother; Leianna, a future lawyer and daughter of a well-known artist and yoga teacher; Ku'ulika, a soccer-playing student of Hawaiian language and culture; Malia, a business major; Amanda, who started pre-med studies at 16; and Alizabeth, a semi-professional hula dancer and the only sister of eight older half brothers.

If you pull down the pageant backdrops of golden sunsets, swaying palm trees, flower leis and grass skirts, what is left is small town America, complete with Wal-Mart, drug problems and big city dreams. Peel back the layers of foundation and lipstick, remove the swimsuit competitions, the smiles, the gowns and well-rehearsed answers to the world's toughest problems, and you will find the real Miss Kona Coffee—and the true story of Hawaii.

BIANCA 18
KAILUA-KONA

I've heard about Miss Kona Coffee since I was a little girl. When I saw her at the parade, my mom told me, "That's Miss Kona Coffee!" and she was wearing a crown like a princess. I wanted to be like a princess, too!

In the future, I want to have my own salon, or do an apprenticeship, or have my own preschool. I'd teach Hawaiian studies, here on the Big Island. Or somewhere else in Hawaii. But I'd also teach them to be patient and say "please" and "thank you" and common good qualities. Children are one of my passions. And the other is cosmetology. I love the art of makeup and hair styling. And then, I love photography.

LEIANNA 17
WAIMEA

I'm always busy. I'm a part-time student, I work and I do this pageant. I dance four times a week. I'm preparing for college and taking classes for the SATs. I want to go to school in southern California; there's a lot to do there, but it's still beach-like. But first, I'm going to go to UH [University of Hawaii] Manoa in Honolulu for a year. That's so I'll be close to my mom, but still in a different place. I've lived in the same town my whole life. I think moving straight from here to a place like Santa Barbara might be a bit too much for an island girl.

In elementary school, and middle school, a lot of people called me haole [Caucasian, usually derogatory], but I always got along with all the local girls and boys. It's only when people got mad, that's when they would say it. I got offended and it made me feel bad, but I've never had any serious trouble. And even I say haole sometimes, when talking about tourists driving around!

AMANDA 17
KAILUA-KONA

We came to Kona when I was 9, on vacation. Then my mom spent a year online, figuring out a way for us to move here. And we did. First we lived in Kohala, in Kapa'au [a very small town on the island's northernmost tip]. Then we came to Kona. But I'm a city girl. I like the lights!

I started pageantry when I was 10. I love it. It's like my hobby. I've done the Miss Cinderella Princess, Miss Hawaiian Tropic, Pacific Island Princess and Miss American Starlet. I get a natural high from doing pageants and I make good friends. My favorite part is the interview portion.

ANUHEA 21
WAIMEA

I thought that pageants were just nothing. I was such a tomboy! But actually, these girls are very intelligent, and it's not all about looks. Learning this made me feel so, so superficial. I had only seen the surface of it. Like Sandra Bullock in *Miss Congeniality*. Pageants are nothing like the way they are perceived. They are so much more than just being pretty girls.

I really want to further my education and stop this loop of just going to work and paying the bills and going to work and paying the bills. I want more out of life than just the basic things. I like learning and this [pageant] can open up so many opportunities.

MALIA 23
KAILUA-KONA

The first time I ran for Miss Kona Coffee, I got 2nd runner up. I didn't feel really prepared, though, and I thought it would be kind of cool to do it again. That was four years ago and I'm 23 already, so it's the last year I'm eligible to run! I think that you have to be what the judges want you to be. I think that when they judge, they are thinking about who would do well in Miss Hawaii, and then Miss America. Auntie Kapina said that my bikini was too skimpy, but like, by only half an inch. I chose it because I saw Miss Hawaii wear one like it, and in the end I said that I didn't want to change it. Auntie Grace said that it was OK. She said she saw something like it at Miss Hawaii, too.

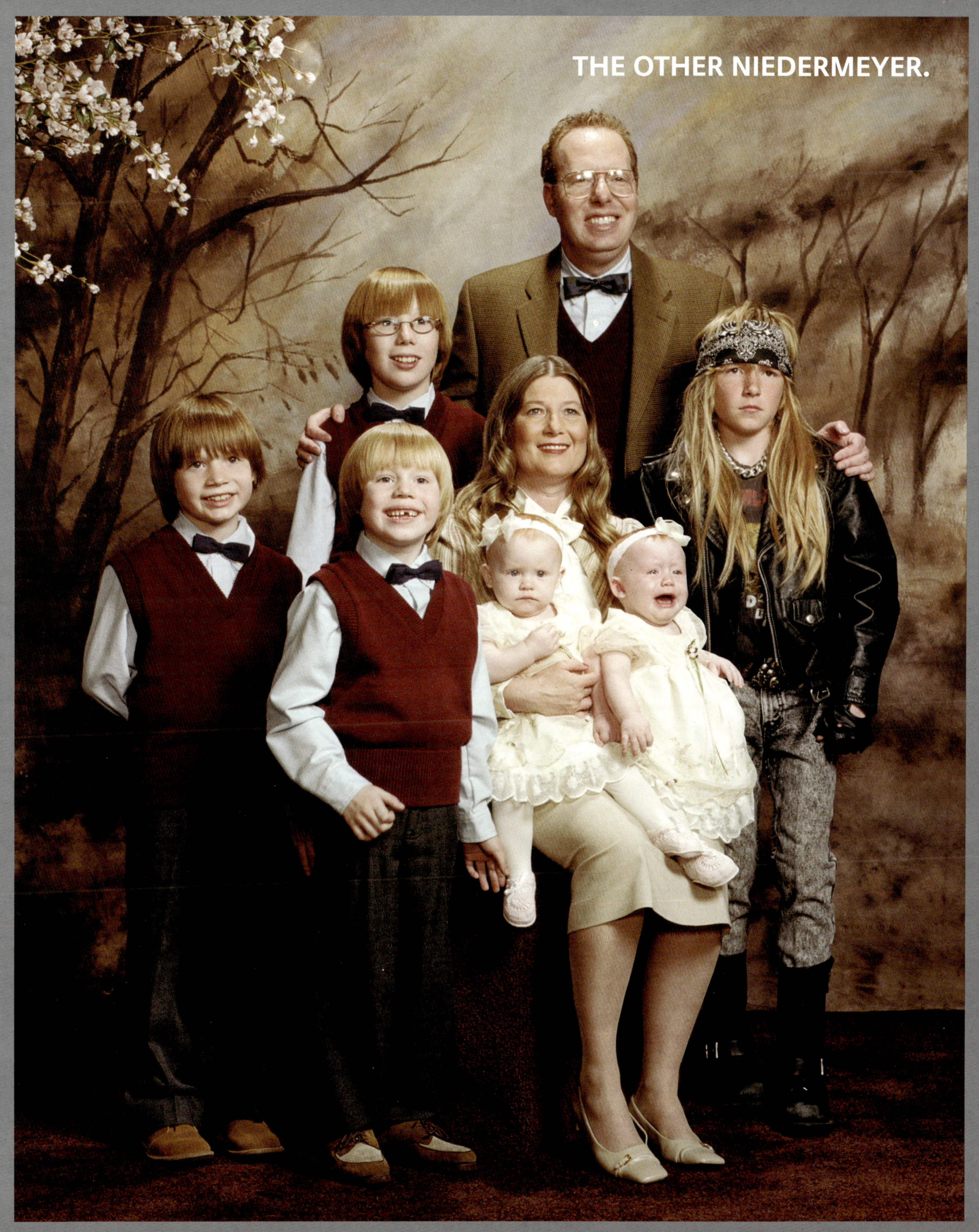

THE OTHER NIEDERMEYER.

I've been to Australia, New Zealand, Tahiti and Spain. Traveling really changes the way you look at things. You realize that in Kona, you're in this bubble. I do love Kona, and eventually, I'll want to live here. It's sad to see all the development. Part of me likes it, but at the same time, you miss the old times. We have lots of new shops and restaurants [including Bubba Gump, Hard Rock Café, and Hooters, all on the town's main ocean-front] and more people. Everything is so expensive now—prices for houses are so high! You don't see local people in town anymore. They're hiding. Things have changed and you realize that the people who grow up here might not be able to call this "home" in the future.

ALIZABETH 22
PAHOA

Pahoa is a small town, and now there are lots of hippies living in the bushes there. My brothers like to go hunting and they always see them. Everyone knows that we have a good welfare system in Hawaii, so people come out here, get a post office box and get on welfare, and they live well.

I graduated from Pahoa High School. It's kind of a rough school. There were about 100 people in my class, and there were a lot of drugs. Everyone is on ice [crystal methamphetamine] in Hawaii—it's a big problem. I don't really know what makes them start taking drugs. I guess they are unhappy. I'm pretty happy. Well, I'm either in denial, or I'm just a very happy person. So far, I've spent about $5,000 for this pageant, but $3,000 of that was for [100] tickets. I have a big family and I want them here to support me. Everyone I know works two or three jobs and is just paying bills, living paycheck to paycheck. Plus, they're in Hilo and they have to come over [to see the pageant], and that's if they have a car that can make it! I'm a caregiver and usually work the 6 p.m. to 9 a.m. shift, and sometimes I'll work 23-hour shifts. Before that I worked 9 to 5 ripping tickets in the movie theatre.

MARY BRITTANY 17
KAILUA-KONA

Both of my parents are from Oahu. My dad is a professional slack-key guitarist and my mom danced hula with the Royal Hawaiian Band. She was cousins with IZ [the popular Hawaiian musician Israel Kamawiwo'ole who died in 1997], and they went all over the world touring. I've never been outside the country, but I have been to the mainland twice.

"Miss Kona Coffee is poised and intelligent. She is not only beautiful, but talented and articulate. We are a scholarship pageant, not just a beauty pageant."

I want to be a good role model for my baby cousin in foster care. I haven't seen her in three years, and I hear she's very kolohe [naughty]. If I were Miss Kona Coffee, maybe she'd see me on TV. Or even at Miss Hawaii. And she'd want to do what I do.

KU'ULIKA 21
KA'U

My [social] platform [a required element for all contestants] is Hawaiian culture education. Our culture is basically disappearing and we need to step up the game. Other cultures are brought into Hawaii and we adapt to them, so our culture gets lost. I'm Hawaiian, so I'm responsible for keeping it alive. The Hawaiian language is not used enough. Most people don't use it at all. I'm fluent in it, and that's because I've studied it. But my little brother has gone to an immersion school.

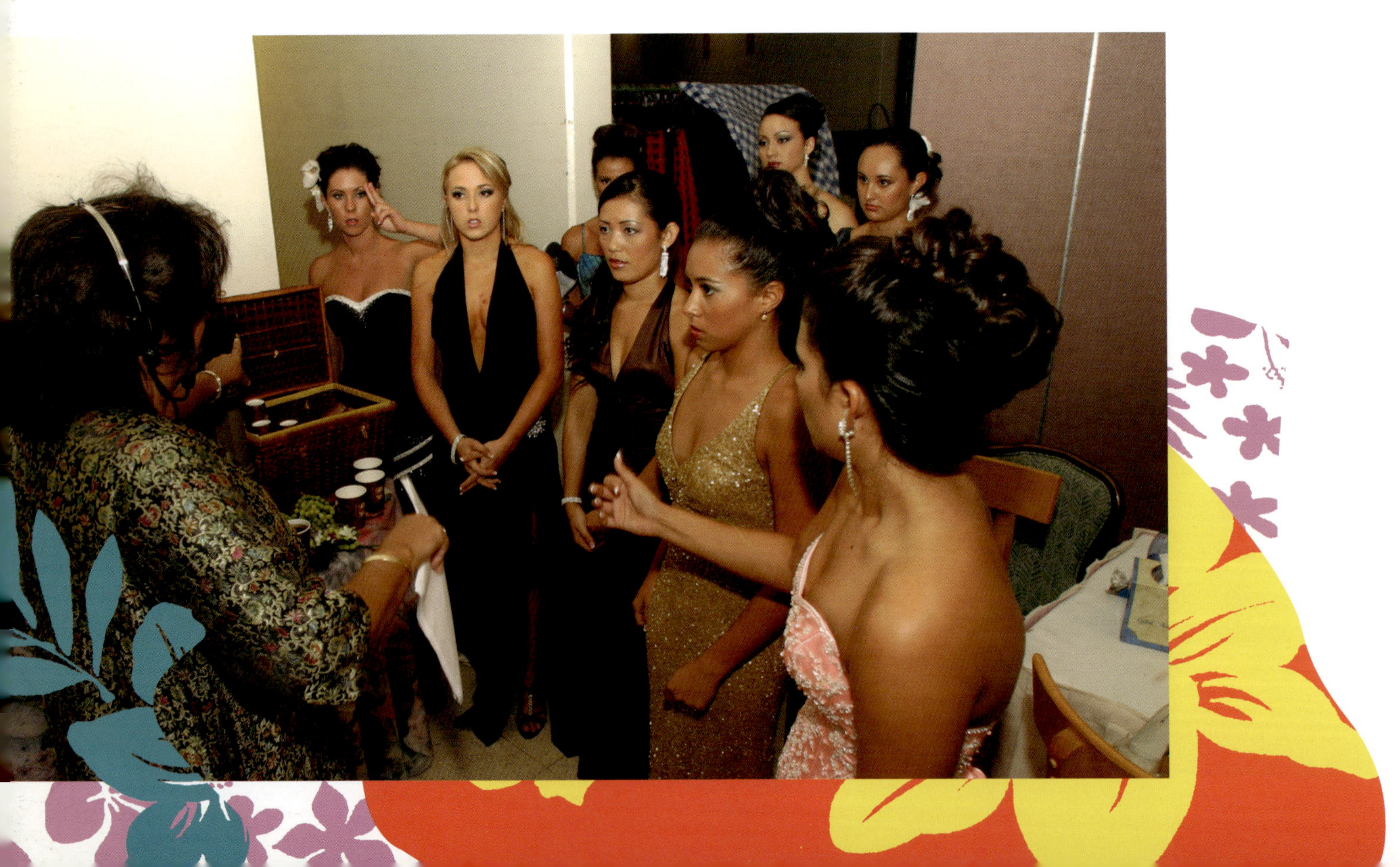

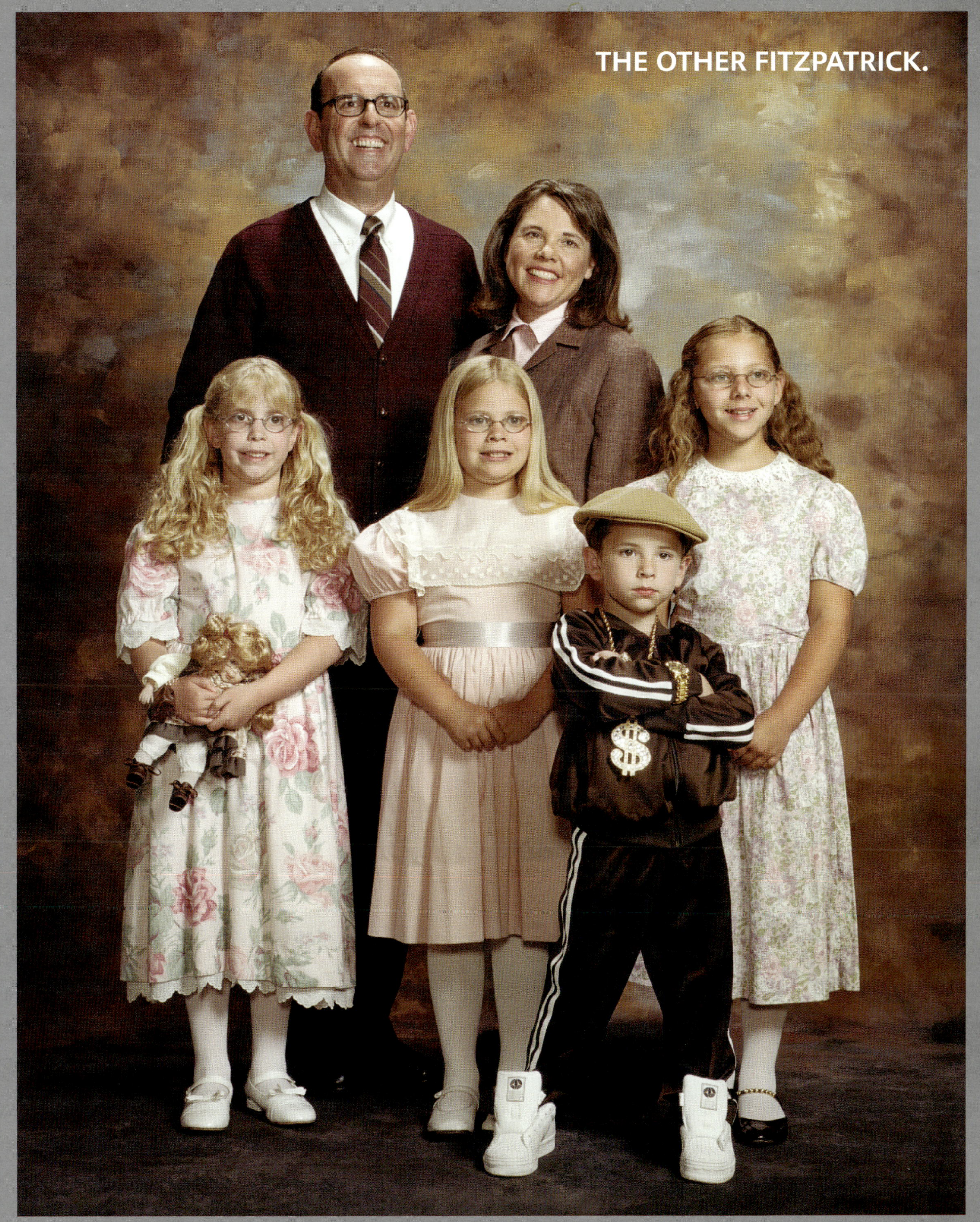

THE OTHER FITZPATRICK.

The lights are hot, the crowd is silent and skin is aglow with tiny beads of sweat—non-icky queenly sweat, of course. With just a few words, it will all be over; no more rehearsals, no more dieting, no more critiques, no more shopping for a bikini top that lifts in just the right place. Saturdays at Auntie Grace's will become a cause for nostalgia, rather than burden, and the heavy gowns and once-worn dresses will be covered in plastic and slipped into the back of the closet—there aren't many reasons for sequins in Hawaii.

Names are called. Third-runner up. Second-runner up. First runner-up. The remaining contestants clutch each other's hands. Their smiles are tired, but firm. Then, Malia wins the crown.

www.konacoffeefest.com

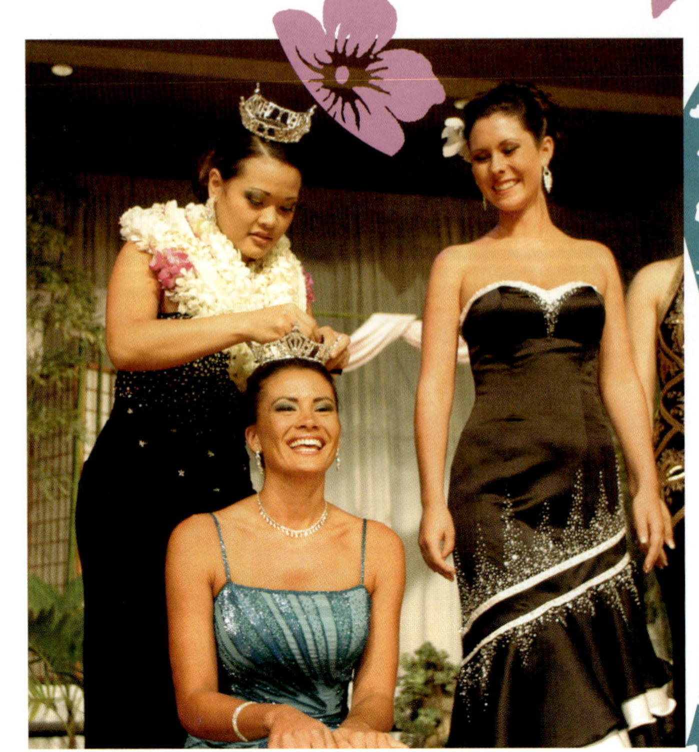

Photo by Regina Tode

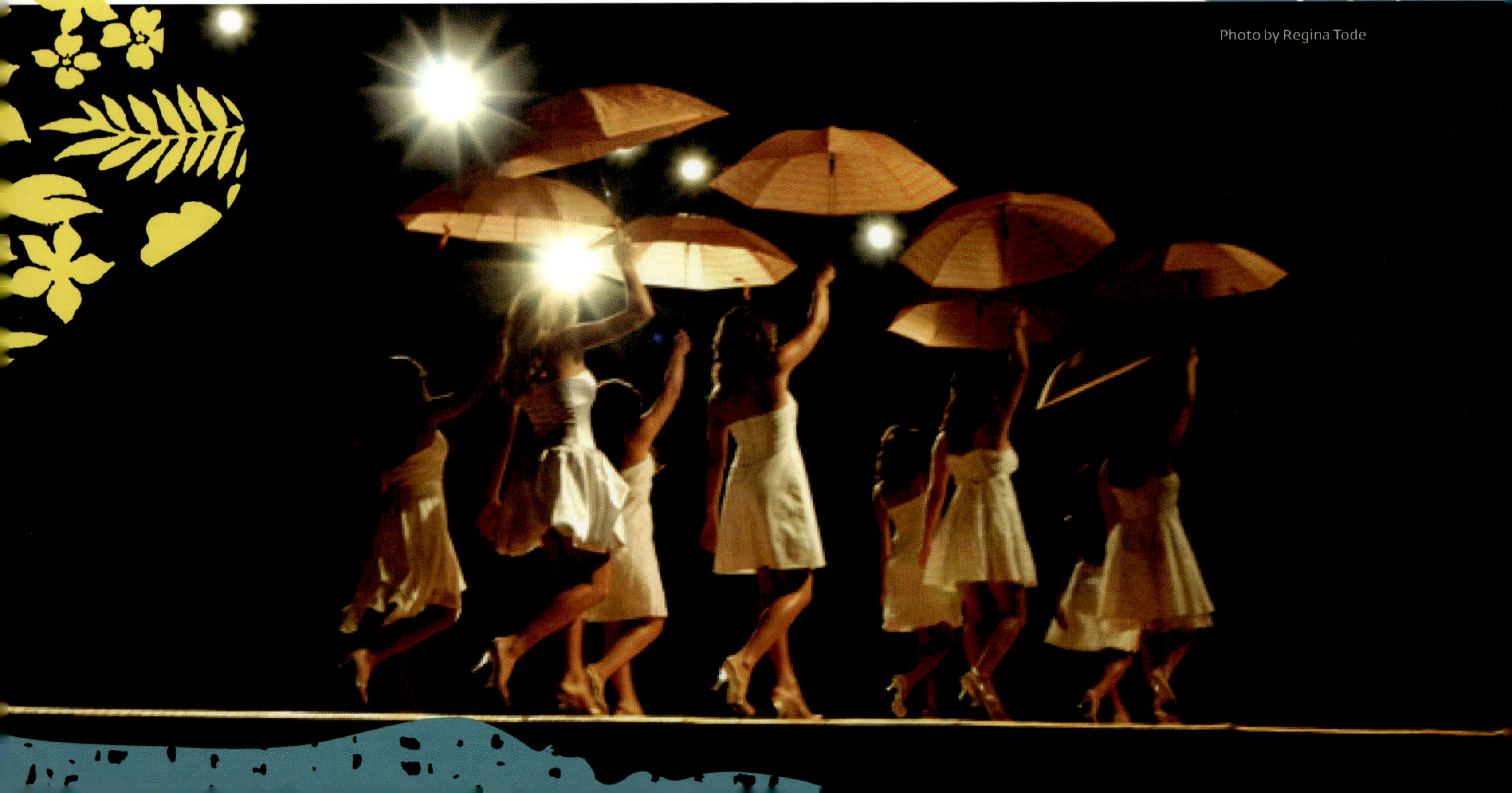

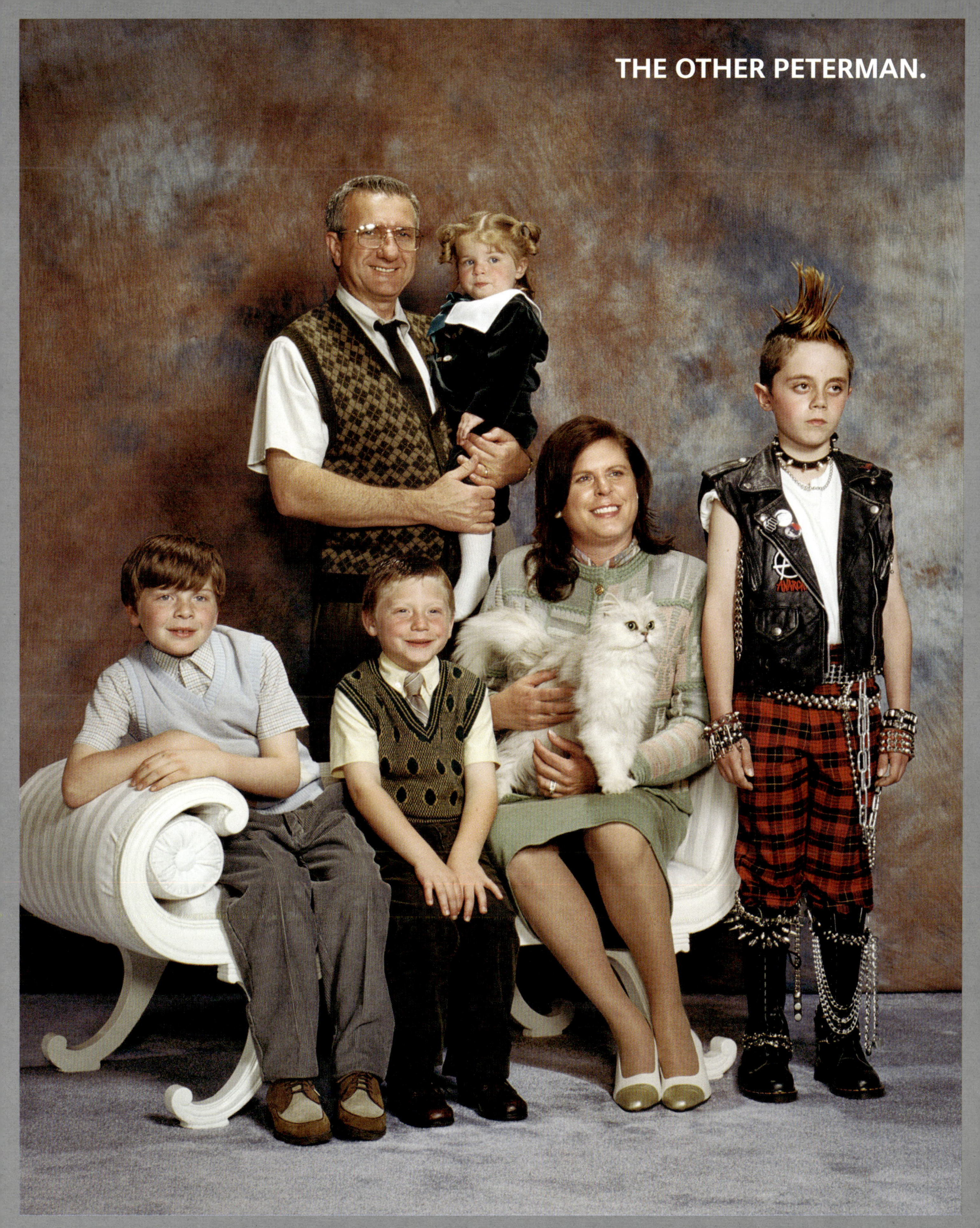
THE OTHER PETERMAN.

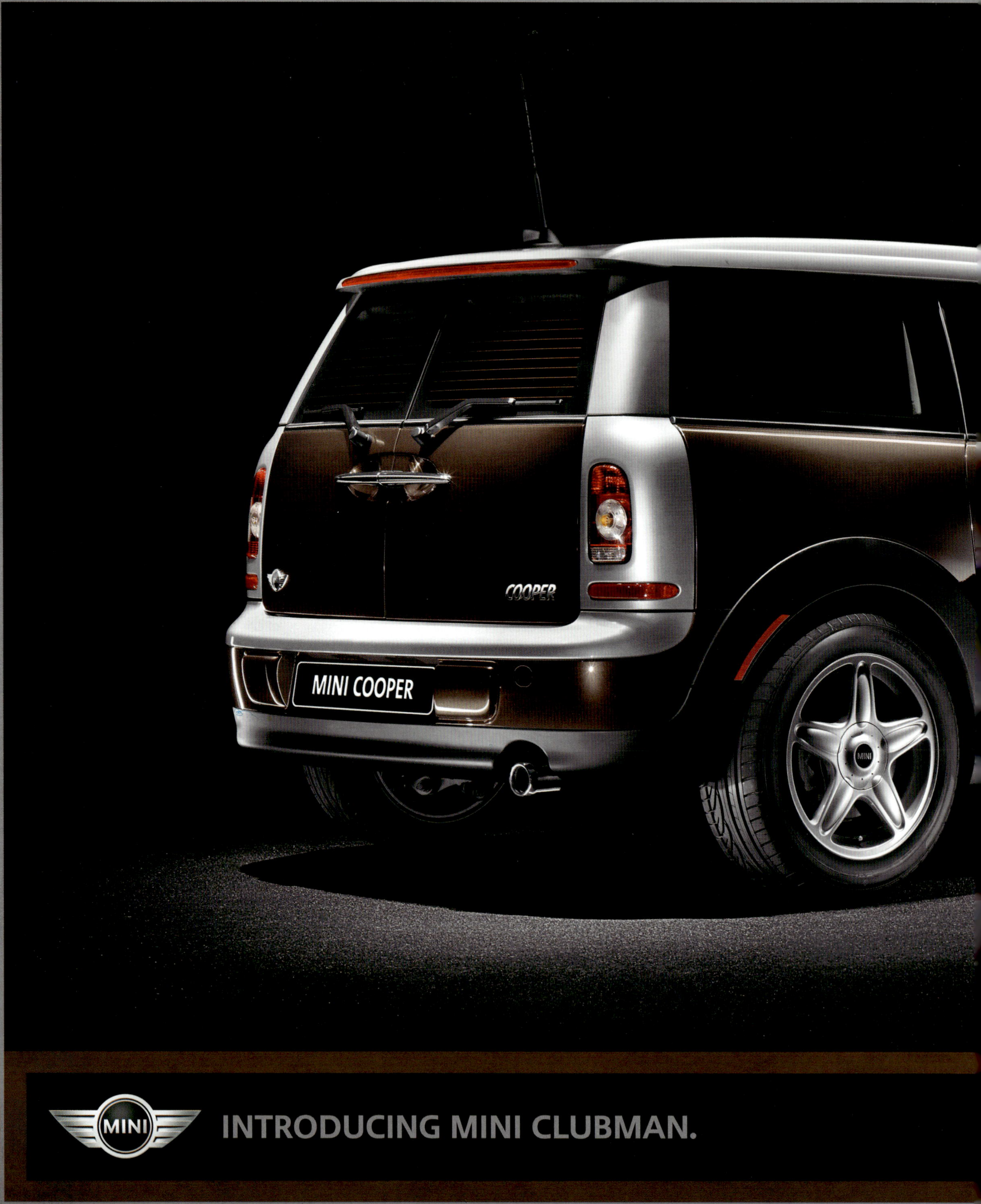

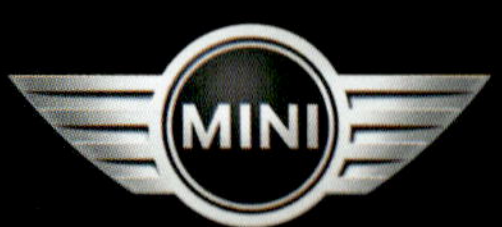

INTRODUCING MINI CLUBMAN.

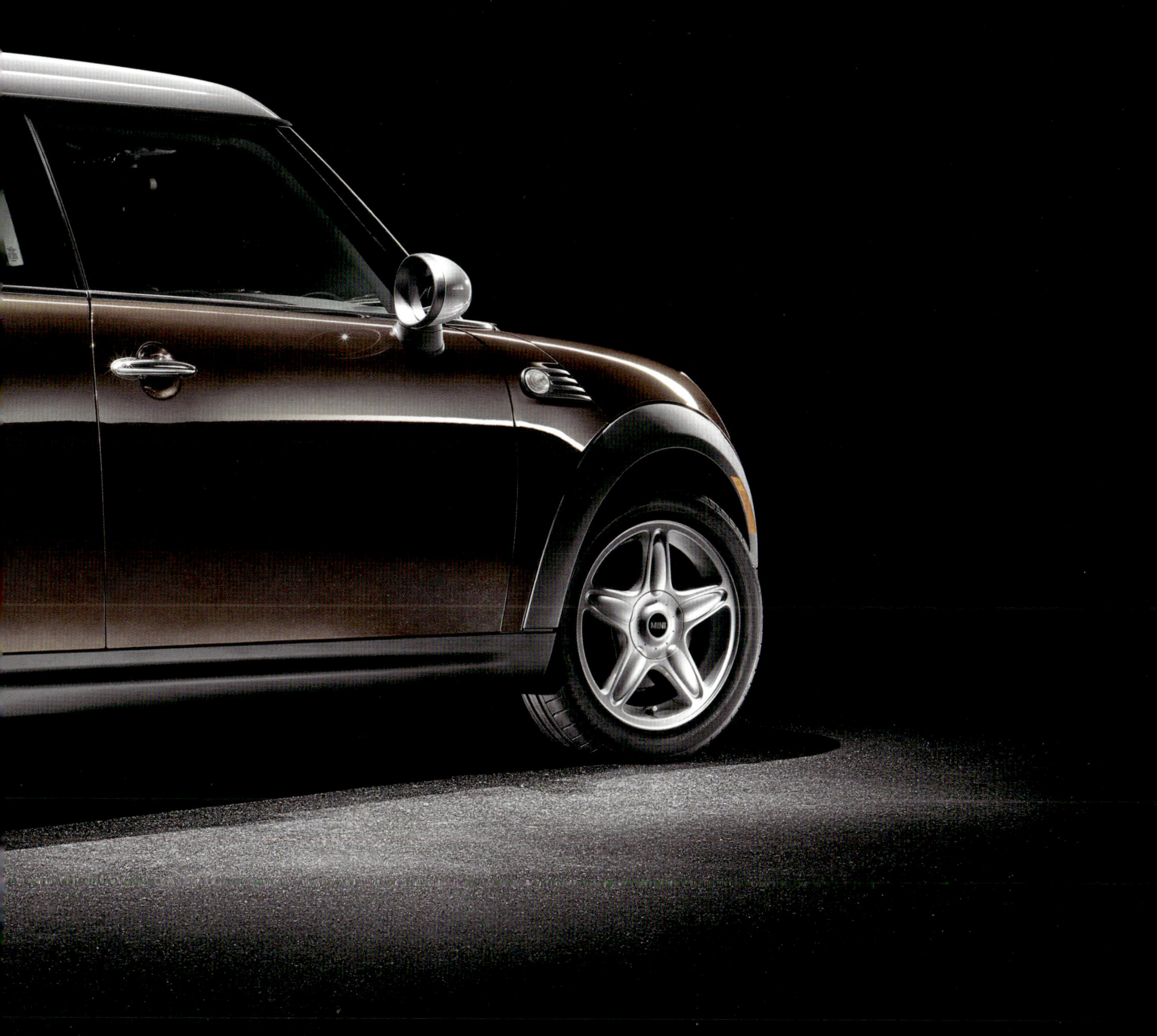

THE OTHER MINI.
MINIUSA.COM
© 2008 MINI, a division of BMW of North America, LLC. The MINI name, model names and logo are registered trademarks.

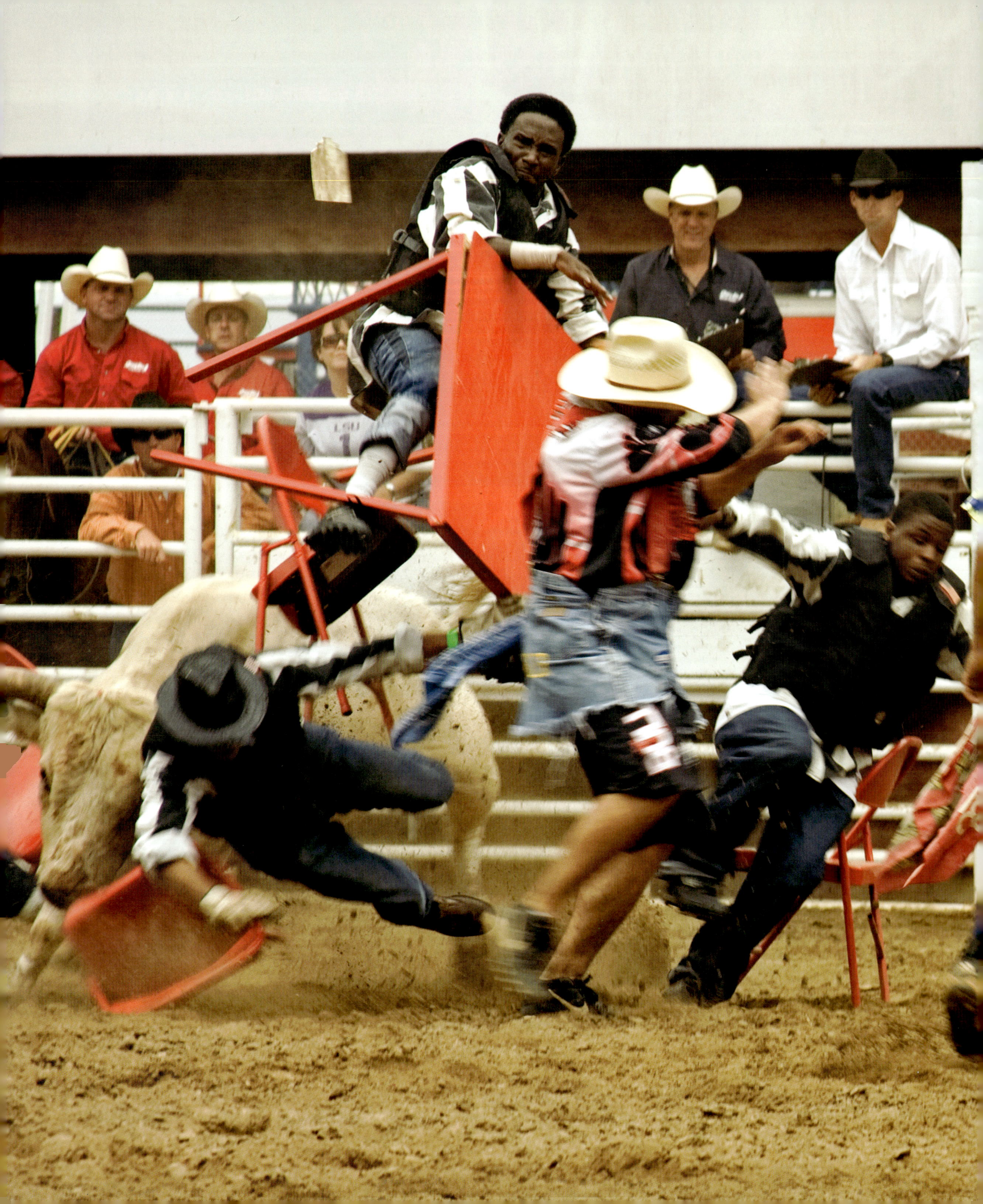

TEXT AND PHOTOS BY TREVOR SNAPP
ILLUSTRATION BY TIM GOUGH

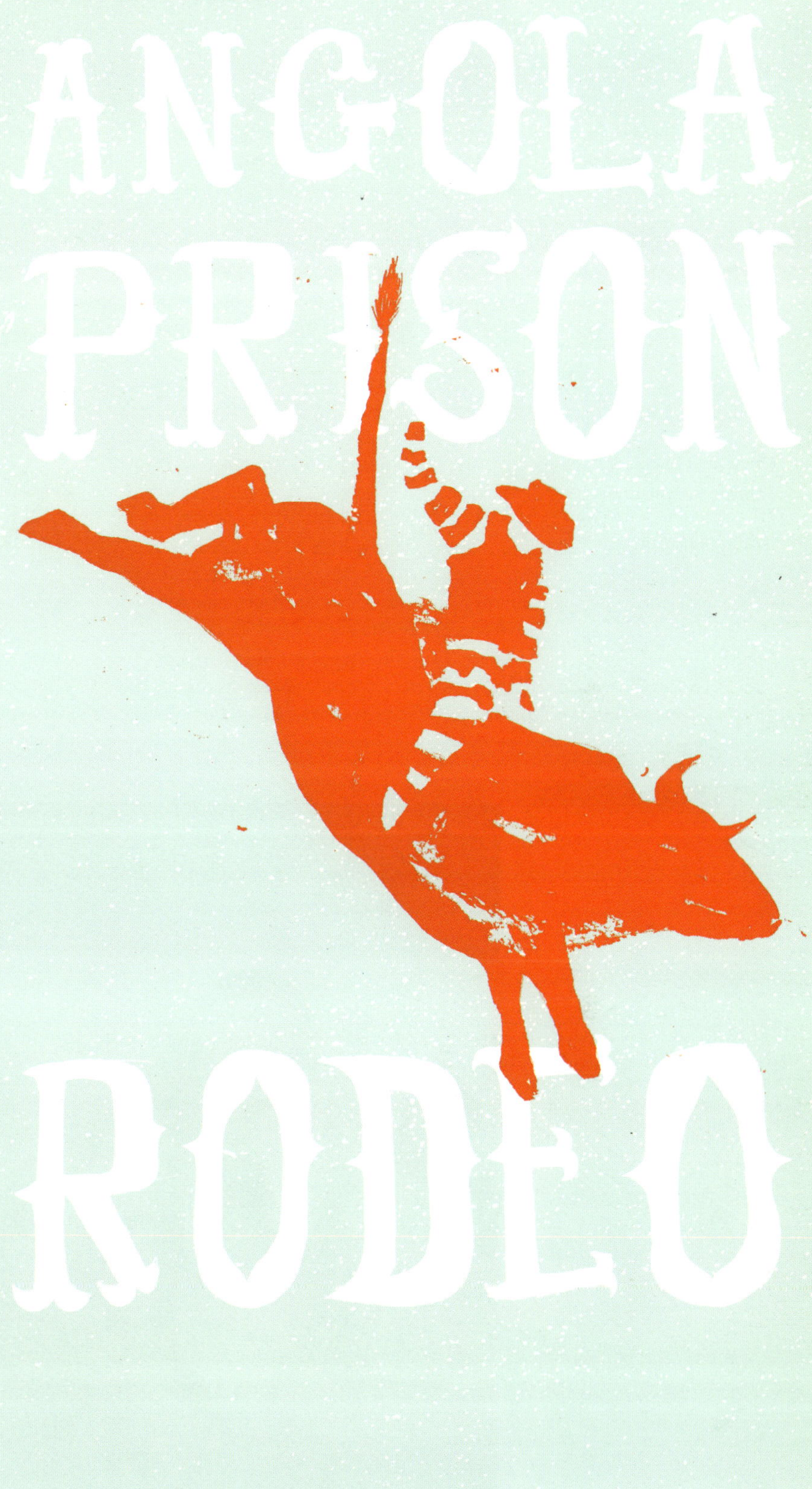

James Blackburn's 54-year-old eyes are a soft muddled blue, his face grizzly, and his mouth sunken around a rack of fake teeth. Dust covers the black-and-white stripes of his shirt, which has "Angola Prison Rodeo" stamped on the back. What did he do to get into Angola, Louisiana's infamous prison for lifers? "Murder," he spits out, followed by a rambling explanation involving a girlfriend getting smart, her lover and her lover's bowie knife. Blackburn's wandering eyes drift into focus and lock me in a long stare. "I took his knife," he says, "but gave it right back to him."

Angola prison is the nickname of the Louisiana State Penitentiary, one of the largest prisons in the U.S. The prison rodeo began in 1965. According to the program guide, "It wasn't much in those days… just staged for the entertainment of prisoners and employees. But it was fun." So much fun that four years later an arena was built to hold the growing public interest in watching criminals getting gored by two-ton bulls. Today, the spectacle has grown to accommodate a crowd of 10,000. Just like 30 years ago, the audience is overwhelmingly White, and the inmates overwhelmingly Black.

The dust on Blackburn's prison stripes comes from riding wild bulls, something he has gotten very good at over the last decade—but not without a cost. "I got my teeth knocked, my shoulder and a bunch of bones broken, lost consciousness a number of times," he says. A senior medic at the prison says, "Most of what we get we call trauma—broken back, concussions, loss of consciousness, loss of wind. Today someone got their tongue cut out by a horse's hoof."

The rodeo opens with a tremendous wail of a horn. Two angels strapped to the top of horses careen into the arena. They are followed by a brigade of evangelical cowboy knights who gallop around the ring carrying flags, bearing phrases like "Jesus is King," "King of Kings" and "He is Here." The music swells and a baby-faced cowboy Jesus enters, brandishing a medieval sword. He lines up the squadron to charge. The crowd roars and Jesus slashes his sword through the rising clouds of dust as they storm back through the entrance. The Christian warriors are followed by the Angola Rough Riders, the only inmates in the rodeo who have any skill with stock. As they canter in circles, two of the African American riders wave Confederate flags. It is hard not to think of the prison's past life as a slave plantation and wonder just how far we have come.

And this is where the moral confusion begins. According to a paper by Anthropologist Melissa Schrift, "The rodeo serves as a forum for the display of animalistic [inmates] who are… subdued by a progressive penal system that… ensures captivity, control, and rehabilitation." She goes on to say that, in the rodeo, the public supports the prisoners by attending—much of the revenue from the event goes to the Inmate Welfare Fund—while the prisoners allow themselves to be pummeled and gored in a Coliseum-like cathartic moment of punishment, thus giving back to society.

The prisoners voluntarily sign up to participate in the rodeo, which offers them the free-world dreams of money, girls and 15 minutes of fame. Most importantly it gives the inmates a chance to earn status that can mean preferential treatment with their peers, guards and, in particular, the master of the prison Burl Cain.

In 1995, Burl Cain was appointed warden of Angola. During his tenure, violence decreased. In 1996 the prison recorded 346 inmate-on-inmate assaults with weapons. In 2004 there were 134. In recent years the U.S. prison industry has held up Cain's Angola as a model prison, focusing on his proclaimed desire to give the prison population of lifers the chance to build a life through work, educational opportunities and church. But mostly church. In Daniel Bergner's book *Rodeo Gods: The Quest for Redemption in Louisiana's Angola Prison*, Cain is quoted as saying, "The prisoners are like my sons." He also compared them to high school seniors.

In the '60s and '70s, Angola was notorious for a convict guard system— prisoners guarding other prisoners to cut costs—that led to obscene abuses and rampant violence. At one point the prison was known as "the bloodiest prison in the south." The convict guard system was abolished in 1972 in a nationwide wave of prison reform. The same year the rodeo agreed to follow the rules of the Professional Rodeo Cowboys Association. The rodeo has grown safer since then. But my minder was quick to state that the inmates still had no training and that the rodeo still deserved its self-described moniker as "The Wildest Show in the South."

For Cain, the rodeo is the pinnacle of his power and proof of his ability to reform the prison's population of murderers and rapists. In a press conference quoted by Schrift, Cain says, "We must give the opportunity for change, because if any are ever released, we don't want there to be any other victims behind any of the people who have done time here... The inmates know that if they were to act up and mess up and cause something to happen during the rodeo, then I wouldn't have the rodeo. And so, therefore, there's tremendous peer pressure to bring out the best behavior in everyone. We won't have any problems today. No one will try to leave, and everything's gonna be peaches."

"I SNATCHED THE BUTTON OFF THE BULL'S HEAD SO MANY TIMES THAT WHEN I CAME IN TO GET MY BUCKLE FOR BEST ALL AROUND RODEO, WARDEN CAIN SAID, 'I GOT SOMETHING ELSE FOR YOU, TERRY. AS OF NOW, YOU A CLASS A TRUSTEE.'"

As the rodeo wears on and inmates are knocked unconscious, thrown into the air and gored by a variety of farm animals, the violence starts to feel like an old cartoon show. The fat black and white prison stripes, a recent addition by Warden Cain, make it easy to disassociate from the reality as EMT's carry inmates out of the arena. But the occasional sheer terror in the eyes of an inmate facing down a 2-ton bull punctures the illusion like a knife.

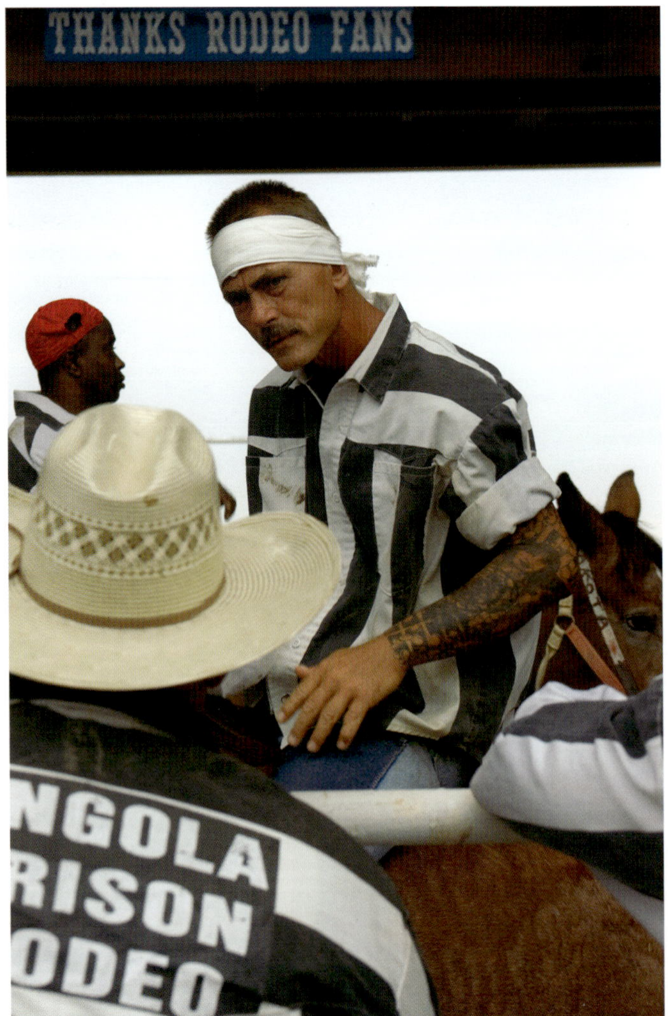

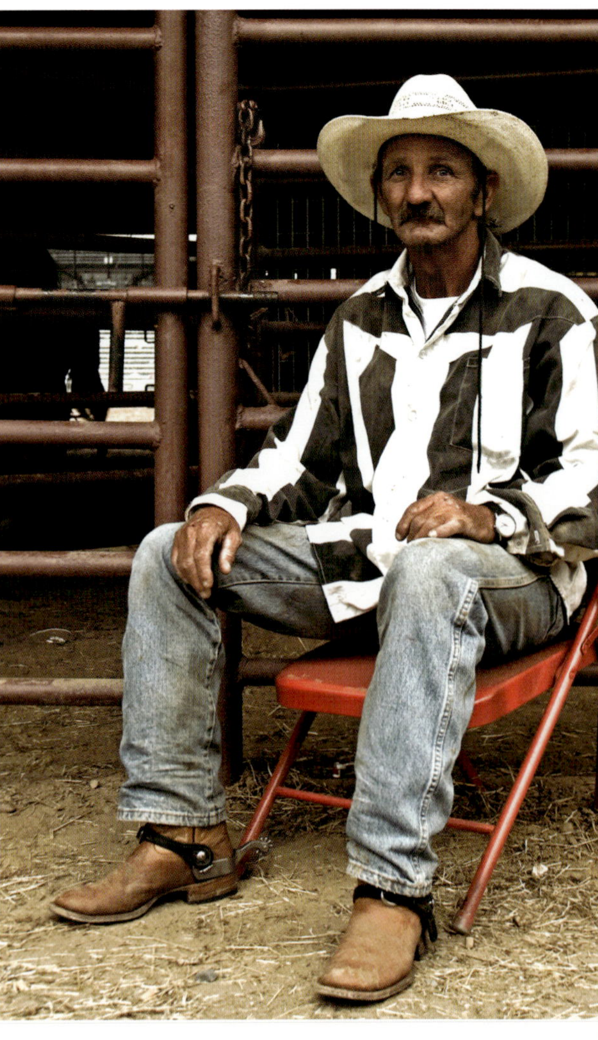

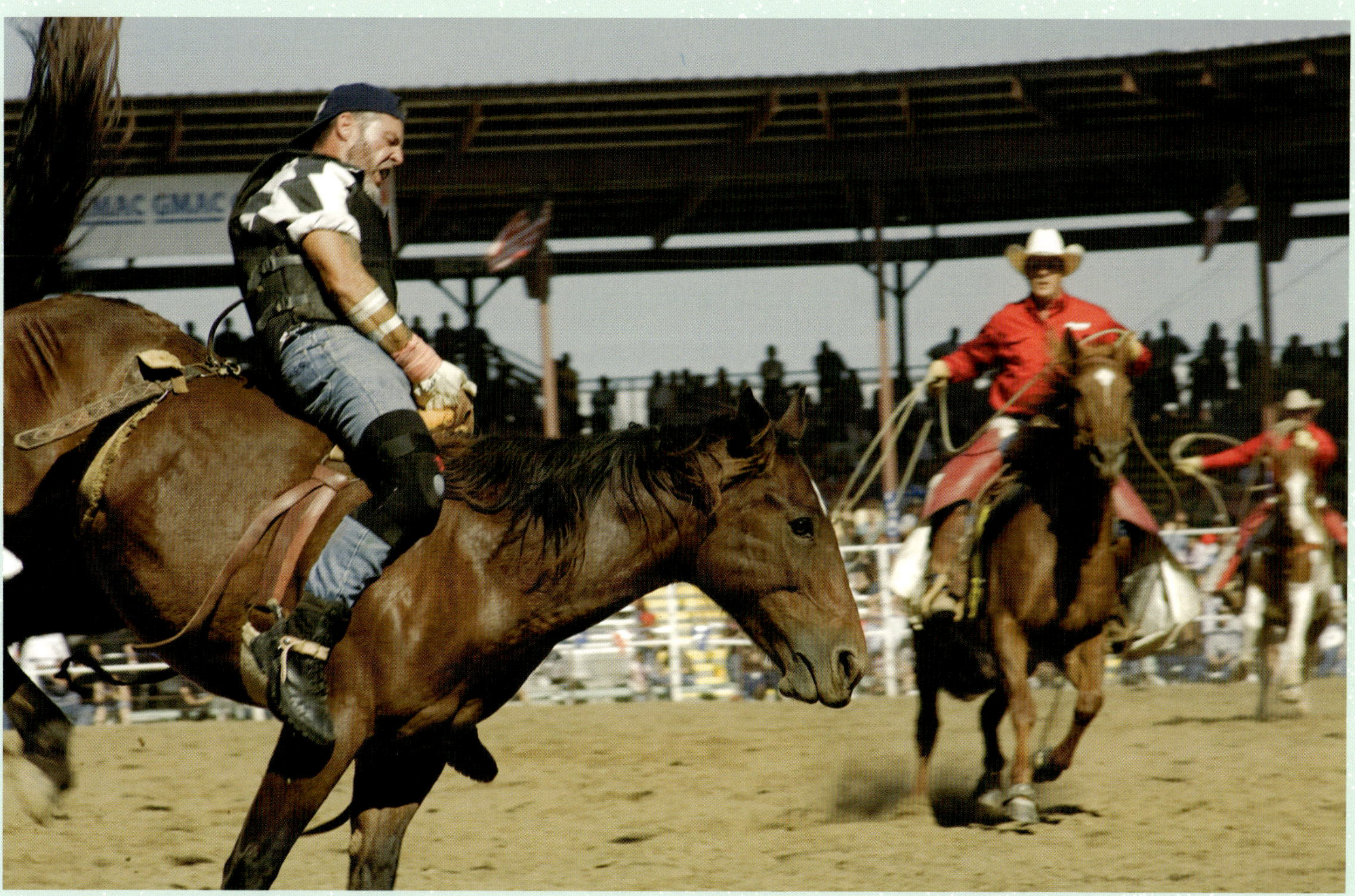

The rodeo climaxes in the Guts & Glory competition in which 15 inmates try to take a red chit from the forehead of an enormous bull. The game results in half a dozen inmates being thrown into the air, before a particularly large man manages to grab the button. The crowd cheers and he pumps his fists. He stares down at the button, writes his name on it and throws it toward the crowd, but it fails to clear the fence and lands in the dust. He has just won $500.

Terry Hawkins is a former Guts & Glory champion—he won Guts & Glory 18 times since he first began participating in the rodeo in 1994. He has been in prison since 1985 for murdering his boss—a butcher—over a racial insult. He says the prison rodeo changed his life. "I been locked up so long my people didn't come see me regular," he says after the rodeo, sitting with his family. "So I figured the only way to take care of myself was to be in the rodeo. I used to make enough money to last from one rodeo to the next rodeo, to buy my own clothes, have my little cosmetics, this and that."

The rodeo attracts a unique group of women. This is how Hawkins met his wife. They married a few years ago and have already had three kids. According to Bergner, sex between inmates and visitors isn't a right at the prison, but for well-liked prisoners, guards will turn their heads.

Hawkins has obtained Class A trustee status, which is what passes as freedom in Angola prison. It usually takes a decade to achieve at Angola, and can be revoked at any time for bad behavior. "I snatched the button off the bull's head so many times that when I came in to get my buckle for Best All Around Rodeo, [Warden Cain] said, 'I got something else for you, Terry. As of now, you a Class A trustee.' Made me trustee right there. I didn't go in front of a board or nothing, and that's what I've been ever since."

Hawkins quit in 2001. "I got my nose broke, my jaw broke, all my teeth knocked out. Riding a bull, [the] bull fell down [and] I stayed with him. When he brought his head up he hit me in my mouth, broke me all up. I quit. Yep, I give it all up." But his family and kids now come to visit him regularly and his life is as close to free as you can get in prison.

As the rodeo comes to an end, an overweight man in a blue latex suit trundles into the arena, followed by goats and four sheepdogs with monkeys tied to their backs. The dogs and monkeys herd the goats into a pen, and the man motions all the animals into the back of a new Ford F-250. The monkeys rest their heads on the shoulders of the dogs, and the man drives out of the arena as dusk settles over the prison. The crowd streams out of the stadium, and the prisoners line up to be counted, searched and led back to their cells.

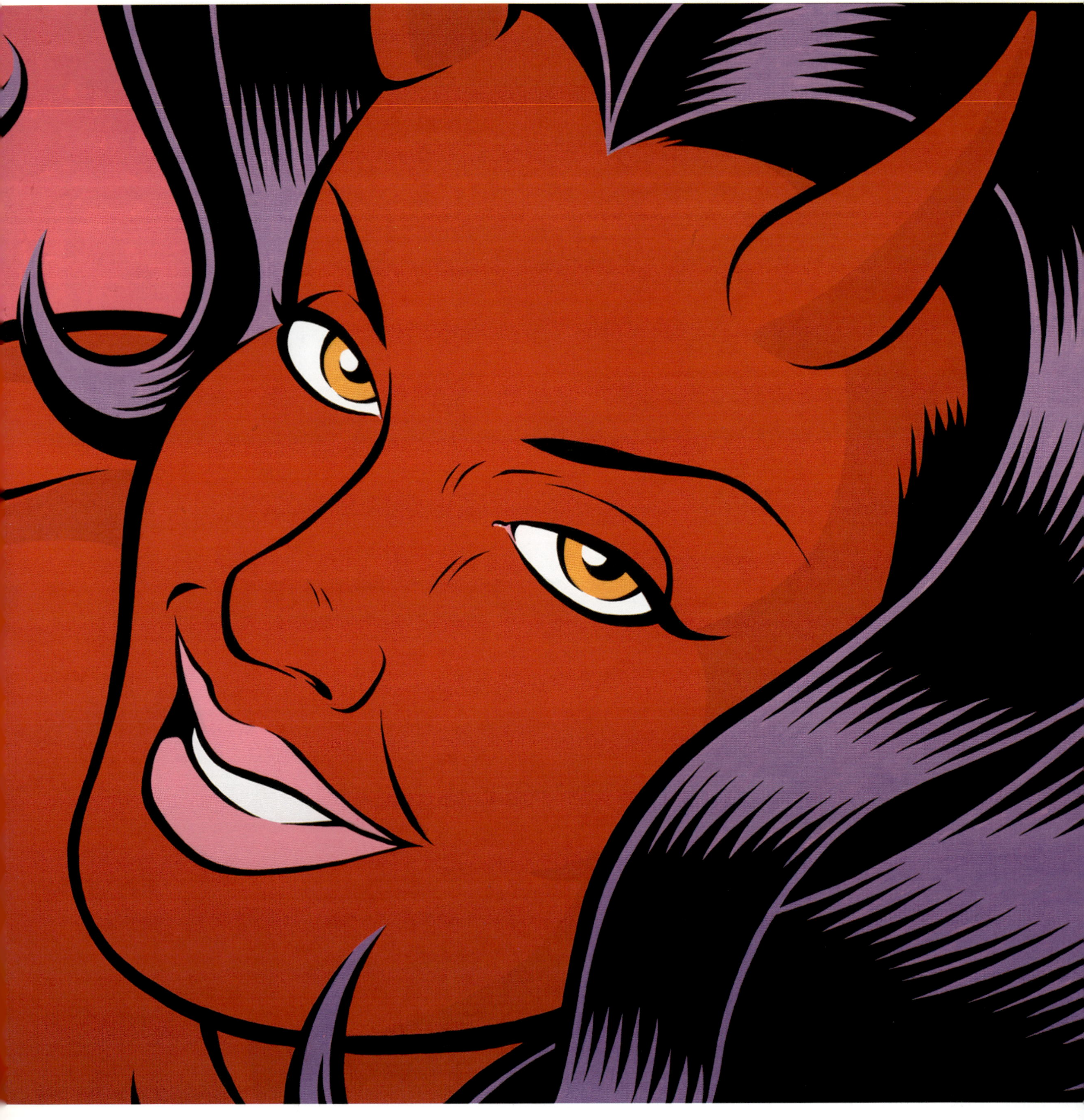

C○○P

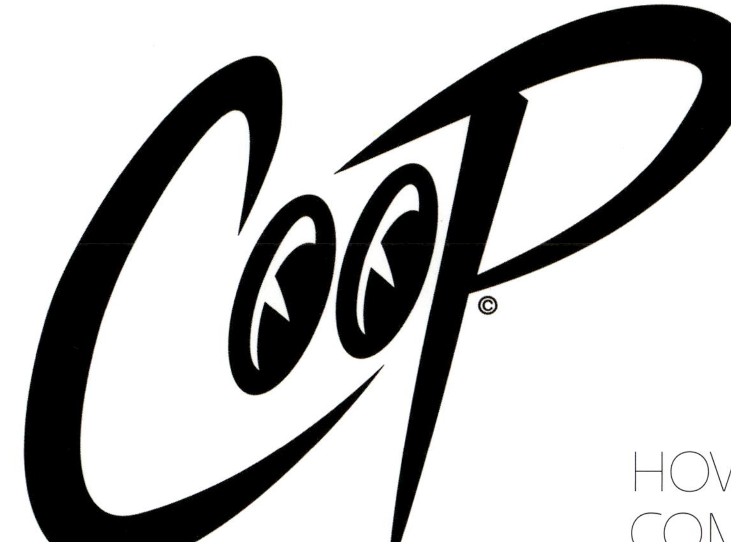

INTRO BY G. BRUNO
TEXT BY COOP, AS TOLD TO CARLOS BATTS
PORTRAIT BY CARLOS BATTS

HOW THE L.A.-BASED ARTIST COMMODIFIED KUSTOM KULTURE

COOP was born Chris Cooper in Tulsa, Oklahoma, in 1968. At 16, he made his first forays into commercial art. He designed an album cover, and got a job making an event flyer for The Flaming Lips. He says that music has been a big influence on his work; as a teenager, he hosted a local radio show that featured punk rock, rockabilly and instrumental pop. At 19, he moved to Los Angeles, where he spent the next decade working as a rock poster artist.

COOP is best known for his iconic image of a cartoonish devil smoking a cigar. Images of the devil are ubiquitous in the so-called kustom kulture—the world of American hot rods and custom vehicles. COOP appropriated this, and it became his signature image. This happened by accident: In 1993, a friend was commissioned to produce a line of Zippo lighters designed by different artists. COOP was called, and he designed the "Smoking Devil" image in less than 30 minutes. He says, "That artwork, it had a life of its own—it started finding a home everywhere."

Perhaps the most iconic image associated with kustom kulture is Ed "Big Daddy" Roth's Rat Fink character, a twisted riff on Disney's wholesome Mickey Mouse. The Rat Fink image was emblazoned on T-shirts and a myriad of other items—it became a product that people bought to represent the bubbling counterculture of the '50s and '60s. It was threatening to the mainstream, and banned in schools. The image stayed in the underground, and did not achieve large-scale commercial success until Rat Fink had a popular revitalization in the '80s and '90s, at a time when COOP creatively came of age, and the infrastructure of commercialization truly took hold. This was a time when the low-brow aesthetic began to encroach on the mainstream, and became part of the increasingly influential branding culture.

After COOP's "Smoking Devil" character appeared on the Zippo lighters, he started selling the image on T-shirts and stickers. "That's been the reason people know my work," he told *Los Angeles Alternative*, "all those devil stickers stuck in the back windows of cars… people were paying me to promote my work, essentially."

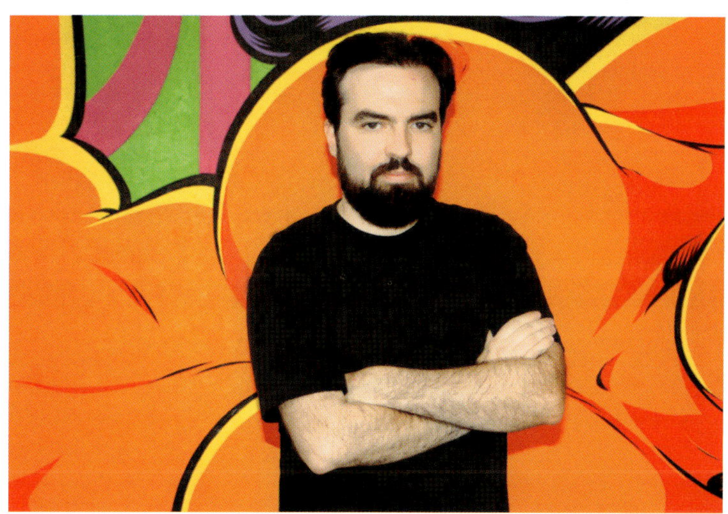

The same year he started mass marketing his creations, he began showing in galleries. His first show was at La Luz de Jesus gallery's old location on Melrose Avenue. In 2006, he held an exhibition titled Brand Recognition at sixspace in downtown Los Angeles. Sixspace billed the show as dealing "with the prevalence of corporate logos in contemporary society and how they have integrated seamlessly into our culture… Combining these easily recognizable corporate images with his own popular brand, Coop touches upon the duality of himself…"

COOP may have gone one-step further. By depicting his motifs alongside timeless logos, he not only commented on consumer culture—he exalted his art as being as commercially viable as capitalist brands like Atari and Goodyear.

COOP took time off from the gallery scene, and when he had his comeback at sixspace in 2007, it was no coincidence that he courted Nike's CEO Mark Parker to buy his entire show. While the artist sits on the fence between commercialism and fine art, he often seems to teeter on the side of corporate culture. Again, in an interview with *Los Angeles Alternative,* he said, "I guess I'm complicit in the same sort of consumer culture I'm trying to take apart." Like pop artists before him, he talks about bucking the system—while being fully embedded in it.

COOP: Everybody thinks of New York City as the nexus of the art world. But L.A. has an incredibly rich art history that people don't think about. One of the greatest artists of the 20th century is Ed Ruscha. He's lived here his whole career. There's more going on in Los Angeles than there is anywhere else in the world right now, as far as art. I think in the next five or 10 years, L.A.'s going to take its place as one of the big art cities in the world.

One of the things I love about living in L.A. is the diversity of people. I particularly love the lowrider culture. For a white kid who grew up in Oklahoma, I didn't have a lot of access to that.

[I draw voluptuous women because] that's my personal taste. You don't see those kinds of women in popular culture except as an object of ridicule. I didn't start out doing it to make a statement… I started out doing it for purely selfish reasons, but now I see that it has some value and importance.

A visual reference point is my dad's stack of *Playboy* magazines from about 1961 to 1970. Those women are great: they're curvy, voluptuous, fleshy and sexy. If you look at the other aspects of how I portray women—their hairstyles, eye makeup and clothing—it sort of reflects that era, too. The photography in those old *Playboy*'s is just so luscious and joyous. [They] have such vitality and look much better than the *Playboy*'s I see on the stands today.

If you look at what's going on in the fine art world now, a lot of artists are incorporating these ideas about mass production and merchandise into their work. And then you have people like myself and Shepard Fairey, who come out of a tradition of silk screening and doing posters, and that's all about multiples.

Before [Warhol] started painting in the first wave of pop art, he was a very successful commercial painter. For 10 years in New York, he was probably the most successful commercial illustrator in advertising and editorial. Jasper Johns and Robert Rauschenberg hated him because they saw him as stepping into their field and pushing them out of the way. A lot of the resistance I've had in the fine art world is the exact same thing. Because of the merchandise and the popular work that I've done, I've made myself very visible and very successful outside of the arena of fine art. When I go into a gallery and try to show my work in a fine art context, there is a lot of resistance, because there's still that [division] between high and low art.

The job of the artist is to engage the culture that they are in, and to reflect and comment on that culture. To not use the tools you're given—the mass media—is foolish. It limits what you can do, as an artist.

I quit showing in galleries for several years, because I felt I had been pigeonholed into this little scene—this hot rod, lowbrow scene. What finally made me come back to [galleries] was, I wanted to make a concentrated effort to do work that by its very nature couldn't be classified in [that] category. I spent about six months thinking about what I could do, how could I change my work to escape that? One of the first things I thought about was pop art. The first wave of pop artists was hugely influential on me, particularly James Rosenquist and Mel Ramos. I started thinking about the things I liked about their work, and scale was one of the things I liked.

So the first thing I decided to do for my first show back, was a big-ass painting. I wanted to do a Rosenquist-size painting like "F-111." I came up with a piece that was [made up of] 13 six-foot by six-foot panels. The piece was 78 feet long. I started looking for somebody to buy it almost as soon as I started painting it. I contacted people who I thought were very serious collectors and patrons, and presented it to them as an opportunity: "Look, I'm trying to change what I do, I'm trying to create something that is really monumental and serious. But in order for it to succeed, I need somebody to buy it. If I can get you, the collector, to commit to buying this piece at this early stage, that allows me to finish the piece, it allows the show to be a success, and you, as the collector—you are my patron. You are going to help me achieve this." [Nike CEO Mark Parker was the patron who bought the giant piece—and the entire show.]

I was very lucky. I found someone who, very early on came to see the work, liked what I was doing and made a commitment to buy the whole piece. Once that happened, I realized [that] this thing that I'm trying to do is working. After that show, painting became my primary focus. I get more satisfaction out of painting than anything else that I do. I love the process; I love all the steps that are involved in the process—from a thumbnail sketch to the final finished piece of art. There's nothing else I'd rather do. If I could just come into my studio every day and [paint] for 10 hours a day, I would be the happiest person in the world.

www.coopstuff.com

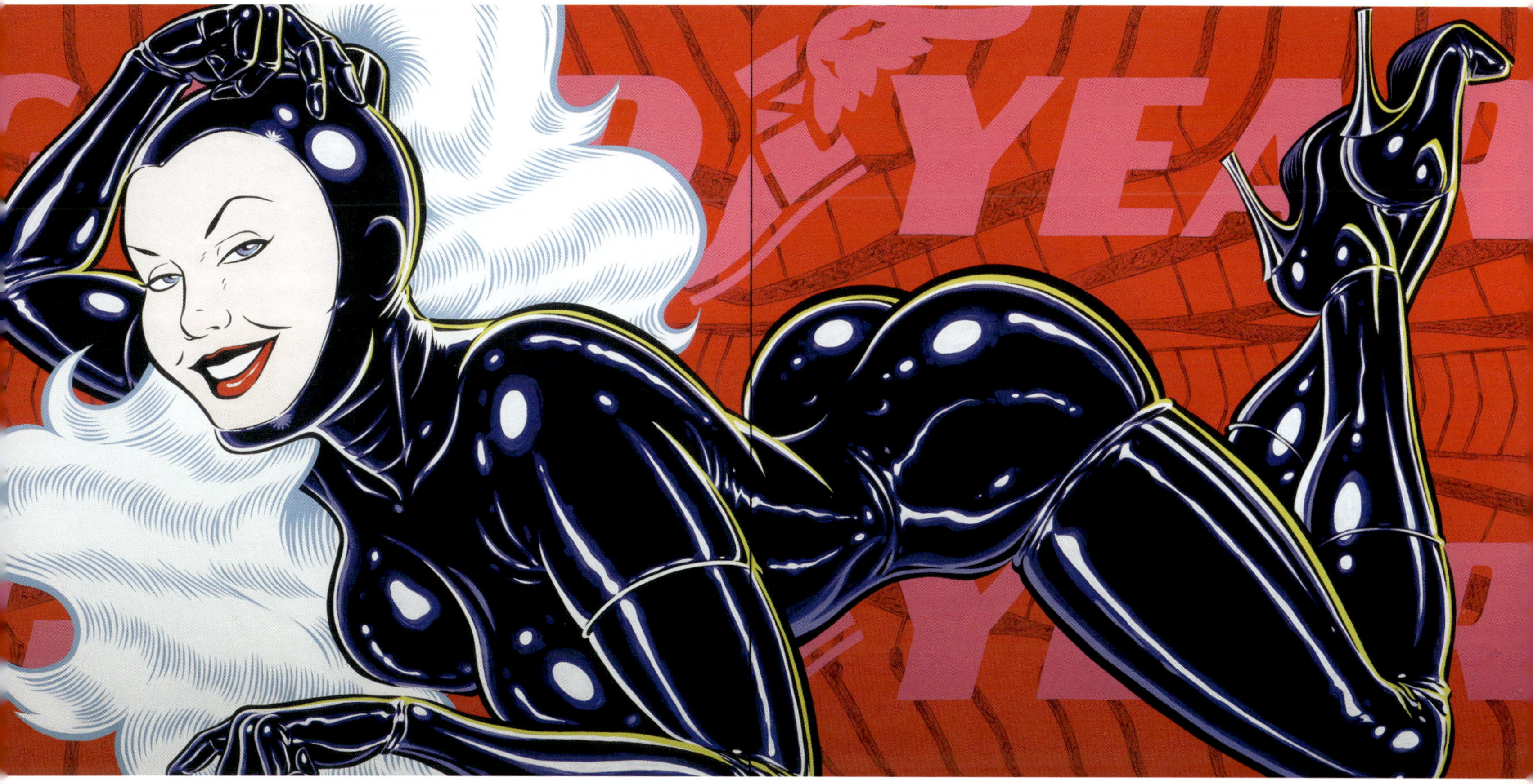

"THE JOB of THE ARTIST IS TO ENGAGE the CULTURE THAT THEY ARE IN. TO NOT USE the TOOLS YOU'RE GIVEN—the MASS MEDIA—IS FOOLISH."

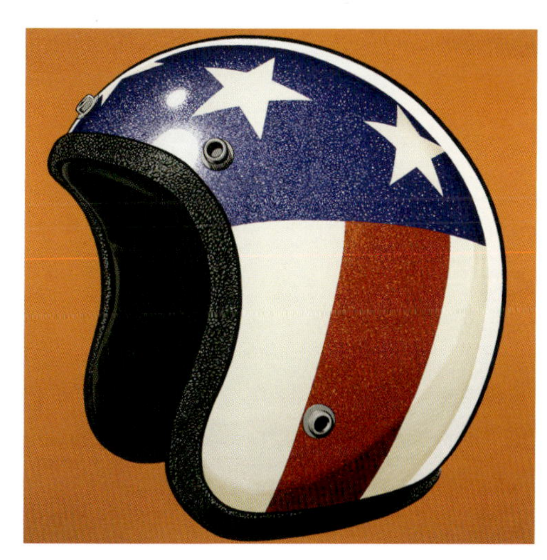

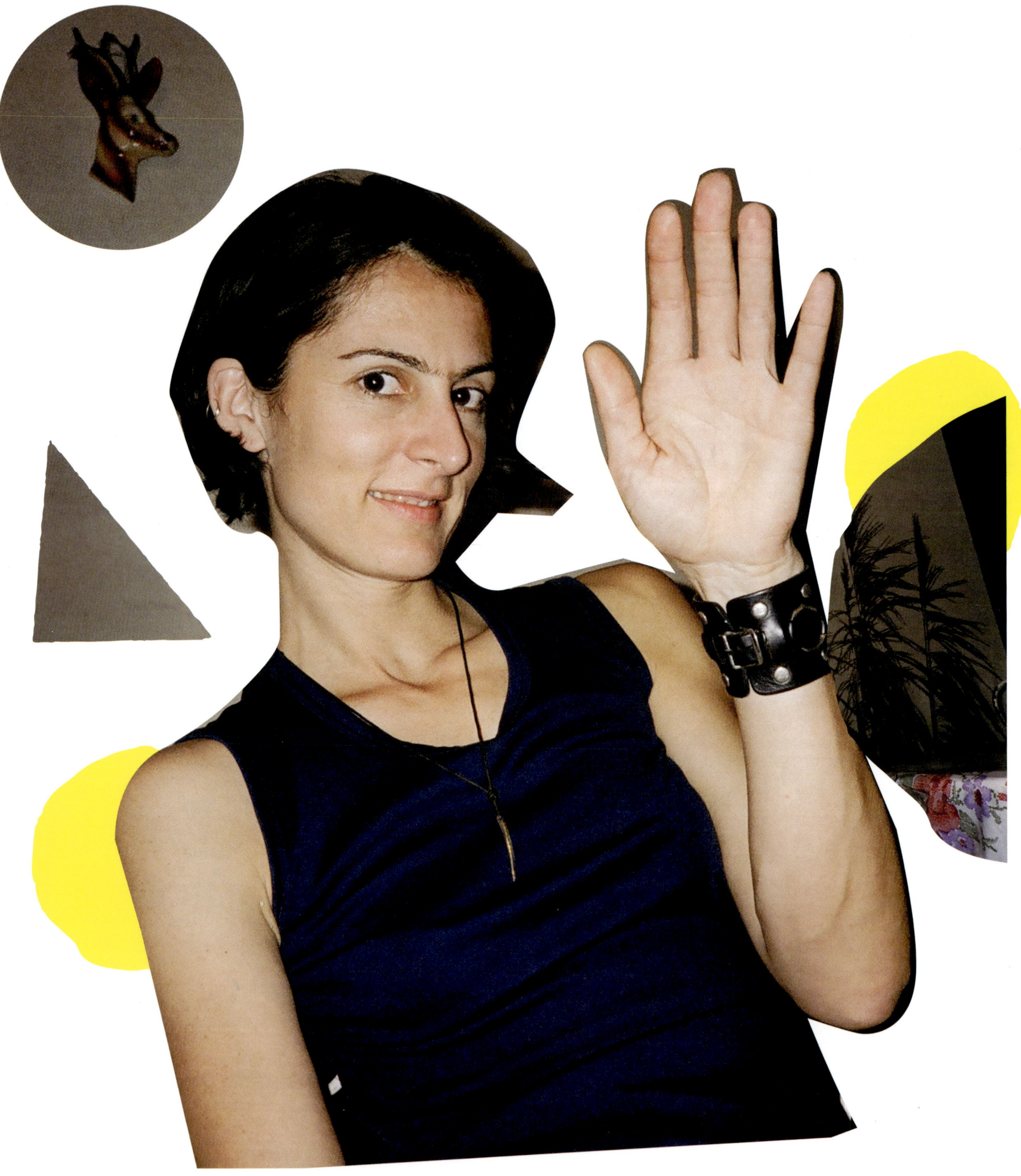

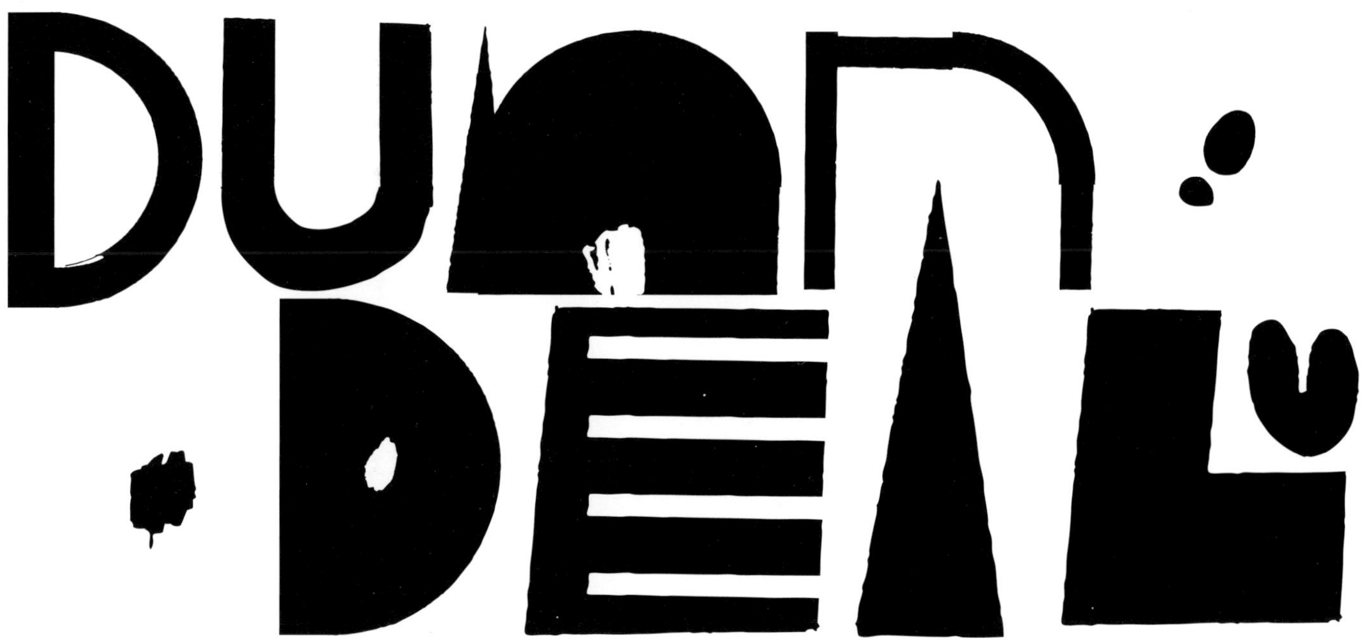

AFTER TWO DECADES OF PHOTOGRAPHING STREET ARTISTS AND URBAN LIFE, CHERYL DUNN FINDS CREATIVE REINVIGORATION FROM AN UNEXPECTED SOURCE

BY SARAH TOMLINSON
PHOTOS BY CHERYL DUNN

Manhattan-based photographer and documentary filmmaker Cheryl Dunn exalts in the kind of gritty street scenes that make tourists pull their children close and cross the street. Not because she has any desire to glorify violence or suffering, but because she sees a truth in these moments. She was recently in Hollywood, where she mounted an art show and screening to benefit her in-progress documentary about the Creative Growth Art Center, an Oakland, California based non-profit that nurtures the creativity of disabled adult artists. The nights before the opening, she saw a man receiving a lap dance in a white Hummer limo as his friends cheered on. She saw another man pawing through the gutter for a phantom rock—right in the shadow of actress Eva Longoria's chic new restaurant, Beso.

Dunn has an angular elegance and her speech is vibrant and profanity-peppered. She talks tough, because she spent most of her career hanging with the guys: her peers in the male dominated art world—many who have invited her to photograph their lives—and the streetwise boxers, graffiti writers and homeless men she has documented. She developed a deep love for New York City during her childhood in Teaneck, New Jersey. She documents the city streets, and the people who strive to leave their mark there, despite having none of the riches and connections upon which the metropolis is built.

In an interview conducted at the Los Angeles offices of her production company, HKM, Dunn says, "I think I'm drawn to really intrinsic, basic humanness. And that's one thing that's a huge thread in the Creative Growth thing, and I think 9/11. Everything else went out the window when that shit went down. It's like, who cares if the Museum of Modern Art has your painting? This could be the end of the world."

CLOCKWISE FROM TOP LEFT:
Fight Man, Las Vegas, Nevada, 1994. "At boxing fights in Vegas, I was blown away by how the fans decked themselves out. Besides the array of celebrities like Jack Nicholson, who was wearing a bright turquoise dinner jacket and fedora with a cigar—and I'm not going to begin describing MC Hammer's outfit—this guy really struck me, because he was head-to-toe tiger like a little boy."

Which Part of Purse Don't You Understand? Phuket, Thailand, 2004. "This was taken in a flea market. Even though this English may not seem to make sense, I thought it made perfect sense. Twenty days after this picture was shot, the tsunami wiped Phuket off the map. The place we stayed in got destroyed, as well as where this shot was taken."

Eviction on 57th Street, New York, New York, 2000. "The signs said this family lived there for 20 years, and the evil landlord was unduly evicting them. I loved the way the tenants used these Christmas lights to spell out their plight, and took their message to the street."

In Front of the Baby Doll, New York, New York, 1997. "This was before Giuliani's lame 'quality of life' campaign, which included the law that banned strip clubs within 200 feet of where children live. This created an exodus of strip clubs to Queens and New Jersey—where way more children live. But the media's not there, so who cares, right!"

Merqui Sosa, Atlantic City, New Jersey, 1991. "This was a classic bullshit boxing situation. This fighter went the distance and fought his heart out. He won hands down, but the decision went with the other guy, because he would be a bigger box office draw."

Artist Dan Miller at Creative Growth Art Center Oakland, California, 2006. "This picture of Dan, with beautiful top light that streams into the studio, represents, to me, the magic and the depths of creative energy emoting from these artists and this place."

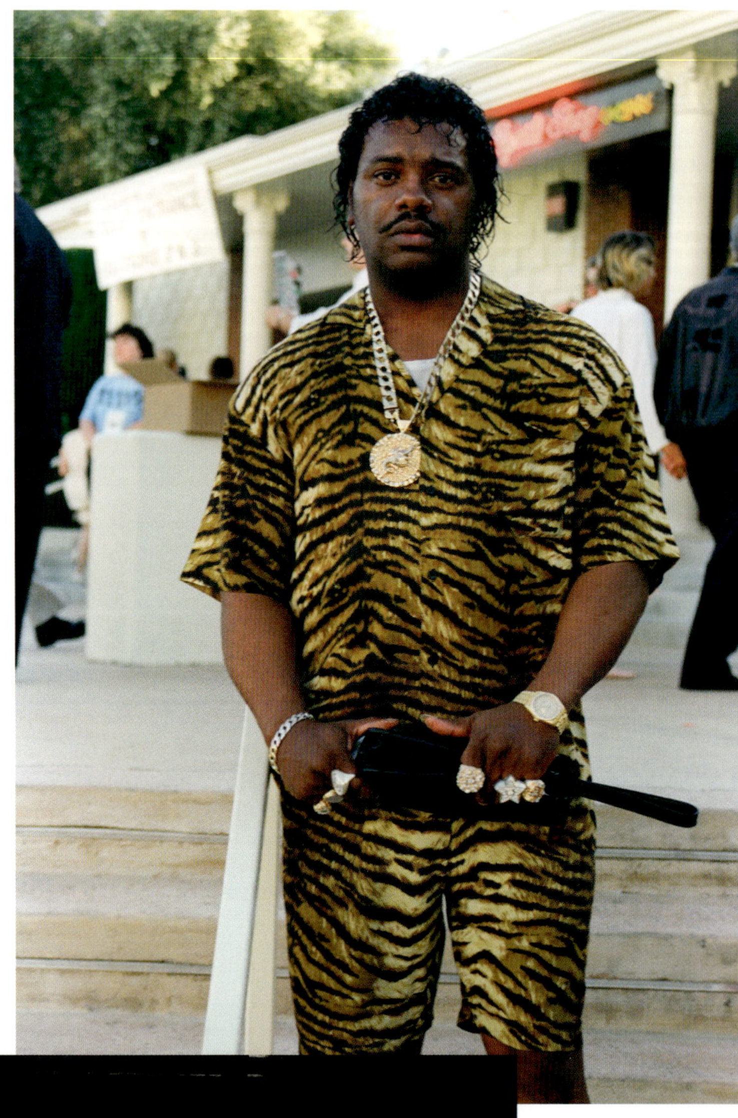

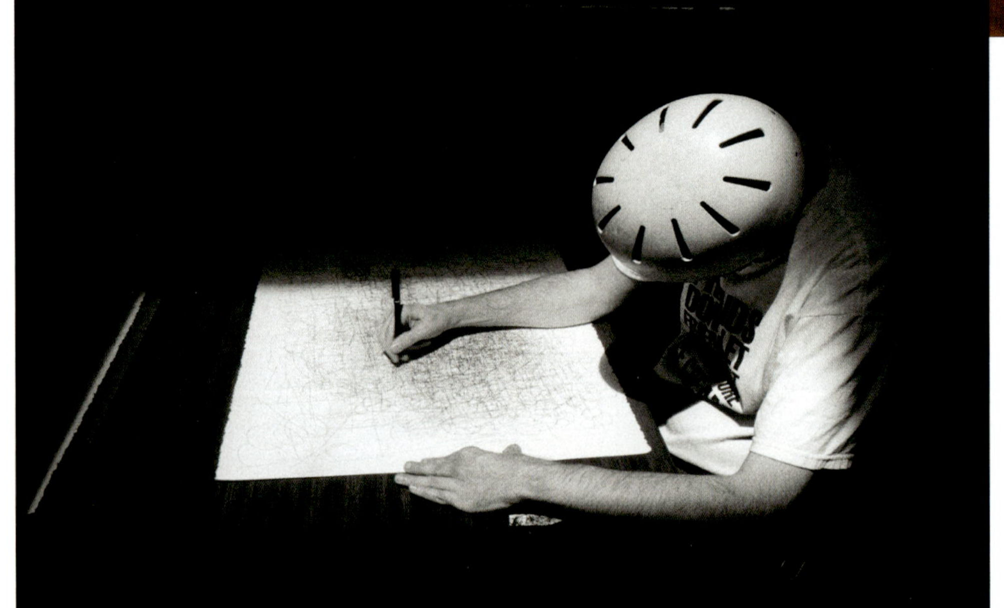

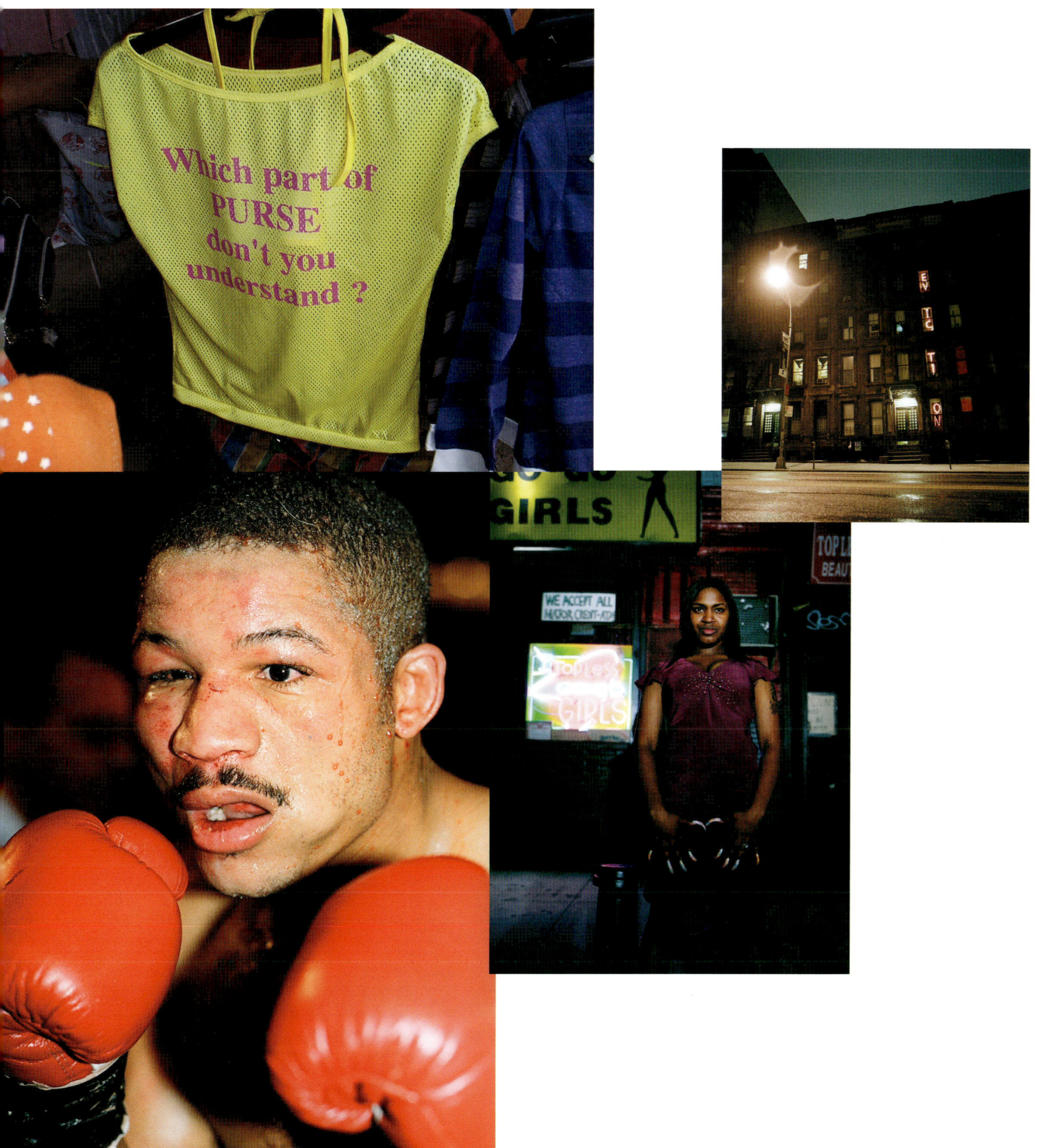
Which part of
PURSE
don't you
understand ?
GO GO
GIRLS
EV IC TI ON
WE ACCEPT ALL
MAJOR CREDIT
Topless
GIRLS
TOP L
BEAUT

For almost 20 years, Dunn has worked out of a studio one block from the World Trade Center. In the aftermath of 9/11, she took her camera into the street, where she was struck by this rare opportunity to capture pure emotion—people shed the pretenses of their day-to-day lives in the wake of this upending tragedy. These portraits were gathered together on Dunn's website in a series titled "A Sad Day."

Dunn has photographed widely varied cultural pockets of American life, as exemplified by her new photo book, *Some Kinda Vocation* (PictureBox, Inc.) The book looks back at the images she has captured over the past two decades—Dunn has documented the career arcs of close friends like Barry "Twist" McGee, his late wife Margaret "Meta" Kilgallen and Chris Johansen. Like Dunn, these artists ennobled the realities of urban life through their own work.

The book is accompanied by a DVD which features *Creative Life Store,* a film that documents the experiences of 13 artists—including the aforementioned McGee, Kilgallen and Johansen—who were invited to Tokyo to launch simultaneous exhibitions in January, 2001. The artists grapple with finding artistic meaning at a time when the contemporary art scene has gone mad for hype, profit and pop culture cachet. Dunn says, of the film, "I just wanted it to be like a painting. When you go to a museum, you don't look at who made the work, and you don't look at who owns it. It's just there, and you feel it, and you take it in."

As a photographer, Dunn has been able to penetrate arenas where women are not accepted as equals. She is acutely aware of the role her personality and appearance played in her ability to create her art. (In *Creative Life Store*, Kilgallen comments on her frustration at being one of the few women in the street art scene.) Dunn says, "I was like some kind of tomboy girl with a camera. I was not the sexy girl, they couldn't put me in a box. I became much more of a fly on the wall. But I was knowledgeable about their sport, so I got a lot of these guys to really open up to me, because they couldn't be vulnerable in front of their peers."

Dunn says she is inspired by people who were born without privilege, but have the audacity to seek notoriety and success. People who try to "somehow figure out how to have a voice, whether it's doing graffiti, or protesting, or whatever… Maybe they're making it, and maybe they're not. But they're not buying into their place, and they're trying to have a voice. That type of character and that type of energy is interesting to me," she says. "I've read *Us* magazine, but celebrity and celebrity culture, I just can't stand. Nobody is better than anybody else… Maybe that's why I was never a very successful commercial photographer."

In 2006, Dunn was an artist-in-resident at the Creative Growth Center. At her recent Los Angeles show, Dunn showed photographs taken there, documenting the center's clients and their artwork. Dunn also screened a trailer of the documentary, depicting the artists of the Creative Growth Center—the film she was raising funds to complete. Of this project, Dunn says, "It brought me back to why I documented artists to begin with. When art and art making… was just about the need to do it, and not infiltrated by the business of art… having the privilege to be around this school and these artists, made me have a whole reawakening. [It brought me back] to how I felt about what I was doing, 10 years ago."

www.cheryldunn.net

> **" I WAS LIKE SOME KIND OF TOMBOY GIRL WITH A CAMERA. I WAS NOT THE SEXY GIRL, THEY COULDN'T PUT ME IN A BOX. BUT I WAS KNOWLEDGEABLE ABOUT THEIR SPORT, SO I GOT A LOT OF THESE GUYS TO REALLY OPEN UP TO ME, BECAUSE THEY COULDN'T BE VULNERABLE IN FRONT OF THEIR PEERS. "**

C-4 Hallway, Tenderoin, San Francisco, California, 1998 . "This kid, at 17 years of age, was up more than anyone in S.F. at the time. He wears a teddy bear hat that his mom made him. I think he is a perfect combination of innocence and outlaw."

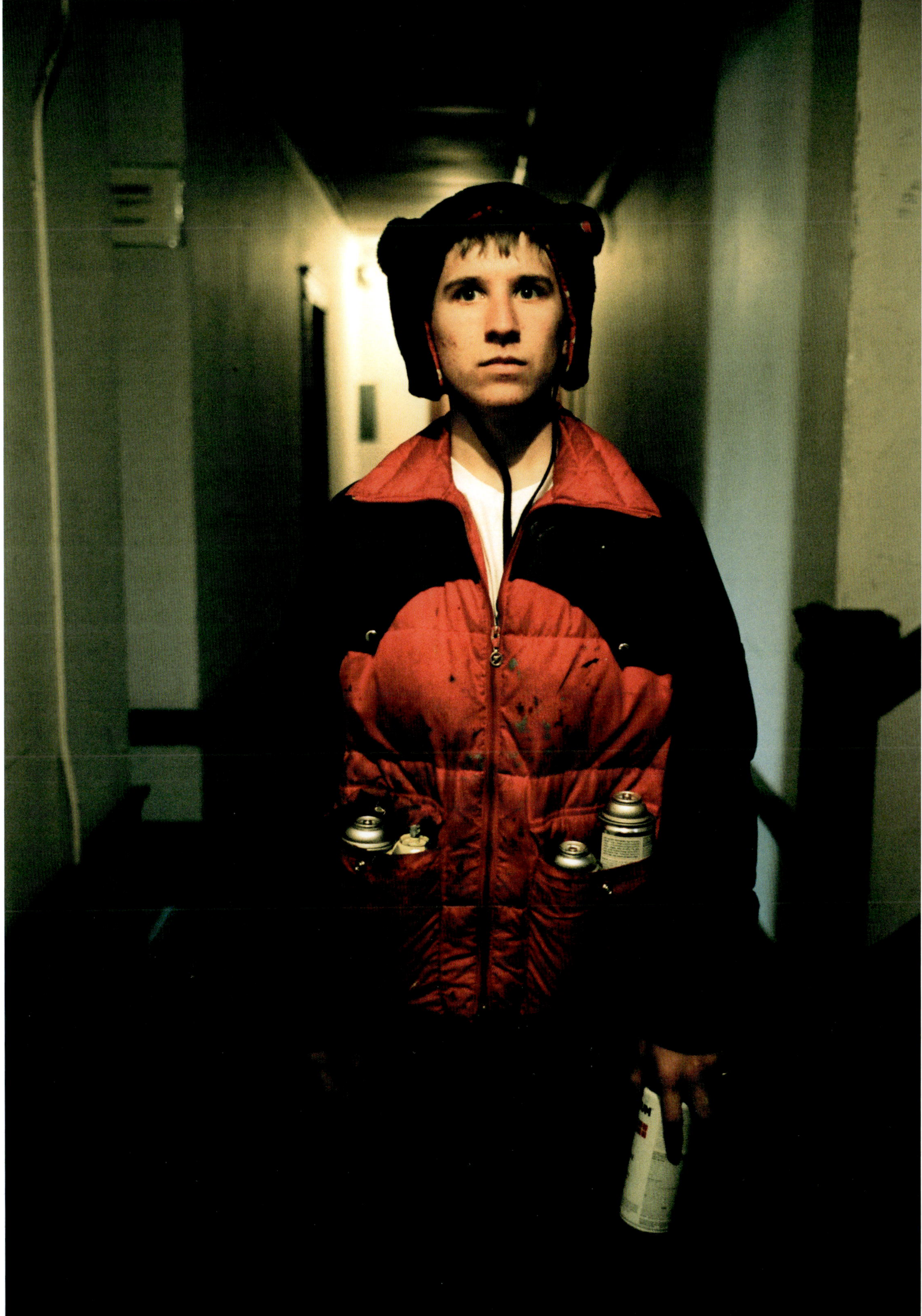

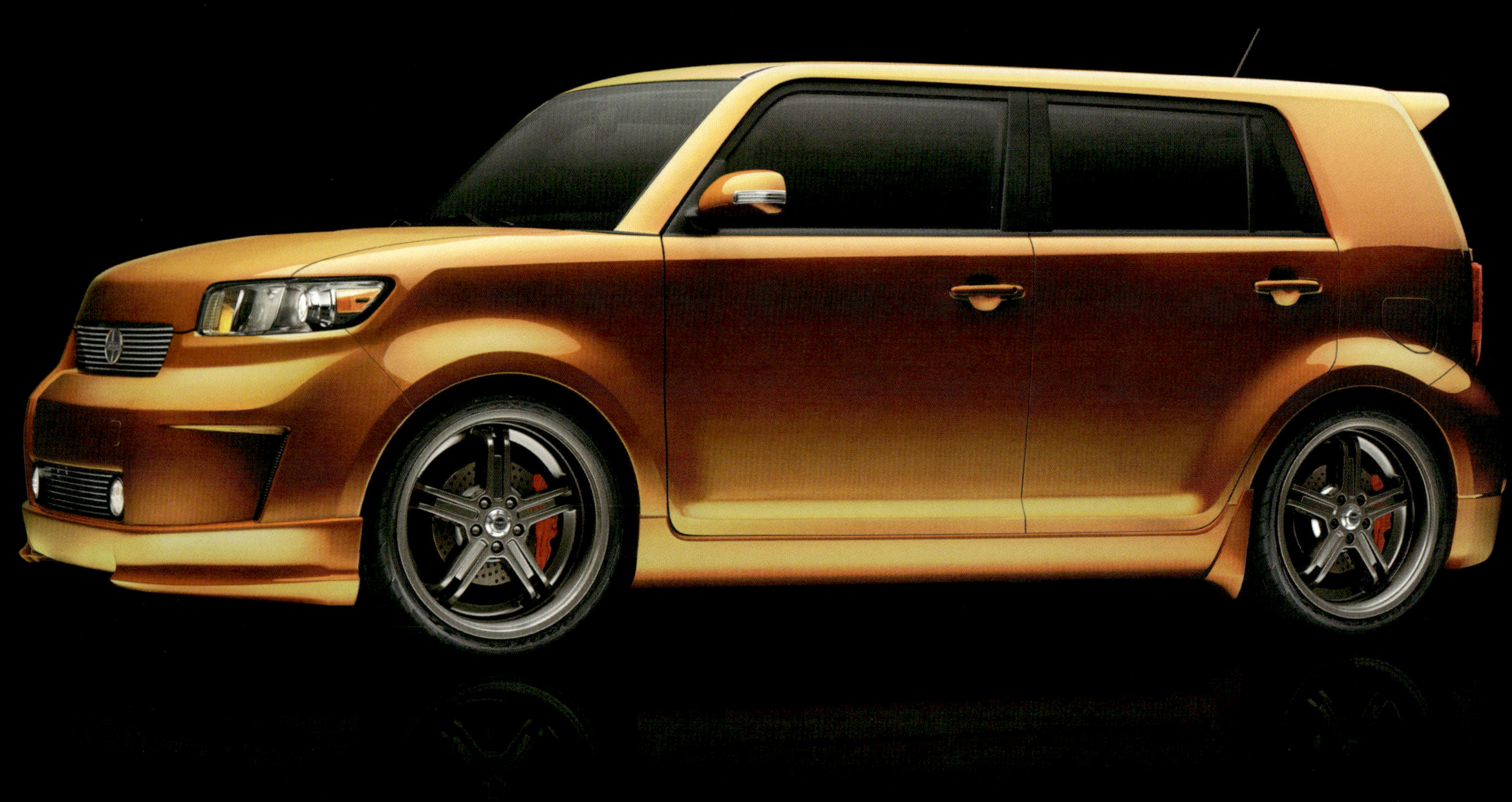

THE 2008 xB.

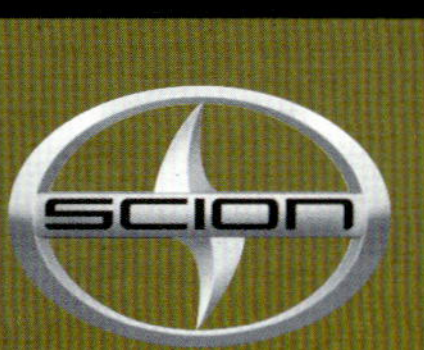

scion
what moves you

FRINGE/ELEMENT

BY MICHAEL R. BLAHA
PHOTOS BY REBECCA MILLER

THIS PAGE:
The "Late 'N' Live" party at the Gilden Balloon during Edinburgh's festival season, 2007.

OPPOSITE PAGE:
Mervyn Stutter, radio and television performer, has attended the Festival Fringe for 22 years.

There is no place on earth like Edinburgh during Festival month. The capital of Scotland since 1437 and the second most populous city in the country after Glasgow, Edinburgh in August is an arts orgy, the world's undisputed culture crack den where 1,000,000 visitors from around the globe converge for their fix.

Edinburgh has no fewer than 12 festivals running in or around the month of August: the Edinburgh International Festival, The Edinburgh Festival Fringe, The Edinburgh International Film Festival (all three celebrating their 61st anniversary in 2007), The Edinburgh International Book Festival, The Edinburgh Jazz and Blues Festival, The Edinburgh Military Tattoo, the Edinburgh Art Festival, The Edinburgh Interactive Entertainment Festival, The International Television festival, The Festival of Politics, The Festival of Spirituality and Peace, and the Mela Festival. Together, they pump over $250 million into the local economy and make Edinburgh the second most popular tourism destination in the United Kingdom, after London.

By far the biggest of these festivals is the Edinburgh Festival Fringe, which started in 1947 when some theatre companies who were turned away from the International Festival unwittingly laid the groundwork for what has become the biggest performing arts festival in the world. In 2007, the Edinburgh Fringe sold 1.7 million tickets, reportedly the most in its history, to 2,050 shows, featuring 18,600 artists in over 30,000 performances in 250 venues. The *Fringe Programme*, which lists every show, concert and event on the Fringe, was 288 pages this year.

RUINED BY GREED?

With so many shows to choose from, it can be hard to figure out which ones to see. You can take the easy way out by opting for a famous name: Ricky Gervais, Henry Rollins, Alan Cummings, Kanye West, The Foo Fighters or Silverchair. You could stick with familiar plays, including countless interpretations of Shakespeare's entire oeuvre, see shows that get four or five stars in *The Scotsman*, or rely solely on word of mouth.

Choosing shows can be tricky. There are rules to follow, to be sure. Mervyn Stutter, an expert on these matters, says, "Anything with the word 'sex' in the title is probably not very good. And anything described in the Fringe brochure as 'hilarious' 'wacky' or 'zany' should be viewed with suspicion."

Stutter, a well-known radio and television performer and writer in England, has been performing at the Fringe for 22 years. In 1992, he began hosting a 90-minute show called "Pick of the Fringe." He sings original, comedic songs and interviews featured performers in front of a sold-out audience. Stutter has witnessed the rapid expansion of the Fringe over the last three decades, and he wonders if it can keep growing at such a pace. "The audience has been stretched too thin," Stutter laments. "If you asked audience members to name their biggest complaint about the Fringe, they'd say it's the cost of tickets." He adds, "If you asked the performers, they'd say it's the cost of the venues."

Alex McSherry, a University of Paisley lecturer who has participated in over 20 Fringe Festivals as an actor, director and writer since 1979, echoes Stutter's concerns. "The Fringe is in danger of being ruined by greed," he warns. "Even into the '80s, the Fringe was still a showcase for new talent, and venues were only charging rent of £150 a week, which in turn allowed the performers to keep the ticket prices to £2 to £3." Now, he says, a lot of locals are reluctant to come see theatre on the Fringe "because of the high prices and the dodgy quality of many of the shows."

Many audience members rely on the reputations of specific venues to guide their ticket buying choices. For example, The Assembly Rooms on George Street has long been considered the premier venue in New Town, while the Pleasance and Gilded Balloon are generally considered to be the best spaces in Old Town. The Traverse Theatre has consistently won an unnaturally high proportion of the Fringe Firsts awarded each year by *The Scotsman* for excellence in playwriting. There is the Spiegelgarden, a beer garden cum circus tent featuring neo-vaudevillian variety shows, often with a burlesque twist, and The Bongo Club, a local favorite.

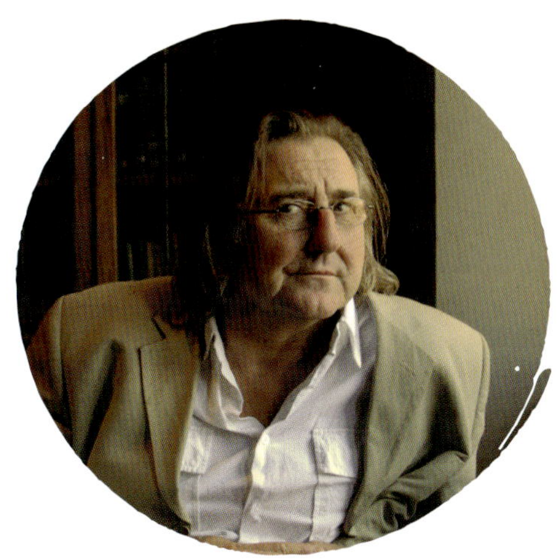

EXPANDING OR DOWNSIZING?

This year, Assembly Rooms dramatically expanded, taking over the programming of four additional, previously independent, venues. One of the spaces Assembly took over was the Aurora Nova, known for its eclectic mix of international dance and physical theatre.

Not everyone was happy about the Assembly's colonization of the other venues. Louise Chantal, the Artistic Director for Theatre at Assembly Rooms for the past three years, acknowledged that she had heard some of the grumblings, but thinks the criticism is unfounded. "One of the fundamental founding tenets of the Fringe is that anyone can do a show, so it ultimately comes down to the venues," she says. "The Festival is getting too big. There are far too many shows competing against each other."

The Gilded Balloon, one of Assembly's friendly rivals in Old Town, shares its reputation for quality, but has a much more active bar scene. During the Fringe, the Gilded Balloon is housed in Teviot House, which, like many Fringe venues, is part of the University of Edinburgh. From its inception in 1985, the Gilded Balloon had been housed in its own building. However, in December of 2002 it burned down, and the Gilded was forced to find a new home.

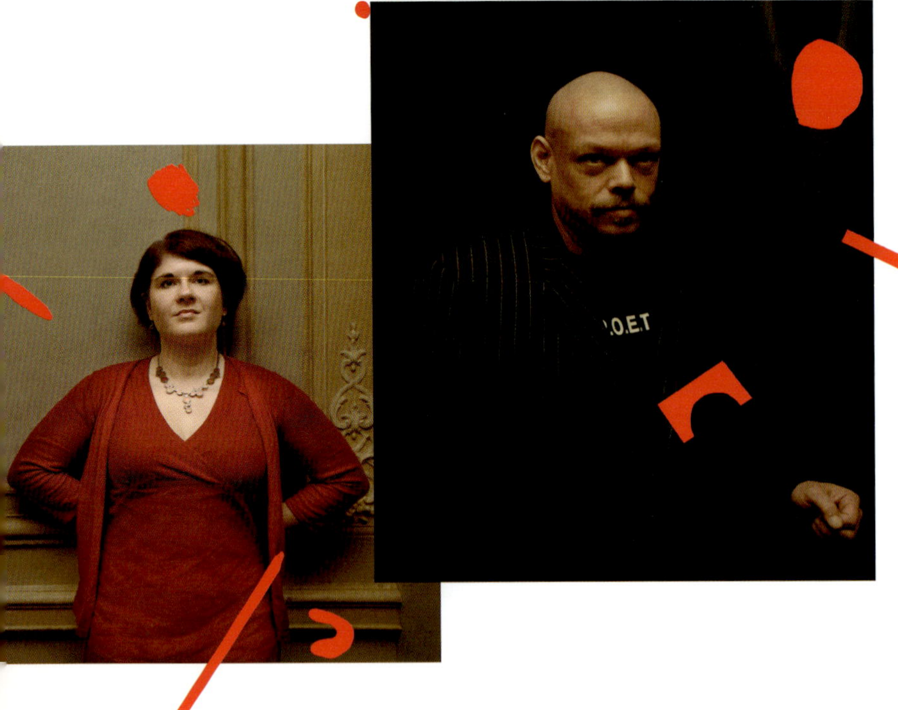

Since 1987 it has hosted Late n' Live, a live stand-up show featuring some of the hottest comedians on the Fringe. The show runs from 1:00 a.m. to 4:00 a.m. nightly, and its well-lubricated audiences have been known to eat comics alive. The Gilded Balloon programs theatre, too, of course, and has won its share of Fringe Firsts over the years.

Karen Koren, who has been the Artistic Director of the Gilded Balloon from the beginning, estimates that 60% of her audiences are locals. She would like to see the Fringe Festival become better known in America and throughout the world. She also laments that its "tough to get visitors to come to Edinburgh the rest of the year."

On the other end of the Fringe spectrum is The Bongo Club, which recently moved to a dedicated space on the eastern end of the city center, just down the way from the Scottish Parliament. Started as an artists' studio in 1996 by the arts and education charity Out of the Blue, the Bongo Club is dedicated, as its manager Ally Hill puts it, to "the weird and the wonderful." Its motto, after all, is "putting the cult in culture."

Because it operates year round as a nightclub, concert venue, theatre and screening room, the Bongo Club is a favorite of local artists. However, it has struggled over the years to expand its audience, for several reasons. For one, as Barney Waygood, its Press Officer points out, "the major Fringe venues all have media partners or sponsors" and the Bongo Club does not. For another, it doesn't have a presence in London like, say, the Pleasance and Assembly Rooms, so Hill doesn't have the same ability to scout out shows there.

The Bongo Club's profile is on the ascension. Last year, playwright Adam Rapp produced "Finer Noble Gases" there, and it won a Fringe First. This year, their offerings included the popular "Comedy for Kids," the cabaret show "Songs for Swinging Leaders," featuring crooners named Saddam Davis, Jr. and Osama Bin Crosby, and the perennial favorite, The Vaudeville Cabaret Club.

No new major venues have succeeded on the Fringe for some time. This year, Calvin Wynter, a former stockbroker turned theatre entrepreneur, opened the Green Room, which presented 30-plus shows in its inaugural year. "The other 'new' venues in recent years were started, seemingly, by people with unrealistic ambitions who thought Edinburgh was about money and capturing the market from other players," he says. "We came as experienced producers seeking to facilitate more work than would be possible as producer/promoters." He acknowledged that there were obstacles in opening a new venue on the Fringe, but the benefits outweighed the risks. "The biggest obstacle was turning a legally and practically unusable space—though a beautiful one—into three venues, offices, production facilities and bars in the unbelievably short period of time available to us," Wynter relates. "We can take shows developed in New York and transfer them effortlessly to the U.K. market via our own facilities and do the opposite with U.K.-originated material, transferring it to New York without delays and interference."

CAPITAL OF COMEDY

All of the bigger venues, including Assembly Rooms, Pleasance and Gilded Balloon, make a significant part of their revenue from comedy. Comedy acts generate the income needed for other program sections—the Children's Shows, Dance and Physical Theatre, Music, Musicals and Opera, Exhibitions and Events. As Assembly Rooms' Chantal points out, "Comedy totally subsidizes the theater program." Without the income from comedy, she goes on, many theatre productions "would simply not be economically viable."

Virtually every well-known comedian in the United Kingdom, and many that aren't but are striving to be, come up to the festival. Although most of the comedians at the Fringe are from the U.K. and Ireland, many Americans have made their mark there. They include Rich Hall (*SNL*, *Not Necessarily the News*) who won the Perrier Award for Best Comedy at the Fringe in 1990 and consistently sells out the Assembly's cavernous Music Hall space; Demitri Martin (*The Daily Show With Jon Stewart*, *Late Night With Conan O'Brien*), who won the Perrier in 2003; and Paul Provenza.

Provenza has an extensive resume spanning more than 20 years, but he may be best known these days as the creator and director of the exquisitely vulgar documentary *The Aristocrats*, which was screened at the Edinburgh International Film Festival in 2005. The Aristocrats featured a "who's who" of comedians telling their own versions of what was quite possibly the dirtiest joke in the history of mankind.

Provenza first appeared at the Edinburgh Fringe in 2003, performing a standup show titled "Myth America" at the Gilded Balloon. He's been back every year since doing stand up and hosting late night talk shows. "I'm addicted to the Fringe," Provenza says. "It's something I would like to do every year if at all possible. It's comedy boot camp. My time in Edinburgh has informed everything I have been doing since I first experienced it."

Provenza says, "My first show at the Fringe was very political, and much of my perspective was fresh at the time for audiences there. My show was reasonably high profile, so I got some attention, and it seemed that hearing an American's critical voice about many of the things that concerned Brits was a bit unusual." Since then, he says,

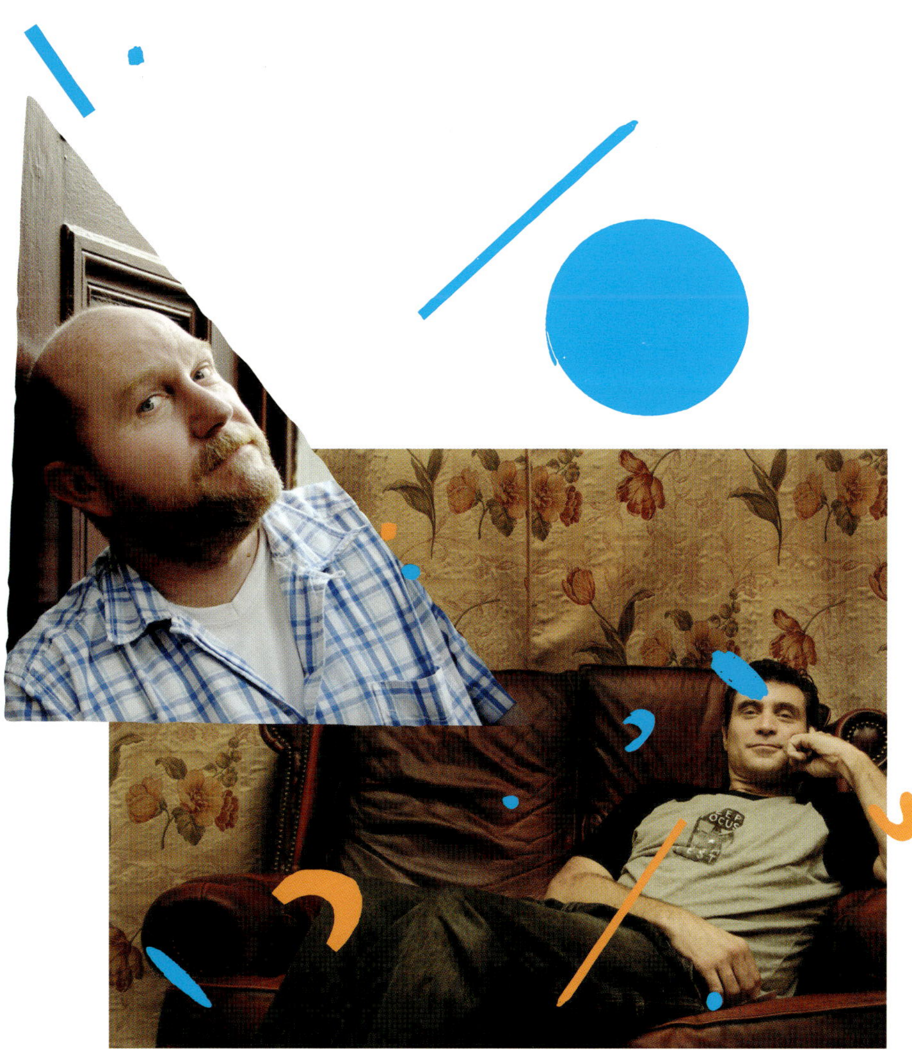

audiences have been exposed to a lot more issues-oriented comedy. This year, there were several shows featuring "Jesus" in their titles, two musicals about Tony Blair, the recently departed Prime Minister of the U.K. and *Jihad: The Musical!* garnered worldwide attention for its depiction of dancing and singing suicide bombers.

When asked if he has experienced an undercurrent of disaffection towards Americans since the start of the Iraq War, Provenza replies, "The audiences start out with the attitude towards an American comedian of 'well… you [Americans] elected him,' but end up with the reality that they are guilty of the same thing—policies and actions on the part of their own government that they don't support either." He goes on, "I also let them know right at the top that their bias against me as an American is as hack as an American comedian getting up and doing the obvious "Bush sucks" jokes. So I try to deal with that tension—which does exist, and can manifest at the strangest times—in a way that brings me and them together against the common foe of powerlessness and no voice in national affairs. We both have that very much in common."

FREE FRINGE — POWER TO THE PERFORMERS

One more noteworthy trend this year is the explosion of the "Free Fringe," a loose confederation of venues that don't charge the audience for tickets—they pay what they can afford or feel the show is worth—or charge the performance any upfront rental. Rather, they make their money from the bar and a box office split with the artist.

Rumors abounded this year that many artists and venues did better financially as part of the Free Fringe, and Stutter says he has heard that some very big names are thinking of making the switch to the Free Fringe approach next year. Not surprisingly, McSherry is a big fan of the Free Fringe because "it gives the power back to the performer."

Provenza says, "If the Fringe as we know it has reached a critical mass regarding paying audience and/or financial stress for the performers, things will change. The cycle will continue. Perhaps the big moneymakers will no longer be immune and some shifts in balance and power will occur, but performers who want to come and do their shows will always come and someone will always welcome them. The Fringe will never disappear, its structure and the way it all happens will simply alter to accommodate new realities."

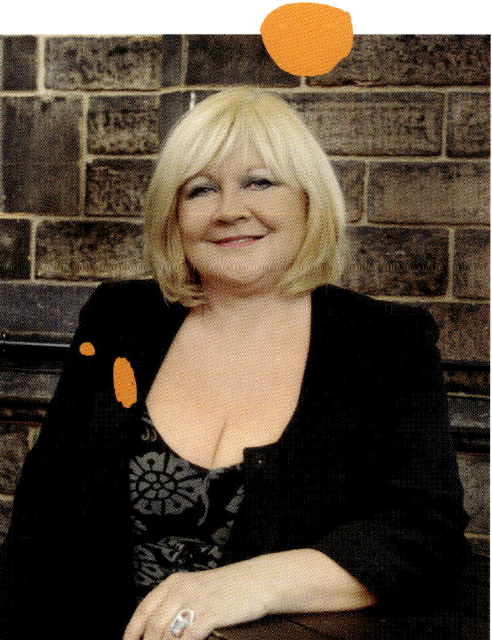

OPPOSTIE PAGE, LEFT–RIGHT:
Louise Chantal, artistic director for theatre at Assembly Rooms; Calvin Wynter, proprietor of the Green Room.

THIS PAGE, TOP TO BOTTOM:
Alex McSherry has participated in over 20 Fringe festivals since 1979; Paul Provenza, comedian and director of the documentary *The Aristocrats*; Karen Koren, artistic director of the Gilded Balloon.

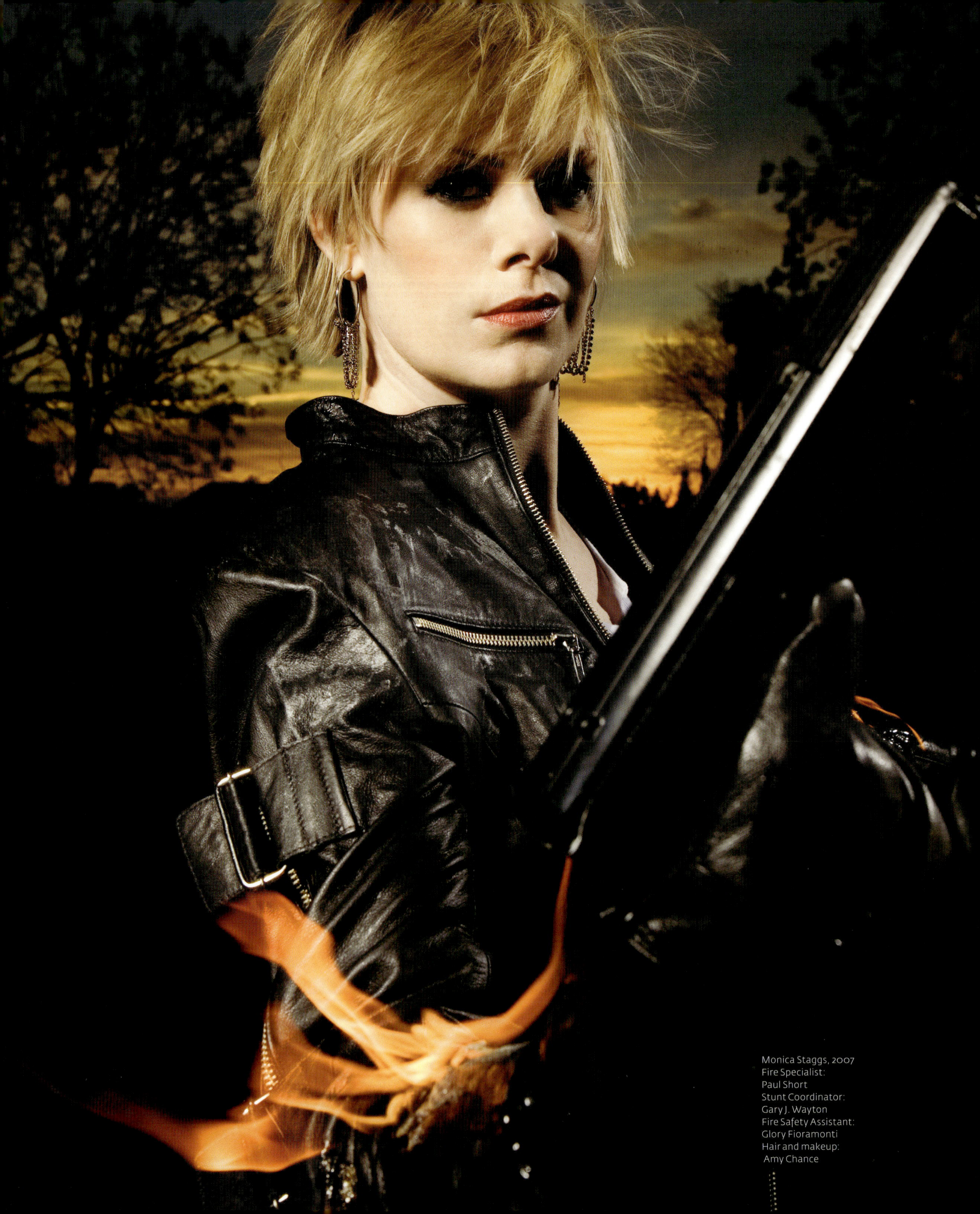

Monica Staggs, 2007
Fire Specialist:
Paul Short
Stunt Coordinator:
Gary J. Wayton
Fire Safety Assistant:
Glory Fioramonti
Hair and makeup:
Amy Chance

BY ANNE KEEHN
PHOTOS BY AARON FARLEY

STUNT COUPLES

Monica Staggs speaks intensely—about her passion for stand up comedy, acting and, perhaps most importantly, her work as a stunt performer—and her hazel eyes get a hardened look. At 26, she moved to Los Angeles with dreams of becoming a famous actress after graduating from the University of Arkansas with a dual degree in drama and creative writing. But the entertainment industry has not always been kind.

Staggs was recently featured in Quentin Tarantino's *Death Proof* as Lanna Frank, a lesbian drug dealer who meets a violent end. But she usually earns her bread as a stuntwoman. Five foot nine, with blond hair and the figure of a fashion model, Staggs has doubled for Rebecca Romijn (*Pepper Dennis*), Charlize Theron (*The Italian Job*) and Sandra Bullock (*Crash*). In 2005, she was honored by the Taurus World Stunt Awards for her work as Daryl Hannah's double in *Kill Bill Vol. 2*. She took the podium with Hannah and Quentin Tarantino, the director of the film who was Staggs' guest for the night.

Staggs broke into the movies when she was still in college. A film crew came to Little Rock and she was cast as the stunt double of the lead actress. Staggs was put into a car that ran off the road and crashed into some trees. The experience was exciting enough for her to pack her bags and jump on an L.A.-bound airplane weeks later. It helped that she fell in love with the stunt coordinator, Gary J. Wayton, who was a veteran in the industry. Today, the couple lives together in Reseda in what she describes as a "big, fat effing house," with lots of space to practice their stunts. (Wayton taught her how to high fall from their roof onto a pile of cardboard boxes. "You count to three, and you jump on three, 'cause if you don't go, you won't go," she says.)

Staggs trained as a dancer, but says she has gone through phases when she works out sporadically. And, she admits, she used to be a hard-partying girl. For this interview, she arranged a lunchtime meeting at a Mexican restaurant in the valley whose bar she used to frequent in the evenings. The place is closed during the day, however, so she suggests another spot down the road. She climbs into her car and peels through a narrow space between traffic cones, takes a hairpin turn out of the parking lot and guns it down the street. "I love driving fast," she'll later say. One of her specialties is in vehicle stunts.

Once in a booth at the restaurant, she announces, "I'm hung over today from two glasses of wine, which means I'm getting older," and takes a swig of water. "On Friday, I'm going to get my head slammed into a car. I'm not looking forward to that." She talks tough; a hardened attitude has helped her survive for over a decade in the high-risk boy's club of film stunts. "You've got to cowboy up," she says. "Rise to the occasion, because you're going to get the shit kicked out of you."

But there is a softness to her. She can break into a beaming Judy Garland smile: her teeth press together, her cheeks pull back and her eyes water up. She is 38, and it is clear that Staggs is no ingénue. But her smile has a childlike eagerness. It is the smile of a film star, disarmingly vulnerable and poignant. "I'm still going to be an actress," she says.

Although stunt performers are getting more and more exposure, they have traditionally worked in anonymity. Many entered into agreements to not divulge that they doubled for a famous actor, lest the star's heroic reputation is tarnished. In 1999 and 2005, the Academy of Motion Picture Arts and Sciences rejected a proposal to create an Oscar category for stunt work. To bolster awareness and appreciation of the craft, the Taurus World Stunt Awards, which premiered in 2001, billed itself as honoring "the movie industry's unsung heroes."

Jackie Chan, who famously implied that he performs all his own death defying stunts, recently came into some controversy when Bruce Law, a Hong Kong stunt professional, blogged about working as the actor's stunt double. Law has been a vocal advocate for stunt recognition. He told CNN that he formed his own production company in the late '80s because "I had already been involved in a lot of movies, but my name hadn't been mentioned in the credits of many of them."

Staggs is a writer—she has worked as a freelance journalist, and is at work on several film scripts. In high school, she harbored dreams of being a stand up comic, and in recent years, she has performed in comedy clubs around Los Angeles. "I have a really blue act," she says. "I do a bit where I talk about having my way with Charlton Heston." She is brash and loud and opinionated. She wants her voice to be heard. Toiling away indefinitely as a faceless "unsung hero" just doesn't cut it for her.

Early in her career, she worked as a stunt double for Leelee Sobieski on *Joy Ride*, a film starring Steve Zahn. One stunt called for her to jump out of a trailer truck moving 15 miles an hour. "The character had to be helped out by the man," she recalls. On hindsight, Staggs says, if she was permitted

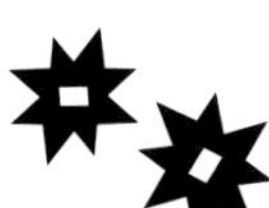

to control her fall, she might have avoided what happened next: she flew against the momentum and slammed her head against the concrete. Her eye socket was cracked, and her skull was fractured in four places.

"When I got carted off to the hospital, they took my wig off, washed the blood out and put it on the next girl," Staggs says. The show went on—whether the stuntwoman had a skull fracture or not. At the hospital, her wound was scrubbed without anesthetic. "I didn't cry. I kept cussing like a motherfucker, because I was in the most horrible pain I had ever experienced thus far in my life. Because I'm obsessed with my nose, I thought I could get a nose job out of it." But no such luck.

Stunts are often filmed on a hurried schedule. It can be difficult for stunt workers to drown out the chaos of the set and focus on the dangerous task at hand. Staggs says, "I almost mule-kicked this [on-set hair stylist] because she was fussing with my hair right before the cameras rolled. I apologized to her after the first stair fall, and guess what? She apologized to me and we all had a smile."

Through her career, Staggs has set herself apart by being willing to charge into high-risk stunts. On her website, she lists one of her skills as "Willing to hit the ground hard." "I got known for being a go-for-it girl, who's tough," she says. During her work on a film called *Sky High*, she was thrown through the air on wires. "I was calling myself a meat puppet," she says. But, as the stunt industry becomes more recognized and stunt technology advances alongside the predominance of CGI, Staggs' survival has increasingly come to depend on her ability to adapt.

Staggs: "If I was a gymnast, with my height, I would be so in demand. I would be driving two Mercedes right now. There are so many more stunt people now. I never even knew there were stunt people when I was back in Arkansas. Now, with all the behind-the-scenes footage on DVDs, everybody knows. [The industry] has become more competitive.

"You have to clock up each set. Sometimes, you don't even know who to be," she continues. Stunt workers are lower on the totem pole than the actors, and because they get no face time, they are fully replaceable. This is mixed with the fact that the industry, as Staggs says, "can be very sexist. Men still run most of the shows." Stuntwomen often contend with issues like "sexist DPs" and "pervs on the set." Out of necessity, Staggs has learned to size up the social hierarchy of every film set she works on.

Organizations like the Stuntwomen's Foundation, which gives financial assistance to injured professionals, and the Stuntwomen's Association of Motion Pictures (SWAMP), which was founded in 1967 by some of the most groundbreaking female stunt professionals—including Jeannie and Stephanie Epper—have been established to solidify women's presence in the male-dominated stunt world. SWAMP is highly selective of its members. Women can only be considered for induction by invitation, then voted in. On their website, the organization says that invitations are extended only "to the

"WHEN I GOT CARTED OFF TO THE HOSPITAL, THEY TOOK MY WIG OFF, WASHED THE BLOOD OUT AND PUT IT ON THE NEXT GIRL."

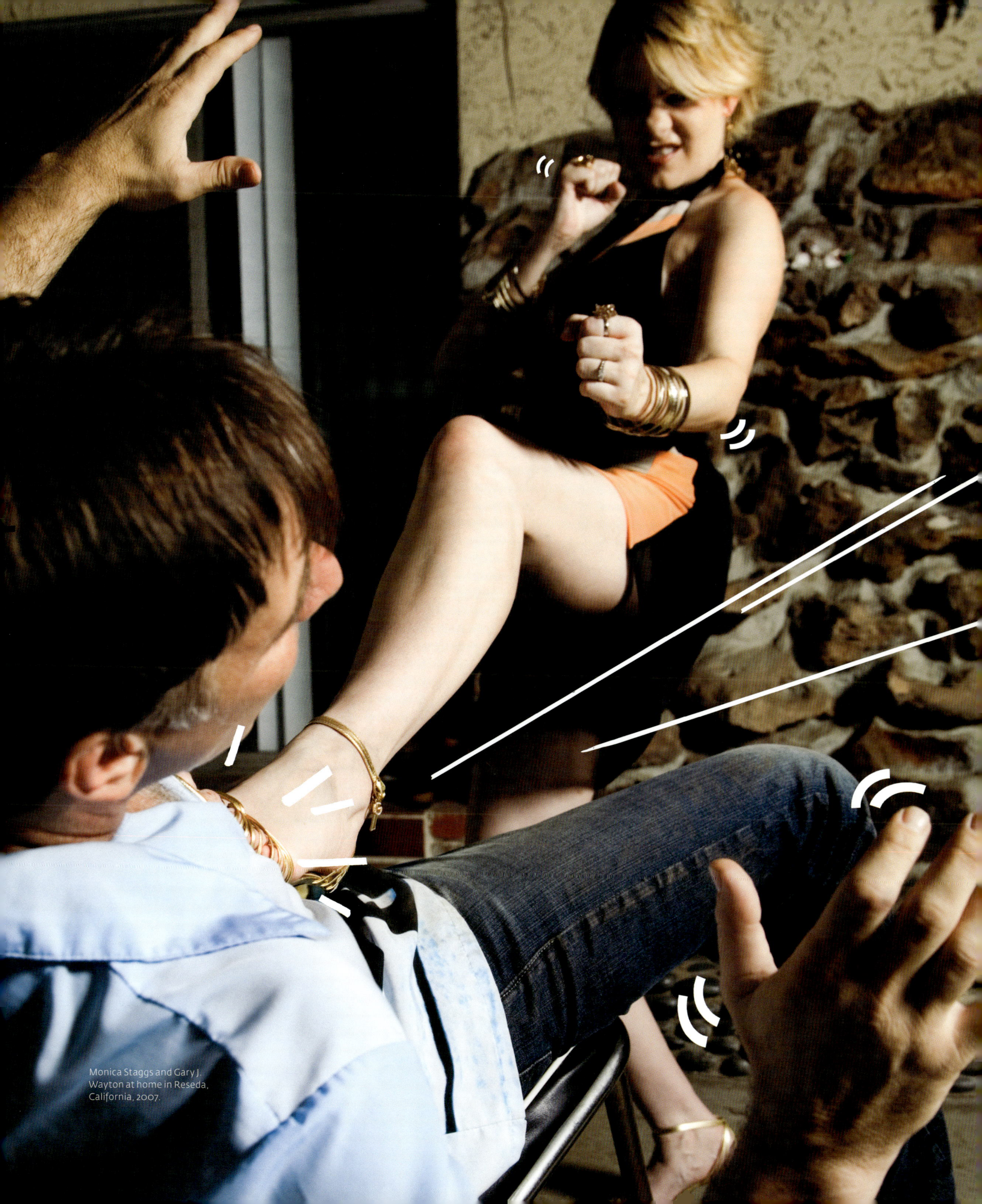

Monica Staggs and Gary J. Wayton at home in Reseda, California, 2007.

top stuntwomen in the industry." Staggs sits on SWAMP's board.

Influential stunt families have historically pre-dominated the stunt industry. The man considered the godfather of Hollywood stunt performers is Yakima Canutt, a former rodeo superstar who became a film actor during the silent era. He specialized in westerns, using his rodeo skills to perform spectacular stunts on horses. With the advent of the talkies, Canutt fell into minor acting roles and worked more and more in stunts, because his voice was weak and unsuitable for sound. Legend has it that Canutt taught John Wayne how to handle horses and act like a real cowboy. Canutt's crowning achievement was his direction of the chariot race in *Ben Hur*—perhaps the most famous action sequence in the history of cinema. Canutt's two sons, Joe and Tap took part in this sequence—Joe doubled Charlton Heston, and purportedly sustained the only injury on set, a gash to his chin that required stitches. (Yakima Canutt was given an honorary Oscar in 1966 for "achievements as a stunt man and for developing safety devices to protect stunt men everywhere." This was the only Oscar ever given for stunt work.)

Another great stunt dynasty is the Epper clan. The patriarch, John Epper was a former member of the Swiss mounted cavalry, who immigrated to California, and ran a business renting horses to film studios. He began performing stunts in westerns, doubling for stars like Errol Flynn and Gary Cooper. Epper raised a brood of children who carried on their father's legacy in the stunt world. Perhaps most notable was Jeannie, who was Lynda Carter's double on *Wonder Woman*, and stood in for Kathleen Turner in *Romancing the Stone*. In 2007, she was the first woman to be honored with a lifetime achievement award from the Taurus World Stunt Awards. All three of her children work in the stunt industry.

Monica Staggs also keeps it in the family. Her husband, Gary J. Wayton has had a decades-long, illustrious career in the stunt industry. He has doubled for Matt Dillon and Kevin Kline, and worked as a stunt coordinator and second unit director—the title given to directors of stunt sequences. Recently, he worked as Harrison Ford's stunt double in *Indiana Jones and the Kingdom of the Crystal Skull.*

But, in recent years, a family emerged that has blurred the division between stunt performers, and film stars. Dwayne "The Rock" Johnson, who rose to fame performing stunt-like work as a pro wrestler for the WWE, emerged as a full-fledged movie star in 2002 with *The Scorpion King.* His cousin, Tanoai Reed—who looks eerily similar to

him—was cast as his stunt double, a position Reed has reprised in every Rock movie since.

The Rock has hosted the Taurus World Stunt Awards, bringing unprecedented star power and interest to the event. He routinely mentions Reed in interviews and pulls his cousin into photo opportunities on the red carpet. "Dwayne was one of the first actors who gave me all the credit," Reed says. "It was unheard of, for an actor to do that."

Reed was a college football star at the University of Hawaii. He came from a football family, and was on track to pursue the sport professionally. But, at 19, he stumbled upon the world of stunts when Kevin Costner's *Waterworld* came to Hawaii. Reed got a job doing grunt work on the set, "as a laborer, doing clean up jobs, etc," he told *laieboyz.com.* He befriended the stuntmen on the film, who helped him get a Screen Actors Guild card, and within days, Reed got himself stunt work on the set.

After that experience, Reed eschewed football camp and moved to Los Angeles to pursue stunt work—and struggled in the entertainment industry for the next half a decade. He lived out of his Chevy pickup truck, and worked sporadically, mostly in TV shows like *Nash Bridges* and *Buffy the Vampire Slayer.* "Stunt people don't have agents," he says. "You get work through word of mouth. And I wasn't very aggressive about putting myself out there."

The Scorpion King was his big break. When he reported to work on set, Reed and the Rock had never met. Reed knew that the two were cousins, but the Rock did not. "It wasn't until he asked me where I was from that I told him," Reed told *laieboyz.com.* "He went home and asked his mother about me, and that's when he found out that we're related."

The Rock was born in California, and grew up moving around the U.S. mainland. Reed says that after he came in contact with the Rock, the actor reconnected with his Polynesian roots. "I got him back into his culture. After [filming] *The Rundown,* we took some time off and went back to Hawaii. That's when he got that tattoo," Reed says, referring to the Polynesian symbols covering the actor's upper arm and shoulder.

In 2004, Reed received a Stunt Award for his work in *The Rundown.* But more importantly, he says, he was inducted into Brand X, an organization of elite stunt professionals. Membership is contingent upon a 100% unanimous vote. Being a part of Brand X has given Reed a sense of validation and community—and invaluable access to a network of high-profile stunt workers.

"There is camaraderie in the stunt community," Reed says. "Stunt guys are like a football team. We have each other's lives in our hands. We are outgoing, love to have fun, love to entertain. We train hard, and play hard."

Reed's association with the Rock has given him an unusual amount of face recognition, for a stuntman. But, he says, "I'd rather be an unsung hero… As a stunt person, you do act. You get lines. But I don't want to become an actor. It's not my passion."

Reed's wife, Suzanne, has also developed a career in the stunt industry. She doubled for Rosario Dawson in *The Rundown,* and Anne Hathaway in *Get Smart.* She is from Kowhai, where, she says, "I grew up living on the beach, surfing, diving. My specialty is in water stunts." Tanoai chimes in: "She's been coined the 'water girl' in the industry. She can stay under water for one minute."

Suzanne became more involved in stunt work, she says, in part, because the long stretches of time that Tanoai spent on film sets, away from home, put a strain on their marriage. Tanoai recalls returning to his family after months away, and feeling heartbroken at how much his young son had grown in his absence. Reed says, "A lot of movies go out of town, to Prague or Canada." Suzanne says, of her husband's prolonged absences, "I missed so much of him."

Recently, the family moved to West Hills, a rural community two hours north of Los Angeles. "We've got a backyard," Suzanne says. "It's like Hawaii. We go on hikes. We entertain friends." As a couple, Tanoai and Suzanne have a quiet intensity—they seem to relish existing in a world of their own, separate from the stress of the Hollywood industry. Their centeredness extends to their approach to stunt work.

"We're not dare devils, we are stunt professionals," Tanoai says. "Don't get the two confused. What we do is calculated risks. People get injured on easy stunts. They get careless. I see a lot of people psyche themselves up before a stunt. But that's not what I do. For me, everything slows down. It's a real peaceful, Zen thing. That's what I love—finding that space. I block everything out. You do your stunt, it's quiet, then, 'Cut!' And everyone claps. All eyes are on you, and it's the best feeling."

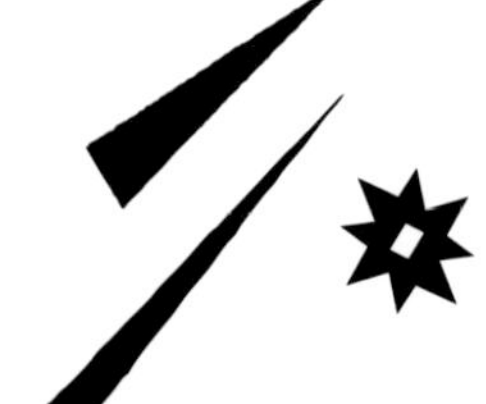

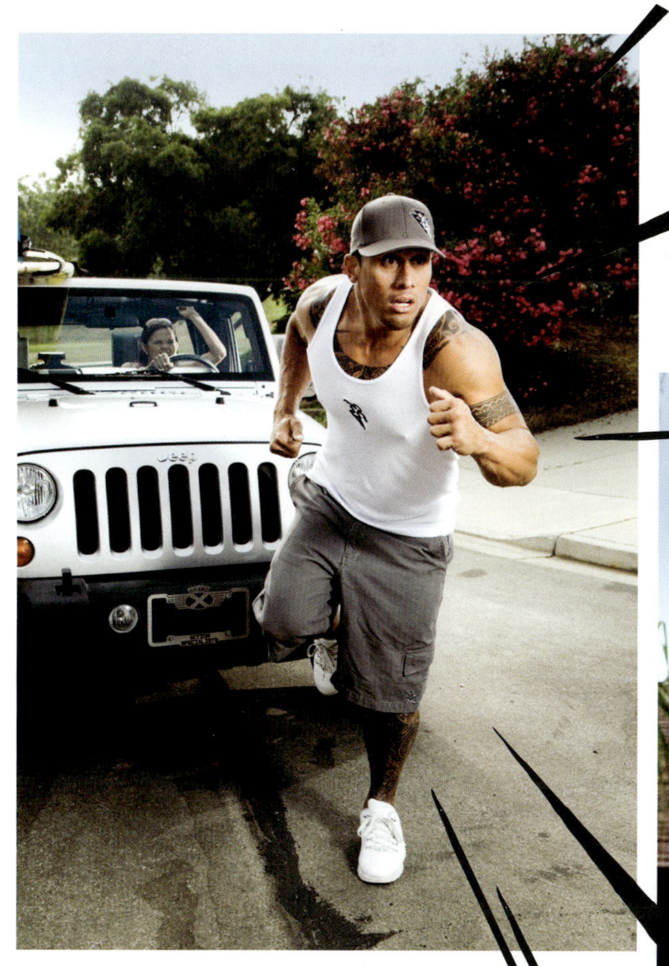

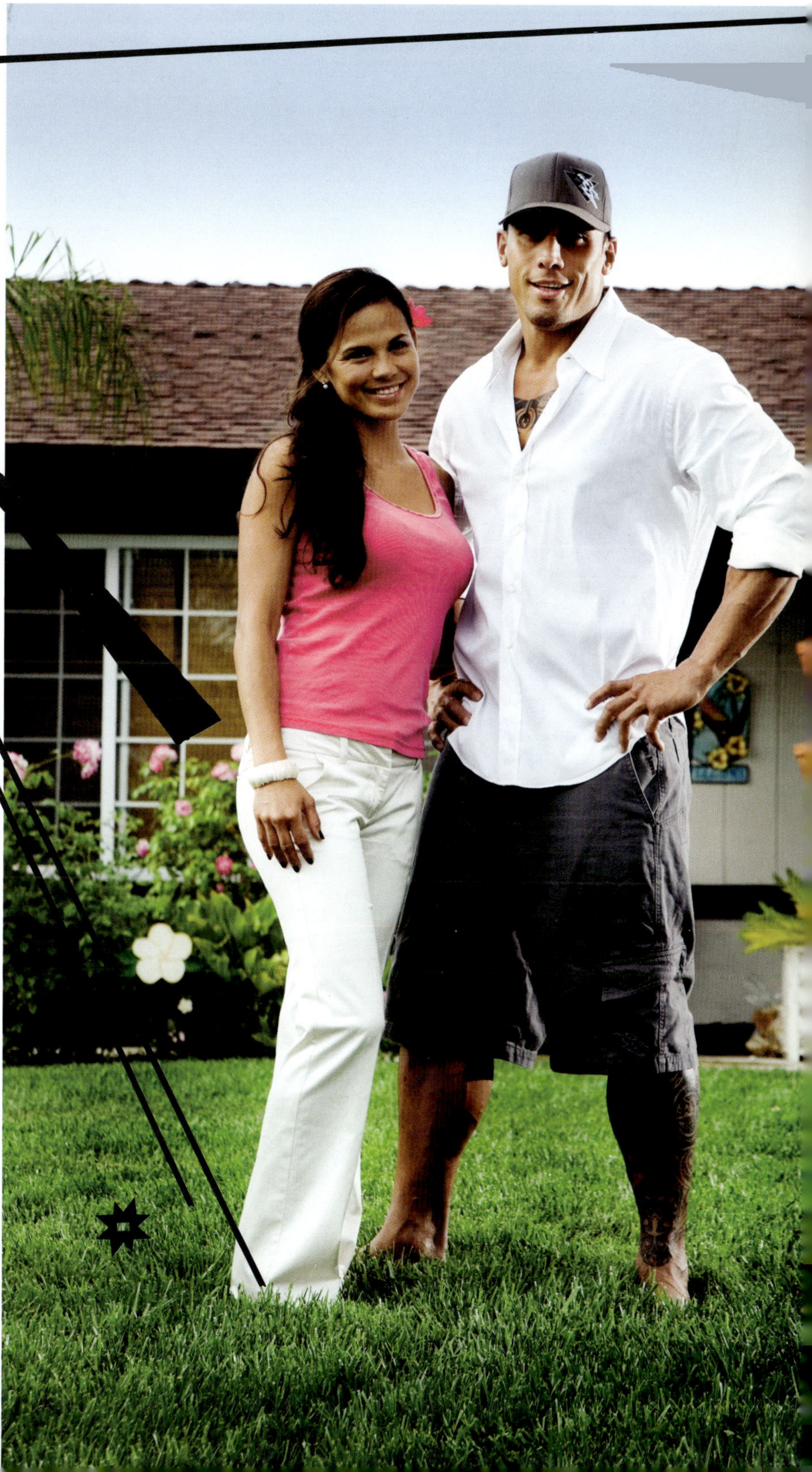

Tanoai and Suzanne
Reed at home in West
Hills, CA, 2007.

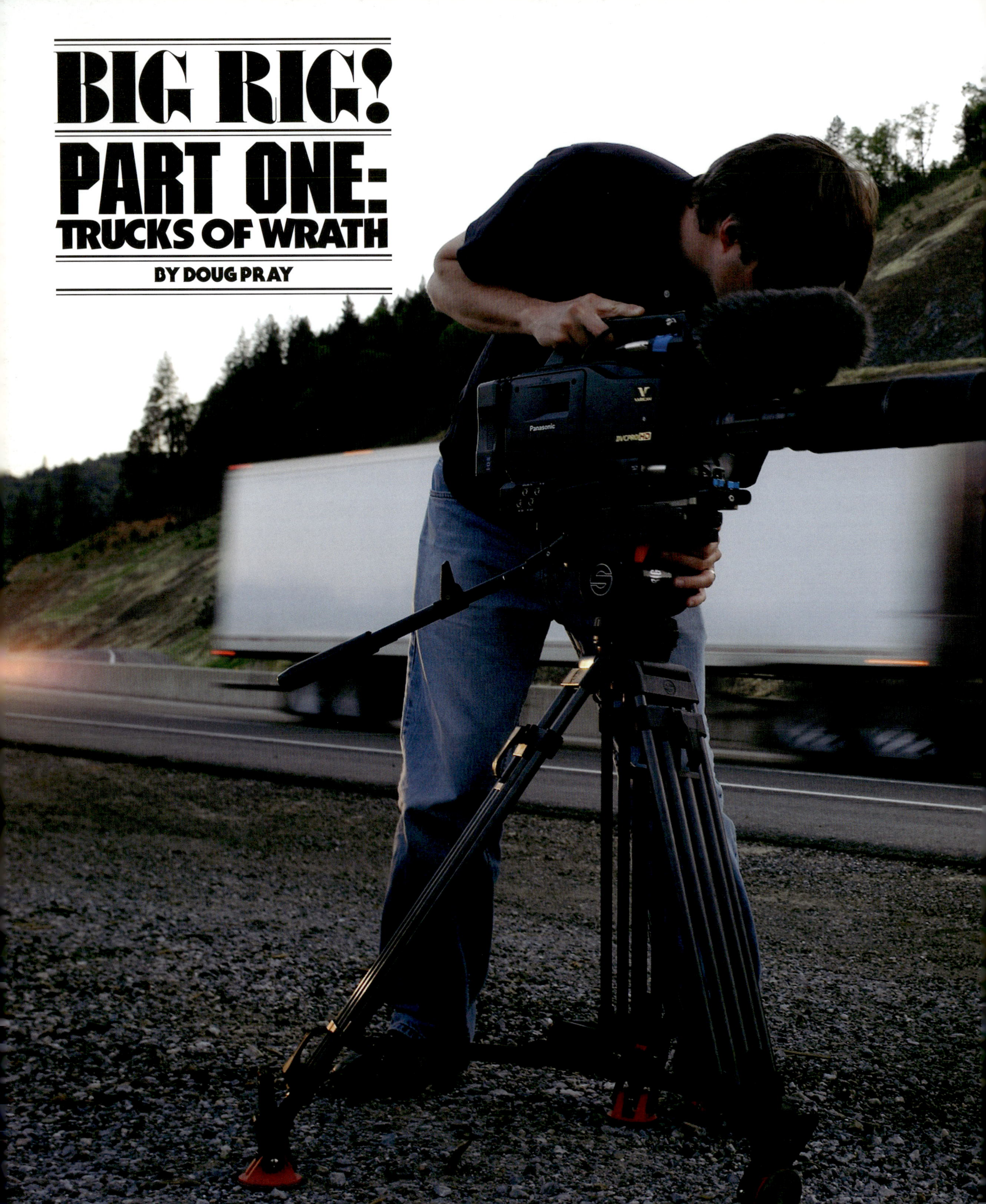

BIG RIG!
PART ONE:
TRUCKS OF WRATH
BY DOUG PRAY

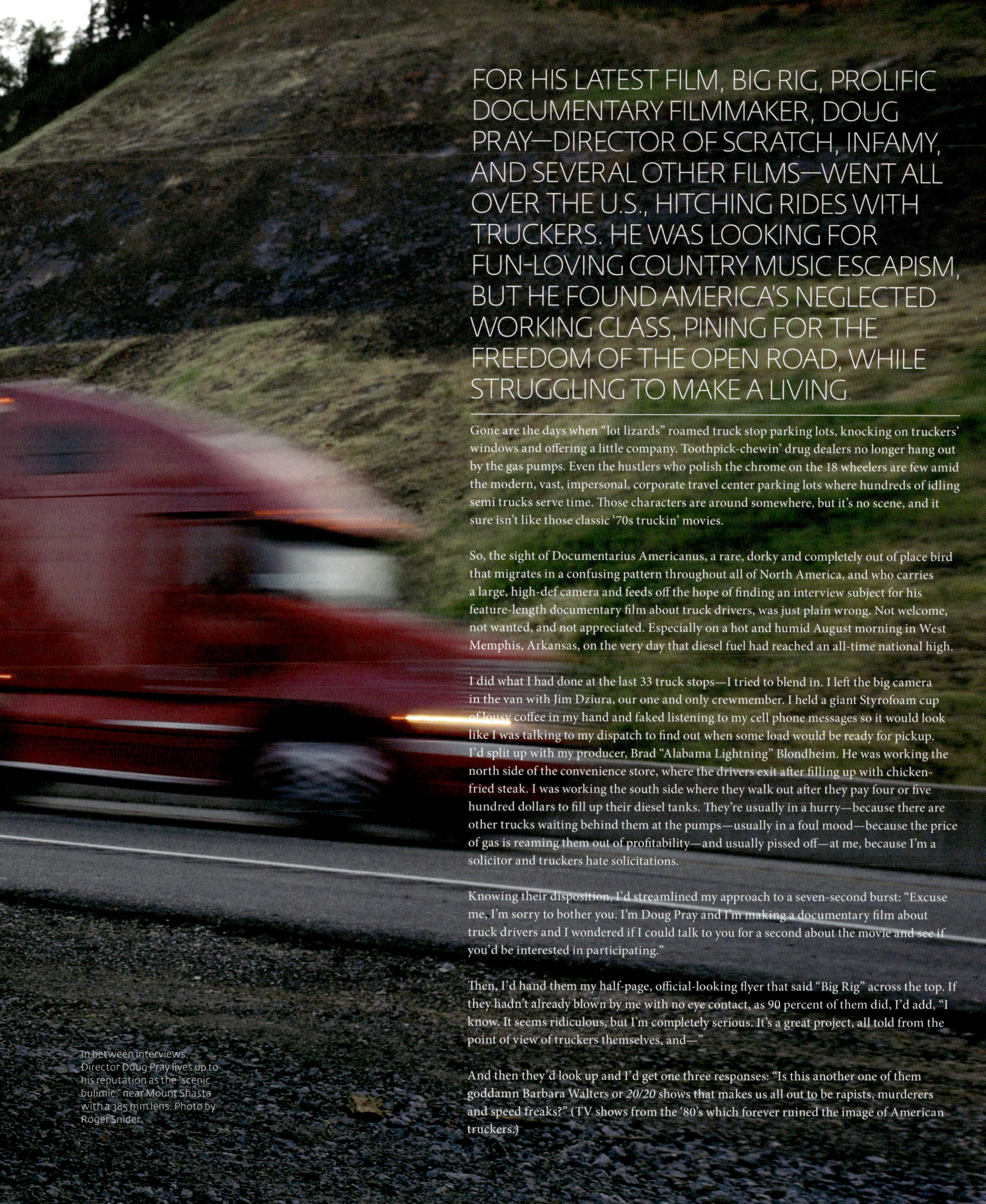

FOR HIS LATEST FILM, BIG RIG, PROLIFIC DOCUMENTARY FILMMAKER, DOUG PRAY—DIRECTOR OF SCRATCH, INFAMY, AND SEVERAL OTHER FILMS—WENT ALL OVER THE U.S., HITCHING RIDES WITH TRUCKERS. HE WAS LOOKING FOR FUN-LOVING COUNTRY MUSIC ESCAPISM, BUT HE FOUND AMERICA'S NEGLECTED WORKING CLASS, PINING FOR THE FREEDOM OF THE OPEN ROAD, WHILE STRUGGLING TO MAKE A LIVING.

Gone are the days when "lot lizards" roamed truck stop parking lots, knocking on truckers' windows and offering a little company. Toothpick-chewin' drug dealers no longer hang out by the gas pumps. Even the hustlers who polish the chrome on the 18 wheelers are few amid the modern, vast, impersonal, corporate travel center parking lots where hundreds of idling semi trucks serve time. Those characters are around somewhere, but it's no scene, and it sure isn't like those classic '70s truckin' movies.

So, the sight of Documentarius Americanus, a rare, dorky and completely out of place bird that migrates in a confusing pattern throughout all of North America, and who carries a large, high-def camera and feeds off the hope of finding an interview subject for his feature-length documentary film about truck drivers, was just plain wrong. Not welcome, not wanted, and not appreciated. Especially on a hot and humid August morning in West Memphis, Arkansas, on the very day that diesel fuel had reached an all-time national high.

I did what I had done at the last 33 truck stops—I tried to blend in. I left the big camera in the van with Jim Dziura, our one and only crewmember. I held a giant Styrofoam cup of lousy coffee in my hand and faked listening to my cell phone messages so it would look like I was talking to my dispatch to find out when some load would be ready for pickup. I'd split up with my producer, Brad "Alabama Lightning" Blondheim. He was working the north side of the convenience store, where the drivers exit after filling up with chicken-fried steak. I was working the south side where they walk out after they pay four or five hundred dollars to fill up their diesel tanks. They're usually in a hurry—because there are other trucks waiting behind them at the pumps—usually in a foul mood—because the price of gas is reaming them out of profitability—and usually pissed off—at me, because I'm a solicitor and truckers hate solicitations.

Knowing their disposition, I'd streamlined my approach to a seven-second burst: "Excuse me, I'm sorry to bother you. I'm Doug Pray and I'm making a documentary film about truck drivers and I wondered if I could talk to you for a second about the movie and see if you'd be interested in participating."

Then, I'd hand them my half-page, official-looking flyer that said "Big Rig" across the top. If they hadn't already blown by me with no eye contact, as 90 percent of them did, I'd add, "I know. It seems ridiculous, but I'm completely serious. It's a great project, all told from the point of view of truckers themselves, and—"

And then they'd look up and I'd get one three responses: "Is this another one of them goddamn Barbara Walters or *20/20* shows that makes us all out to be rapists, murderers and speed freaks?" (TV shows from the '80's which forever ruined the image of American truckers.)

Or: "You don't wanna hear what I have to say!" Then, they would break their own rules and go into an enraged tirade about the fuel prices and us disrespectful four-wheelers, and the asinine government regulations, and the stupid log book rules, and the corporate take-over of truck stops, and the lack of parking and the hundreds of unpaid hours they have to wait at the loading docks, and how they're losing money, and how lame the speed limits are in most states, and how poorly trained the younger drivers are these days, and how they used to be heroes of the highway but are now feared because the media has given them a bad reputation, and how profane all the idiots are on channel 19 of the CB radio—the mode of communication truckers use to speak to one another—and how there aren't any more "real" truck stops, and how the country is going straight to hell, and how they want their left lane back!

Or, they'd look me over, see how absurdly out of place I was, and say, "Sure." And, within seconds Jim and I would climb up into a giant Peterbilt truck, clip a wireless lavalier microphone onto the driver's shirt, slap a small suction-cup mounted Kino Flo light onto the inside of the windshield, hit the "record" button on the Panasonic Varicam and ask, "So what's your name, what are you hauling and where are you headed?" And off we'd go into America,

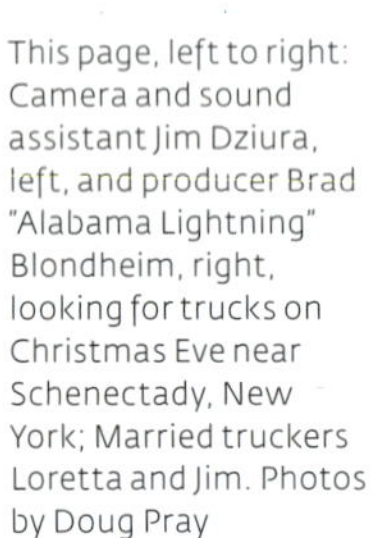

This page, left to right: Camera and sound assistant Jim Dziura, left, and producer Brad "Alabama Lightning" Blondheim, right, looking for trucks on Christmas Eve near Schenectady, New York; Married truckers Loretta and Jim. Photos by Doug Pray

for two to eight hours, talking about trucking, taxes, music, marriage, war, life and death, while the countryside flew by.

This particular morning the fish weren't biting, and time was running out. Usually, after about an hour of wandering the lots an employee would spot us and immediately kick us off the property. We were one of the three banished "P's": Pushers, Prostitutes and the Press. I became used to this treatment—I had been run out of dozens of truck stops. But I had also gotten dozens of rides and some great interviews. Today, however, I was stunned with an unexpected twist: another camera crew was coming around the corner.

My heart sank. There's another crew, making another trucking documentary? Then, my ego kicked in. Will I need to have a head-to-head battle with these perpetrators? Crew to crew, camera to camera, jousting with the boom poles, strapping on battery belts and tackling them on the pavement as we fight for interviews

and rides to Nashville? I challenged them with a friendly wave, and found out they were here from a local news channel to cover truckers' reactions to the highest gas prices in recorded history. No battle necessary, but the odds of getting a ride were a lot worse with the other camera around—and the truck stop manager was now angrily accosting them, about 30 feet away. The last thing the truck stop wanted was bad press about their gas prices. No cameras allowed.

My producer, Alabama Lightning and I were about to bail, when a beautiful rose-colored Freightliner with a feisty, blond female driver, wearing mod, Jam-style shades pulled into fuel island #2. Alabama and I looked at each other with a knowing nod: she looks like a great character. We need more female interviews. We're about to get kicked out of here—let's get that truck now!

This woman had apparently been approached by countless other aggressive jerks at other truck stops, and she rolled her window up tight, in sync with my approach.

I wanted her.

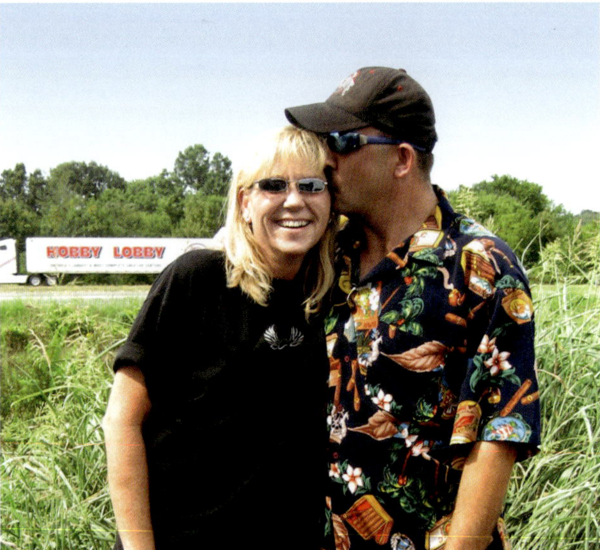

I knocked on the tinted glass and could see her shaking her head "No!" I looked at Alabama. He shrugged. I knocked on the door again and held our flyer up to the window for her to read. After a hot, noisy, exhaust-filled eternity of standing in the precarious no man's land between dozens of slowly rolling 80,000-pound loads, she cracked her window a bit and yelled, "You gotta talk to my husband." On cue, a guy in a Hawaiian shirt hopped out of a blue, matching Freightliner and introduced himself as Jim, and asked me what I wanted with his wife. Alabama quickly negotiated, and it was agreed that if we first rode with Jim, he'd consider letting us interview his wife, Loretta.

I signaled to my assistant to quickly bring the gear around, grabbed the camera and started loading it into the big rig—when the truck stop manager descended on us. The manager had just gotten rid of the news crew, and she was furious to see that now I had a camera, and was also soliciting her customers. Two evil henchmen were by her side, one wearing rubber gloves and the other holding a mop

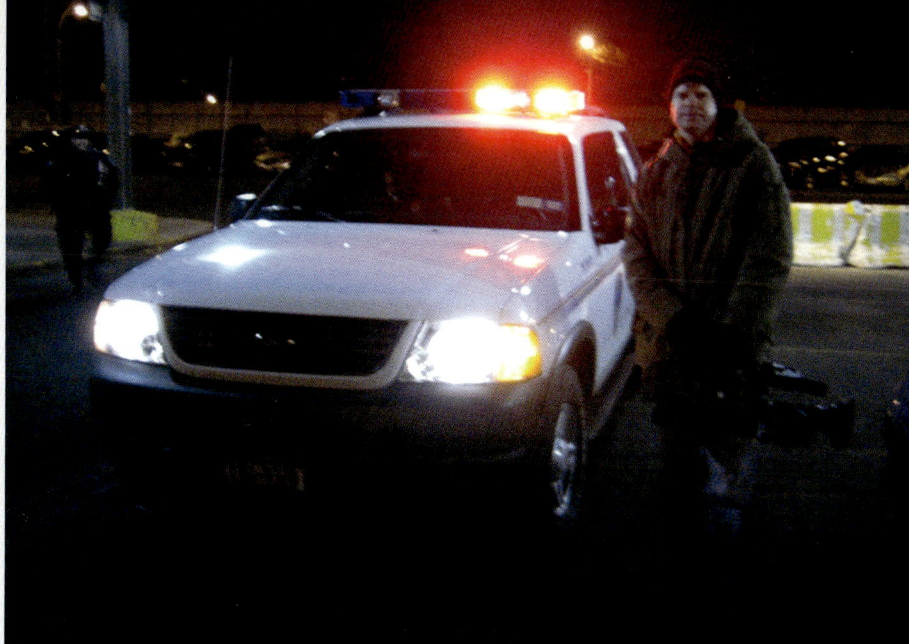

like a weapon. I tried to convince her that I had the full permission of this driver to board his Freightliner, which I continued doing. She said the police were on the way, and forced me to remove the camera from the truck—Alabama threw it back in our van—and leave immediately.

I didn't want to lose my double interview, so I asked Jim if I could ride with him off the property, and get my camera later. Rather amused by all this, he agreed, and we tried. But on our way past the security gate, two police squad cars, the angry manager, and now four large thugs stopped us. They forced me out of Jim's truck, and in a bizarre public crucifixion, jabbed their mops toward me. One of them—I kid you not—said, "You'll hang for this!" while the cops grabbed my license.

I have been in many weird situations with my camera. But, I am not a war journalist. My films are not known for their danger—unless you count being hit by flying chards of shattered vinyl from DJ Swamp's turntables. Until now, I have never been told that I was going to be hung for being a documentary filmmaker. It was a defining moment.

And, it ended as absurdly as it started. The lead cop actually believed me when I told him that we had driven from California and had nothing to do with the local news crews or the rage against fuel prices. "Good luck with your movie," he said, and the truck stop manager and crew scowled and walked back to the overflowing fuel islands.

I climbed aboard Jim's big truck, feeling safe and above it all. We drove to the interstate onramp, and we were back on our way, along the Trooper John Gregory Mann Memorial Highway towards Nashville. I got the camera and started filming.

The whole idea of this production was to travel through the entire country—essentially hitchhiking—in whatever direction the interviews would take us. I had always noticed how open and lucid people are on long road trips. Something about the physics and psychology of traveling great distances and driving while talking makes people reflect on their lives. I wanted to make a road film filled with deep conversation, and juxtapose it against roadside scenery from every interstate. Fields, onramps, cities, white dotted lines and dark clouds, next to drivers talking about their lives.

In four two-week trips, we drove 25,000 miles through 45 states, visited about 115 truck stops and shot about 60 interviews—of which at least half were substantial, in-depth character portraits. When I was in the trucks, Alabama followed behind in our camper van, talking on the CB. Other times, when we couldn't find interviews, we'd just drive together in the van to the next truck stop and I shot scenic vistas out of the passenger window along the way. My nickname became "The Scenic Bulimic" because I developed an obsessive habit of yelling, "Stop! Stop!" as if I wanted to vomit, and, even before we'd fully stopped, jumping out of the van with my camera to film anything remotely interesting: a road sign against the blowing wheat, or a frozen view of Pittsburgh, or a glistening collection of backlit "Pee Bombs"—you know all those half-filled iced tea bottles you see scattered along the roadsides? They aren't filled with iced tea.

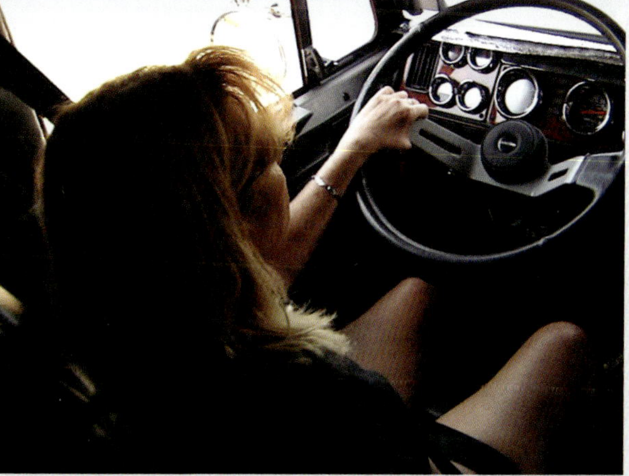

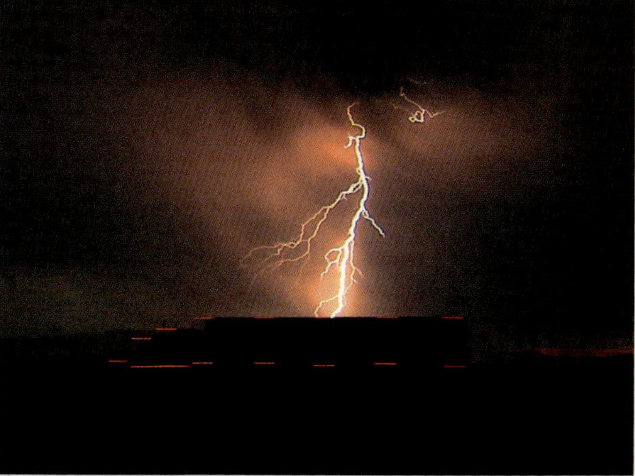

This page, top to bottom: Doug Pray, at 3:30 am in Hunts Point, Bronx, New York. Photo by Jim Dziura; Loretta hauling 21 palates of honeydew melons along I-40. Still image from *Big Rig*, shot by Doug Pray; Lightening strikes behind a big rig in the desert near El Paso, Texas. Still image from *Big Rig*, shot by Doug Pray.

At nights we'd park at the truck stops, review our footage on a little monitor and crash out in the camper van. In the morning, we'd take nine dollar truck stop showers, drink truck stop coffee and fish for trucker interviews, starting with the guys seated around the counter.

I had a naïve idea that making a documentary film about truckers in modern America would somehow be like *Convoy* or *Smokey and the Bandit*. I idolized the 1970s movie image of American trucking culture. I loved listening to classic trucker tunes like "Six Days on the Road" and "White Lightning Express," and in my big city stupidity, I figured *Big Rig* would be a kick-ass anthem to the dangerous, fun side of America, just filled with wacky, chrome-lovin', country-listening characters, like a giant episode of "Hee Haw" on speed. It seems incredible to me now, but when we set out on our first shoot, we even brought along a little barbeque and a guitar so we could hang out by the trucks at night, cook brats, drink beer, meet drivers and… What a joke.

What we actually found was more like *Grapes of Wrath*: 40 days and 40 nights with America's neglected working class. Broken dreams. Empty wallets. Rolled up windows and suspicious looks. America is going to hell. And the truckers are the first to know it.

Loretta was no exception. "I think we oughta all block the entrances to the fuel islands and shut these highways down!" she said, in regard to the fuel prices. About the inability of independent truckers to truly organize and stage a strike, she said, "It's crazy!" Like most, Loretta wanted to be a truck driver because of the independence and freedom of the job. "When I'm sitting up here behind the wheel? It's my world," she said.

She loves being a truck driver. But when we park at a Petro, she shows me a lipstick case that conceals a razor sharp knife blade. She carries it at all times, for fear of being attacked. "I have to carry a weapon with me, and at night, my doors stay locked." There is a desperation in her voice, and it goes beyond a basic fear of violence against women. It's a feeling of loss of respect—it's a feeling that comes from the daily sight of four-wheelers cutting you off and giving you the finger, as if you're to blame for all the traffic congestion; from getting a $350 ticket for a tail light that went out, while others speed by; from having the Department of Transportation dictate when you can and can't sleep (they instated an "11 hour rule" which mandates the amount of uninterrupted hours you have to remain idle vs. driving); or paying at least 50 cents a gallon more for diesel fuel than unleaded, when everyone knows that unleaded is derived from diesel and it should be the other way around. At every turn and every transaction, you are reminded that you are not really in control, and nobody really cares—even though you have driven 100,000 safe miles this year, and transported Playstations, apples, paper, Coke, steering wheels, socks, shower curtains, insulation, DVDs, toothpaste and SWINDLE magazines to keep the nation alive.

But Loretta, like most drivers I interviewed, was honest and funny. She spoke about how she learned to drive a truck in the Navy, how she'd lost custody of her three kids down in Georgia, and had been homeless for a while. She told me how she met her new husband, Jim, and almost lost him to "another woman." Throughout the interview, Jim checked in on the CB from the other truck to alert her of cops or tell jokes. He'd pass her and they'd wave, husband and wife in tandem trucks, hauling along I-40. When they stopped, she'd open up the doors on the back of her trailer and check the temperature of the 27 palettes of honeydew melons. Her "reefer" (refrigerator unit) was having issues. Keeping produce at the right temperature is a driver's responsibility. If her melons aren't in the right conditions, they won't be accepted at the loading dock, and they'd have to be thrown away.

We drove about six hours with Jim and Loretta, and shot four hours of tape. We said "goodbye" at another set of fuel pumps, somewhere just north of Nashville. I pulled the camera out of Loretta's truck to get a shot of her checking the oil and kicking her tires—but we got booted out of the truck stop by another manager, saying "Get out with that thing." And so we did.

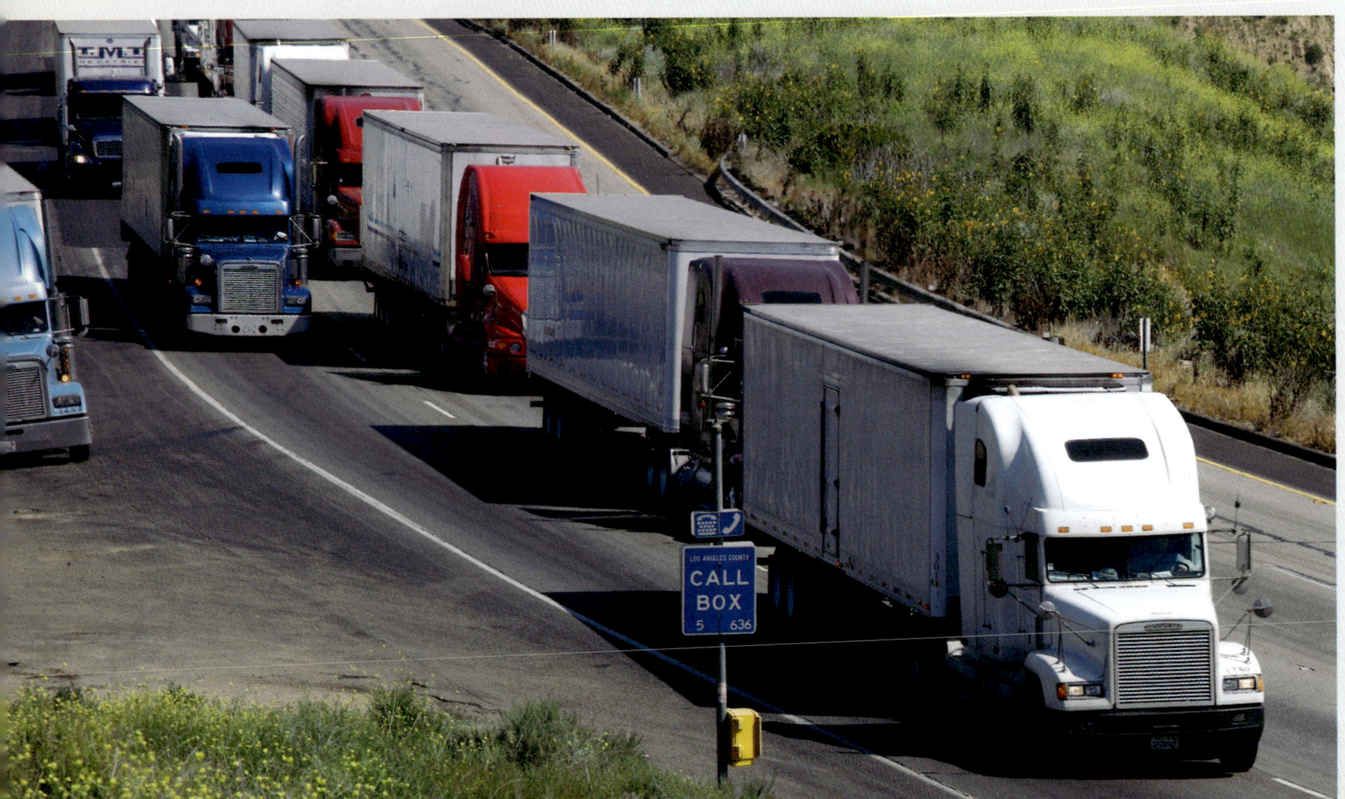

Just a few of the thousands of trucks that climb out of the L.A. basin everyday via "the grapevine" near Gorman, California. Photo by Roger Snider.

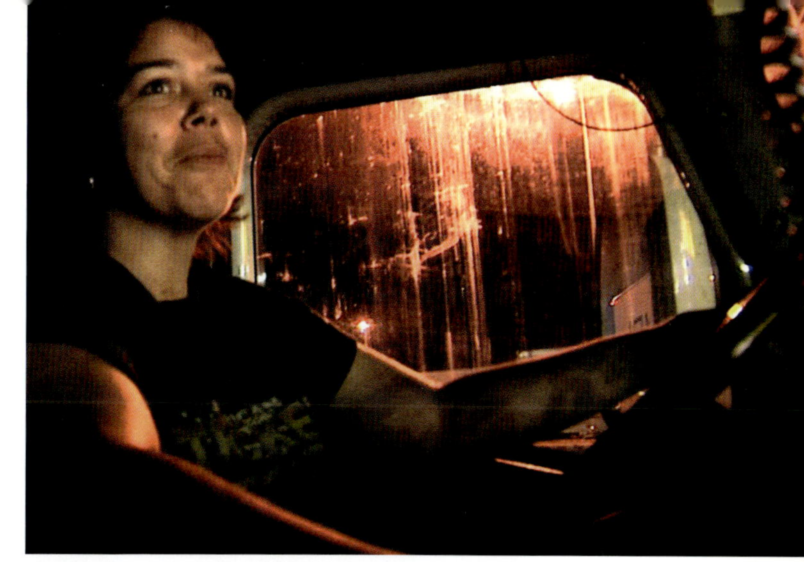

Heading north to Cincinnati, the "Scenic Bulimic" got shots of Kentucky horses, tobacco fields, a Louisville skate park off I-65 filled with teenagers and a giant black billboard that said "Hell is Real," under an orange, full moon.

In Mississippi, I rode with Jessie, who was hauling cypress wood, and talked about his son in Iraq. In upstate New York, we met Jerry, a fiercely anti-government veteran, hauling cabbages through a blinding snowstorm. In Nevada, we rode with John in a Kenworth truck who was hauling pigs to their death. In Maryland, I filmed the most spectacular sunset ever while riding with Jeff who was hauling post-Christmas Wal-Mart returns. In Oregon, we met Ron, a Native American who had an upside-down U.S. flag in his window, and had just dropped off a load of vinyl flooring in Seattle. In the Bronx, we pulled an all-nighter filming produce trucks unloading at Hunts Point to feed the entire Northeast. In Lebanon, Tennessee, we ate damn well at Uncle Pete's, one of the last, true, great, independent truck stops, and interviewed Uncle Pete himself. On the grapevine in California, we met Jacek, a Polish immigrant from Chicago who loved everything about America, as he grooved to Warsaw disco.

They all smoked. All of them. Many of them were vets. Most were fiercely independent souls with great stories. Other than that, none of them fit a single trucker stereotype.

Over the next year, I edited about a dozen stories together with all my scenic shots and fused it with the killer beats, haunting music and spoken word lyrics of Buck 65. We premiered the movie at SXSW in Austin, Texas, where all the drivers showed up and freaked out when they saw their faces on the 50-foot screen. *Big Rig* will be out this summer. If you're still looking for a chrome-hookers-n-speed flick, rent an old truxploitation movie—they're great. But if you want to hitch a ride with a bunch of real truckers who are out there right now, hauling your shit, check out our film. And next time you're about to flip off that 18-wheeler in the number two lane, remember what they all say: "If you bought it, a big rig brought it."

Look out for "Big Rig! Part II" in SWINDLE #17. We'll explore the subculture of suped-up show trucks, featuring the photography of die-hard big rig appreciator Roger Snider.

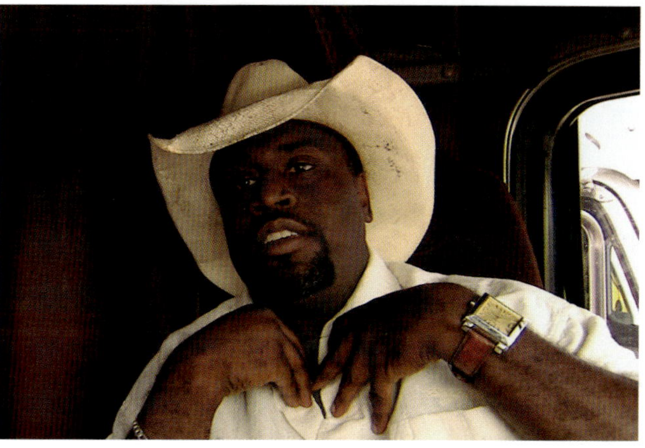

From top to bottom: Doris Lee, hauling an MRI unit near her hometown of Pascagoula, Mississippi. Still image from *Big Rig*, shot by Doug Pray; Claude Eric Walker, Sr. in his Peterbilt truck, Montgomery, Alabama. Still image from *Big Rig*, shot by Doug Pray; Al "Tiny" Marshall, waiting for a load, photo by Roger Snider; Ron Belgard, a Native-American driver being filmed by Doug Pray. Photo by Roger Snider.

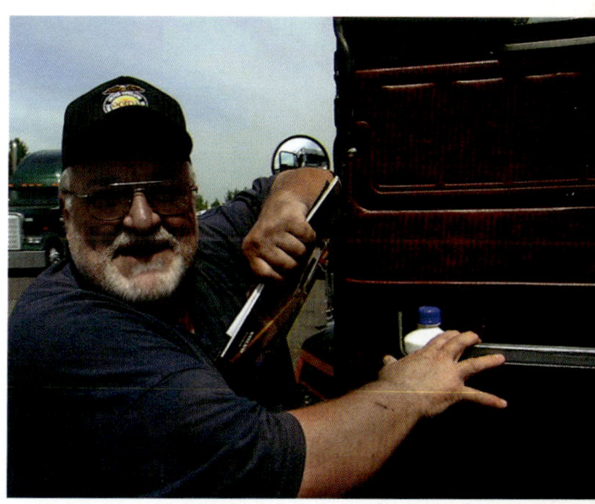

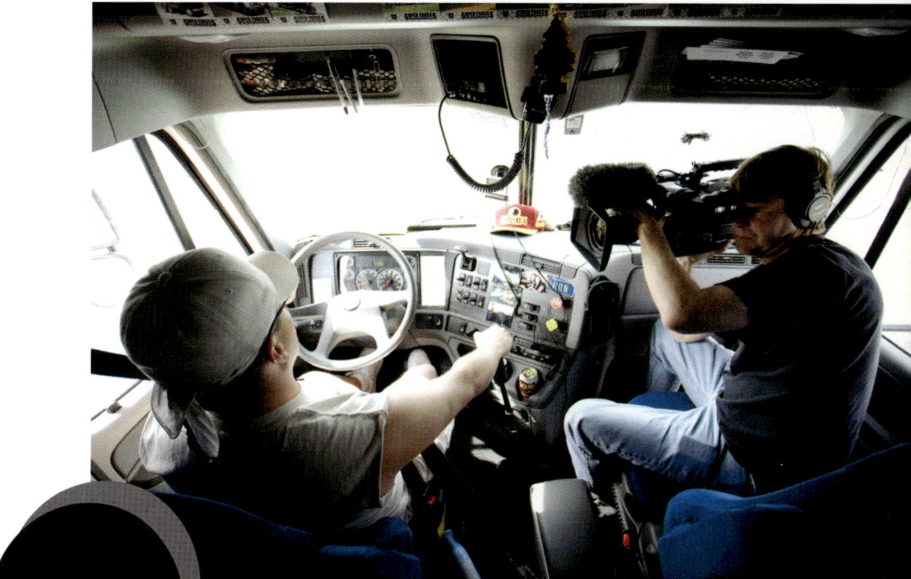

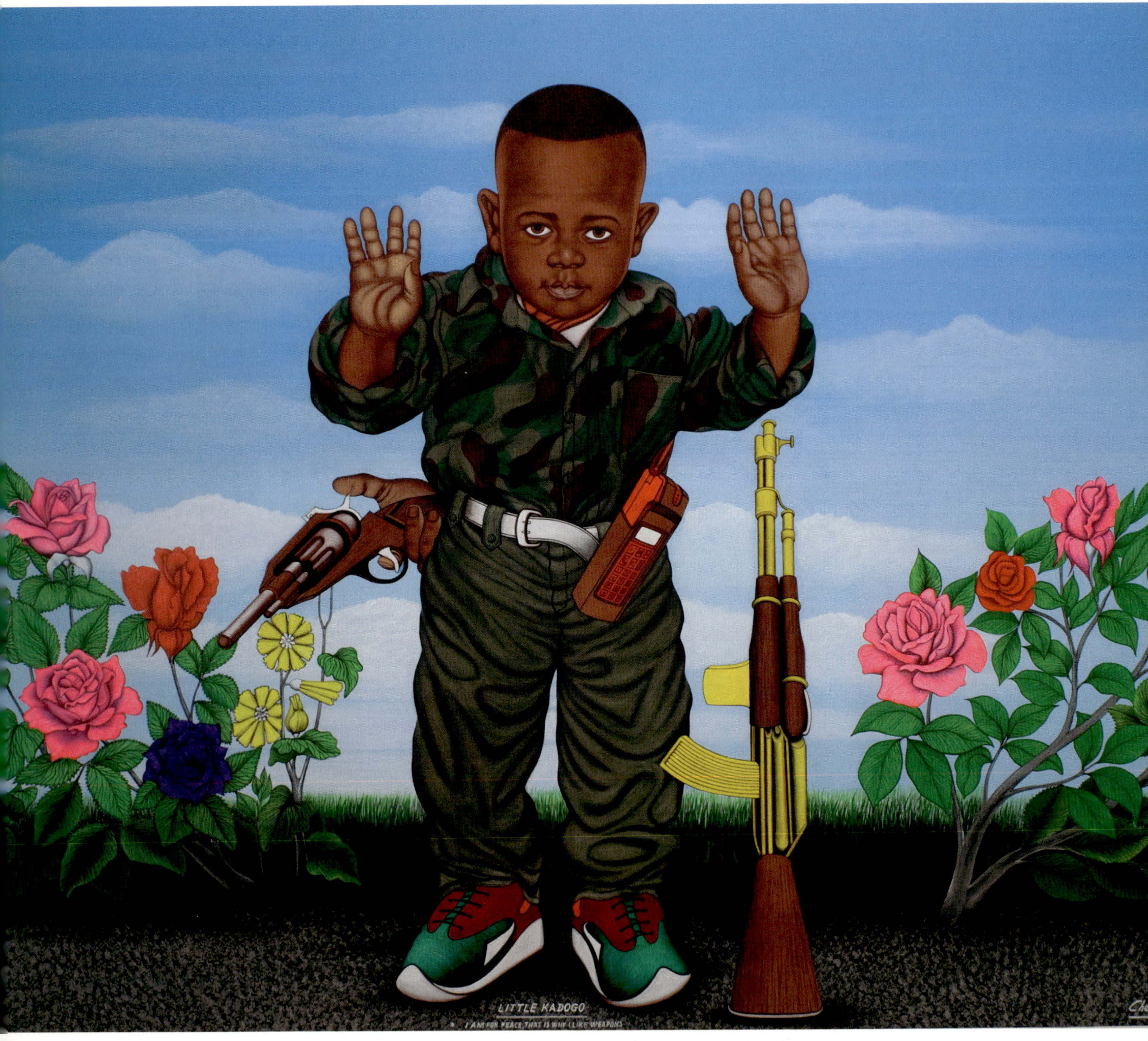
LITTLE KADOGO
I AM FOR PEACE THAT IS WHY I LIKE WEAPONS

STRENGTH IN NUMBERS

AN ELITE GROUP ᵒ CONGOLESE ARTISTS SHOW ᵗʰᵉ WORLD ᵗʰᵉ VIBRANT URBAN CULTURE ᵒ KINSHASA

BY CAMILLE LOWRY

The Democratic Republic of the Congo has been long associated with war, corruption and destruction. From the megalomaniacal regime of Mobutu to the devastating fratricidal war of the last decade, this sub-Saharan African country has suffered economic ruin, and for its people, hunger, disease and death.

In December *The New York Times* reported that the Congo is on the brink of another civil war. As a result of the burgeoning conflict, 425,000 people have been displaced from their homes, and others are experiencing severe hardships. In contrast to these harsh realities there has existed a rich local artistry which reflects a thriving spirit and vibrant culture.

Chéri Samba, Moké, Bodo, Chéri Chérin and Cheik Ledy are the five men collectively known as the School of Popular Painting. The members of this group, founded in the mid-1970s by Samba, have served as both pioneers of Congolese contemporary art and unofficial cultural ambassadors for their country.

Little Kadogo
2004
Acrylic and glitter on canvas
204.5 x 245.5 cm
© Chéri Samba
Courtesy C.A.A.C.
- The Pigozzi Collection, Geneva

These artists were born in the '50s and '60s, and their work deals with themes of urban existence—violence, illness, sexuality and technology. They all share the same source of inspiration, the capital city of Kinshasa. Mostly self-taught, they use the skills they acquired as billboard and sign makers to make large scale acrylic paintings in vibrant colors, often incorporating text.

Due to a lack of local museums or galleries in the Congo, this artwork was first exhibited in the street, on the walls of the artists' studios or even hung from mango trees, which attracted crowds to view and discuss the artwork. The artists' careers progressed and they exhibited in important international venues. But the group continued to hang their art in the street, where the public could have immediate access to the work—the paintings were about the public, for the public.

Samba, Moké and Bodo were the trailblazers of Congolese popular painting. Their careers took off after they were included in the 1978 African art exhibition "Art Partout" [Art everywhere], in Kinshasa. In 1989 Samba brought international attention to the art movement when his creations were shown alongside major contemporary artists like Francesco Clemente at the Magiciens de la Terre [Magicians of the Earth] exhibit at the George Pompidou Center.

Since then, a number of the artists have exhibited internationally. Jean Pigozzi, a renowned art collector, and curator Andre Magnin have purchased their works, including them in the largest private collection of contemporary African art in the world, titled the Contemporary African Art Collection. Recently, the Tate Modern exhibited eight pieces from the Congolese School of Popular Painting in a show called States of Flux.

International exposure has brought a new dimension to the artists' work. Tate curator Sheena Wagstaff says, "The School of Popular Painting [was] primarily geared towards the local [Kinshasa] market. But, of course most of [the artists] have sold internationally, and so their scopes have broadened, and therefore so have their themes."

New themes that have emerged are cultural tourism, and a self-reflective examination of these men's lives as successful artists. In one of Moké's works, "Untitled," the artist is depicted standing before several paintings wearing a dapper suit that is in stark contrast to his simple surroundings.

Wagstaff explains, "A lot of them have moved into a very self-reverential, wry take on the artist as celebrity, or people wanting to collect the artist as opposed to collecting the work." Samba illustrates this in "Une Peinture a Defender" (A Painting to Fight For), in which he stands as if crucified before a painting, shielding it from collectors.

Chéri Samba, who is credited with coining the term "popular painting," is the most well known artist of the group. He first found success as a witty comic strip illustrator, and his biting humor has translated into his fine art, which are cinematic in scope. In a review of Samba's work, *The New York Times* said that the artist "portrays the difficulties and hypocrisies of everyday life with a combination of tenderness, humor and bitterness that cuts through language barriers."

History of the Congo

1482
Portuguese explorer Diogo Cão becomes the first European to navigate the Congo region.

16th-17th Centuries
The slave trade spreads to the Congo.

1870s-1880s
King Leopold II of Belgium sets up a private colony, known as the Congo Free State.

1908
Belgium annexes the territory from Leopold's private control, in light of atrocities committed under the king's reign being publicly exposed. The region is renamed the Belgian Congo.

1960
Independence. The fiercely anti-colonial Patrice Lumumba, 35, becomes the first prime minister, Joseph Kasa-Vubu becomes the first president. The Congolese army mutinies, causing civil unrest. Lumumba seeks financial assistance from the Soviet Union. The CIA backs a coup d'état, orchestrated by Colonel Joseph Mobutu to oust Lumumba from office.

1961
Lumumba is assassinated, likely killed with the consent of Belgium and the U.S.

1963
Moise Tshombe, leader of the separatist Katanga region, agrees to end secession.

1964
President Kasa-Vubu appoints Tshombe prime minister of the Congo.

1965
Joseph Mobutu becomes president after he seizes power in a bloodless coup.

1971
Mobutu renames the country the Republic of Zaire, changes his name to Mobutu Sésé Seko Kuku Ngbendu Wa Za Banga, which means "The all-powerful warrior who, because of his endurance and inflexible will to win, will go from conquest to conquest, leaving fire in his wake."

1974
Muhammad Ali and George Foreman's famous fight, "The Rumble in the Jungle," is held in Kinshasa, Zaire. Mobutu Sésé Seko puts up $10 million to finance the fight.

1996-1997
The First Congo War breaks out. Anti-Mobutu forces, with the backing of Rwanda, Uganda, Burundi and Angola form the Alliance of Democratic Forces for the Liberation of Congo-Zaire (ADFL)—and successfully ousts Mobutu from his 32-year presidency. Laurent-Désiré Kabila becomes the new president. The country is renamed the Democratic Republic of the Congo (DRC).

1998
The Second Congo War breaks out.

1999
The Lusaka Ceasefire Agreement is signed by six nations embroiled in the war: Angola, the DRC, Namibia, Rwanda, Uganda, Zambia and Zimbabwe. Two rebel groups, the Movement for the Liberation of Congo (MLC) and the Rally for Congolese Democracy (RCD) also signed the treaty.

2001
Kabila is assassinated. His son succeeds him as president.

2003
The end of the Second Congo War.

2005-2006
A new constitution is approved by parliament and democratic vote; the first free elections since Mobutu came to power are held. Joseph Kabila continues his presidency.

2008
As civil unrest continues, peace talks take place between the government and General Laurent Nkunda, leader of rebel forces in eastern Congo.

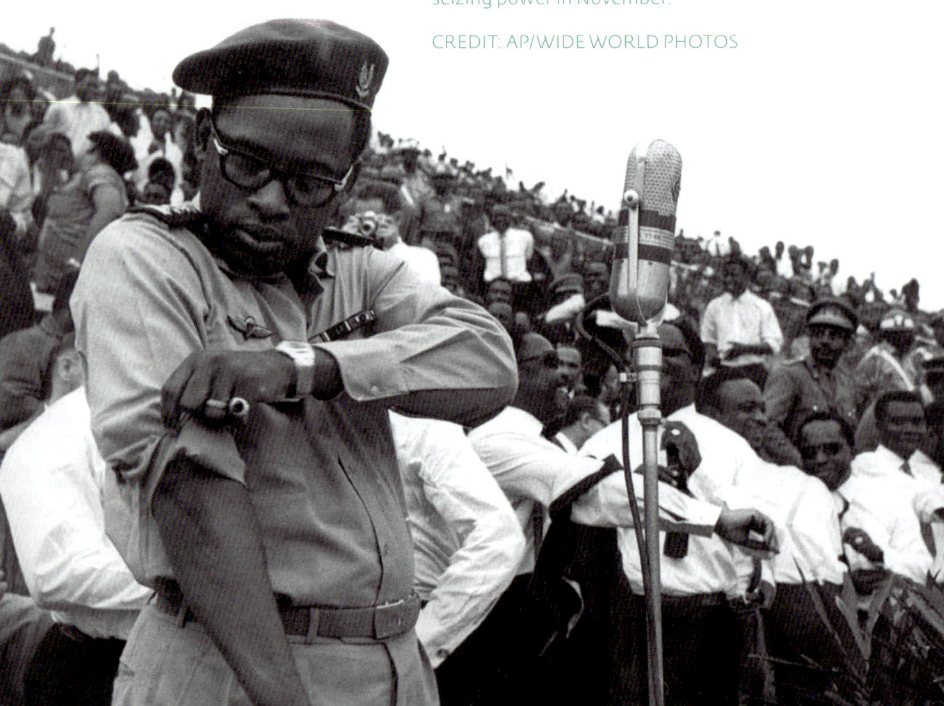

Below: Coup leader Joseph Mobutu, later known as Mobutu Sésé Seko, rolls up his sleeves during a speech in December 1965 in Leopoldville (now Kinshasa), Congo, after seizing power in November.

CREDIT: AP/WIDE WORLD PHOTOS

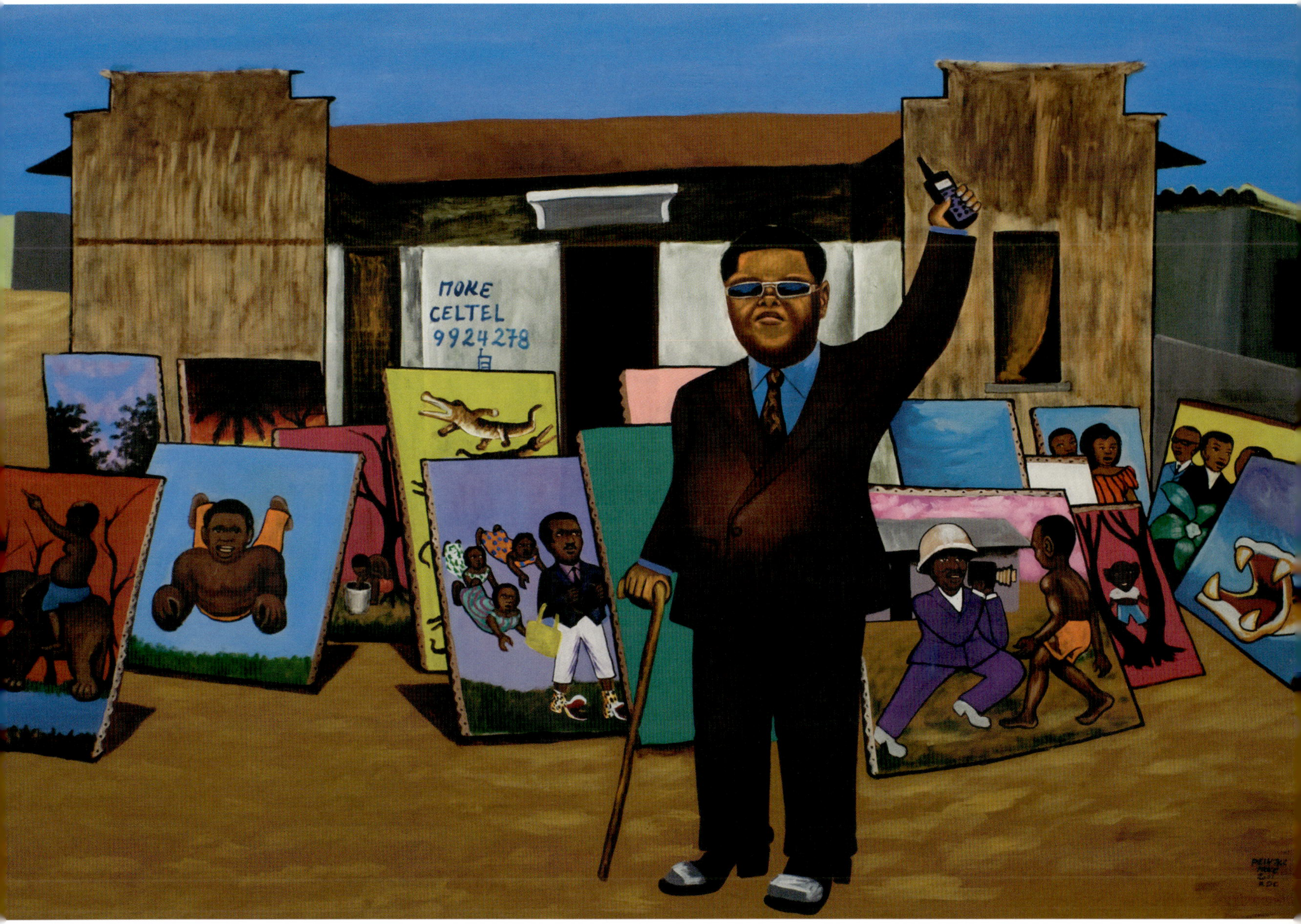

Untitled
2001
Acrylic on canvas
200 x 293 cm
© Moké
Courtesy C.A.A.C.
– The Pigozzi Collection, Geneva

Je suis un rebelle
1999
Acrylic and glitter on canvas
146 x 204 cm
© Chéri Samba
Courtesy C.A.A.C.
- The Pigozzi Collection, Geneva

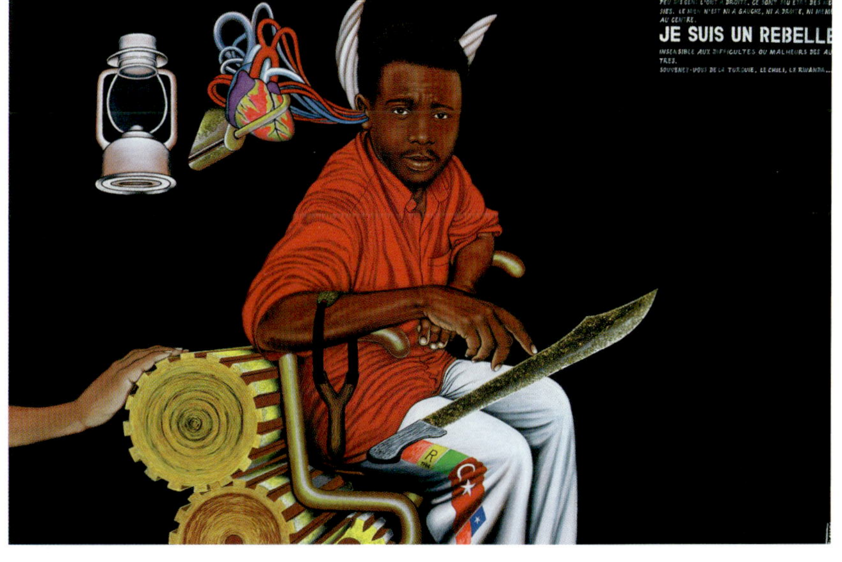

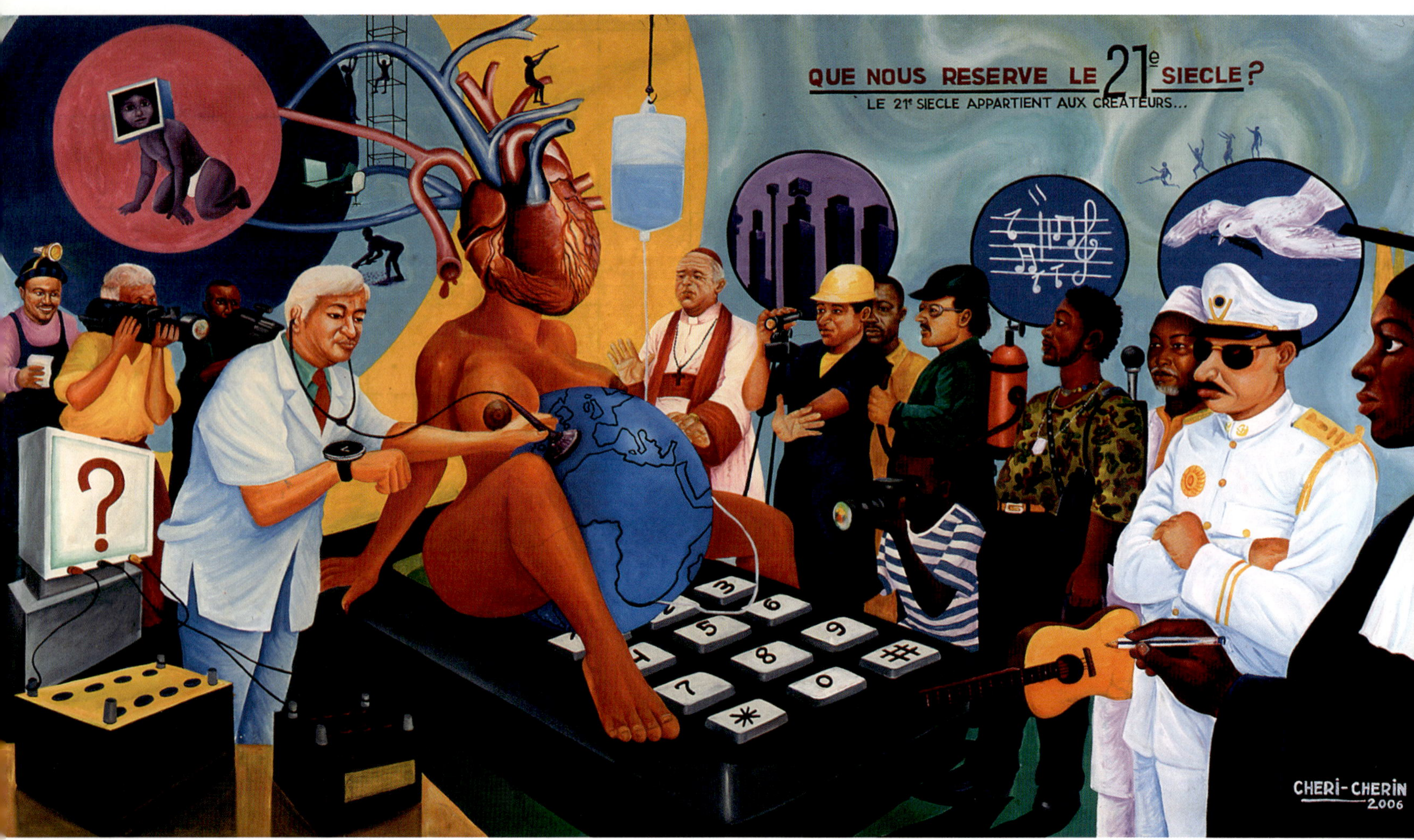

Que nous réserve le 21ème siècle ?
2006
Acrylic and oil painting on canvas
200 x 370 cm
© Chéri Chérin
Courtesy C.A.A.C. -
The Pigozzi Collection, Geneva

Défilé de modes
2006
Acrylic on canvas
168 x 440 cm
© Bodo
Courtesy C.A.A.C. -
The Pigozzi Collection, Geneva

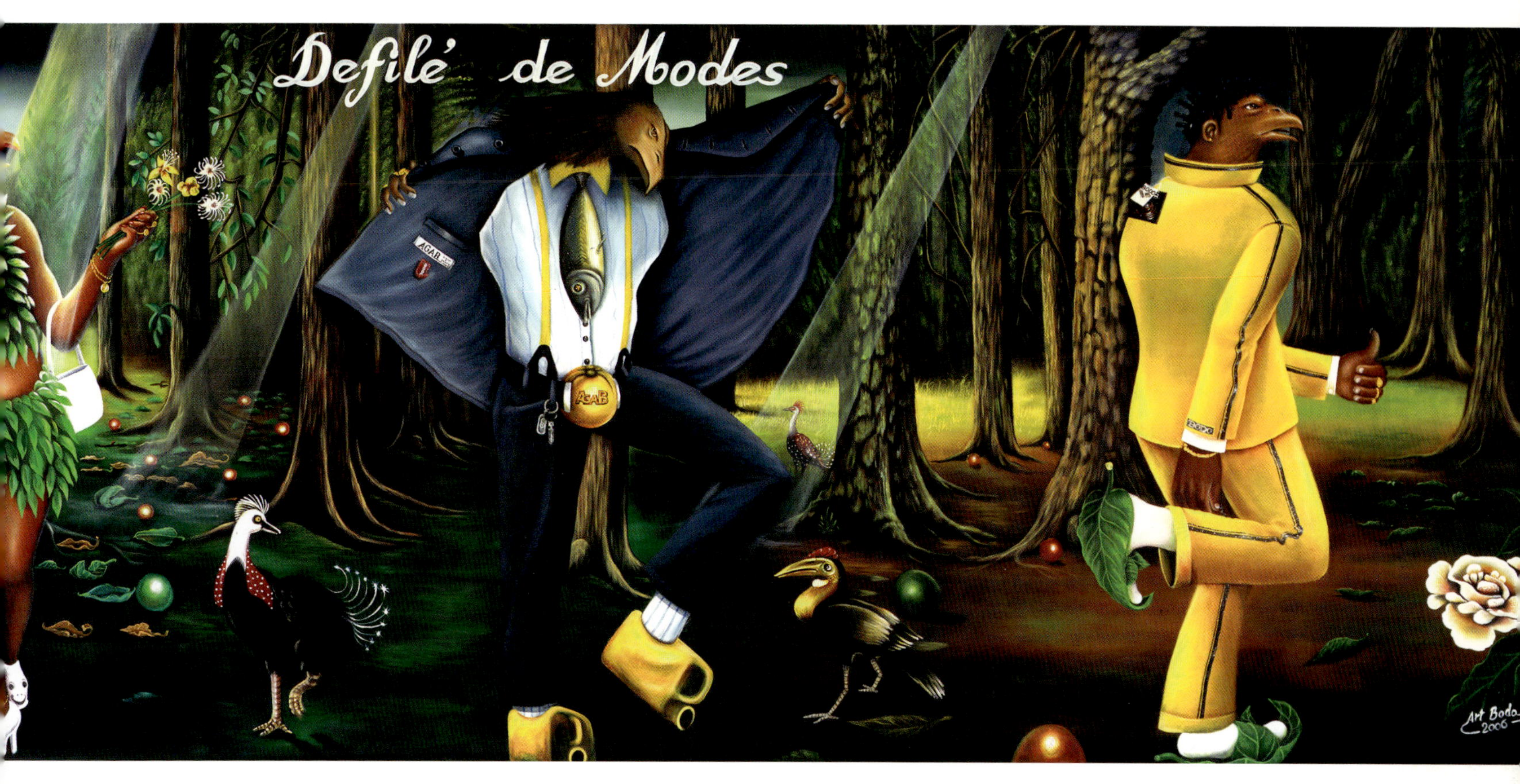

"MY POPULARITY MADE ME QUITE A HIT WITH THE LADIES. I WAS PROUD OF MY CONQUESTS. I WAS THE LADIES' CHÉRI, AND I ALSO WANTED TO BE THE ART LOVERS' CHÉRI, AND THE CHÉRI OF THE GODS."

-Chéri Samba

Samba says, "I favor a direct style to convey messages that speak to everyone, both the initiated and the uninitiated. And the term 'popular' seemed the most appropriate to me." It should be noted that the word popular translates to "common" in French, the official language of the Democratic Republic of the Congo.

Samba is known for his use of text, a practice he utilized to make his work stand apart from his peers, and engage his audience. He says, "I noticed that people in the street would walk by paintings, glance at them and keep going. I thought that by adding text, people would have to stop and take time to read it, to get more into the painting and admire it."

" AFRICAN ART IS A WEAPON AGAINST PREJUDICE... SUCH ART CAN HELP KEEP THIS HUGE, BUBBLING CONTINENT PROUD AND VITAL. "

- Jean Pigozzi

He sees himself as not only a painter, but also an educator. His works are morality tales that transmit the socio-political issues of his home country to the greater world. "Little Kadogo" features a boy in fatigues raising his hands in surrender, with a third arm, brandishing a gun emerging from his back.

His paintings also exhibit a brazen sexuality, featuring ripe, curvaceous women. Chéri Samba acknowledges this with the cheeky statement, "My popularity made me quite a hit with the ladies. I was proud of my conquests. I was the ladies' Chéri, and I also wanted to be the art lovers' Chéri, and the Chéri of the gods."

Unlike the other self-taught popular artists, Cheik Ledy was a skilled painter, having trained under his older brother Chéri Samba for 10 years. He mimicked his brother's style of using text in his work and using humor to address grave topics. Andre Magnin described Ledy's work as "an exhortation" to his countrymen "to take responsibility" for the conflict and corruption predominating their nation. Ledy died of AIDS in 1997.

Moké differs from the other artists in the group by focusing on the lively world of the local middle class—who were the patrons of his work. He painted street scenes, bar life, celebrations and portraits of the Kinshasa bourgeoisie.

Magnin says that Moké painted characters "without concern for likeness or perspective. Instead, he celebrated the painterly aspects of his art, using a rich palette and vividly animated compositions." The artist did not rely on text to convey his messages—the images were strong enough. Some of his paintings were so beloved that, that local admirers reproduced them by the thousands. The artist passed away in 2001.

Bodo, who is an evangelical Christian pastor for the Pentecostal church, creates artwork that is more internally reflective than the work of his compatriots. He says, "I express everything that happens to me, so that I am no longer focused on specifically African topics and address myself to the entire world."

In 2002, the surviving members of the School of Popular Painting, along with some emerging artists, formalized their fellowship, by creating the Association of Painters of Popular Art (AAPOOO). The group's slogan is "Unity Makes Force." The School of Popular Painting has garnered the admiration and "participation of ministers and government officials," Bodo says. "We have been admired by the people."

Jean Pigozzi says, "African art is a weapon against prejudice... Africans produce art that is as good and as creative as any other region in the world, and such art can help to keep this huge, bubbling continent proud and vital."

The artists of the School of Popular painting have broadcast a purely Congolese perspective to the world. Unified, they have created a formidable, internationally recognized voice for the Democratic Republic of the Congo.

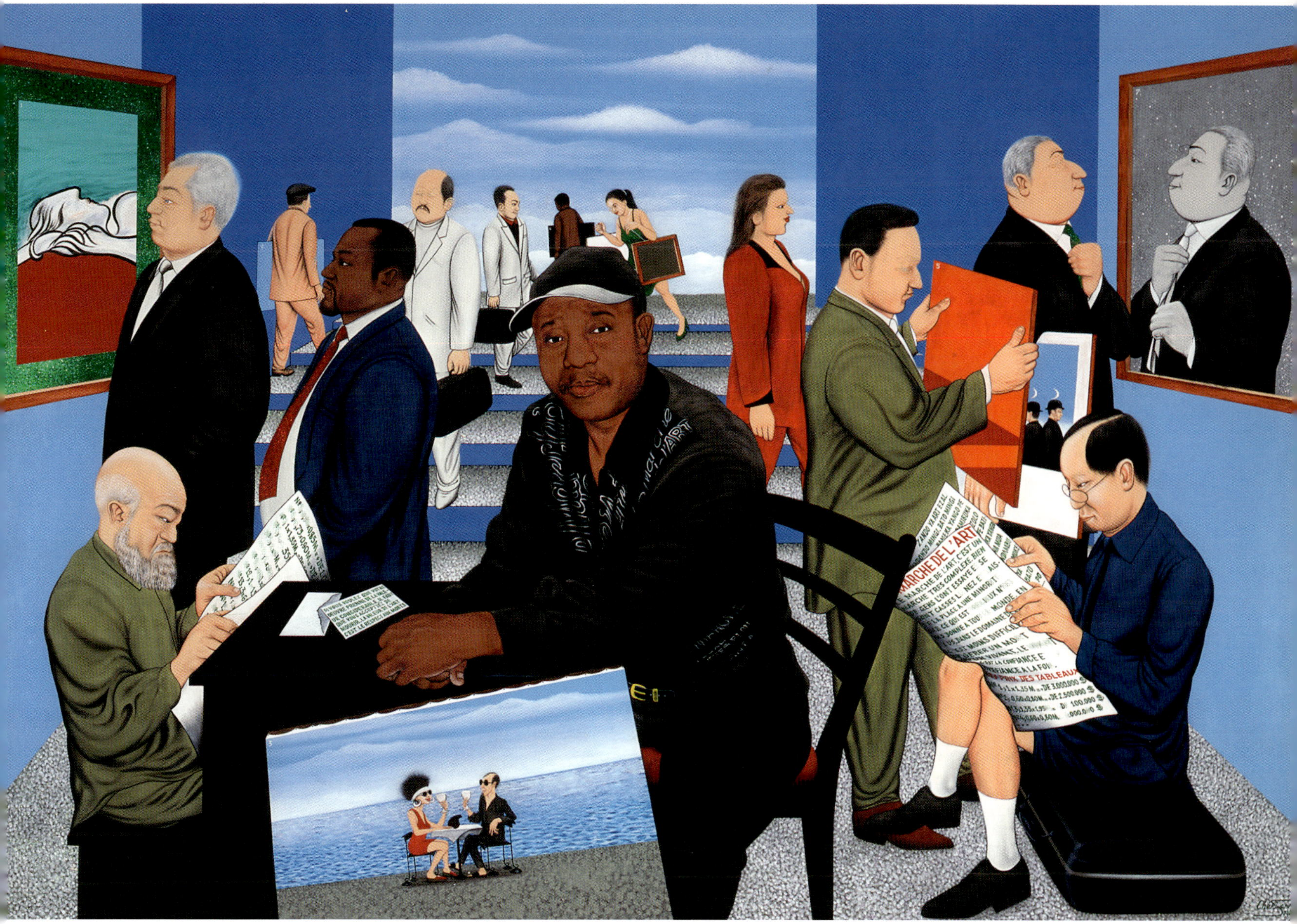

Le marché de l'art
2006
Acrylic and glitter on canvas
200 x 289.5 cm
© Chéri Samba
Courtesy C.A.A.C.
- The Pigozzi Collection, Geneva

Où va le monde ?
2006
Acrylic and oil on canvas
149 x 370 cm
© Chéri Chérin
Courtesy C.A.A.C.
– The Pigozzi Collection, Geneva

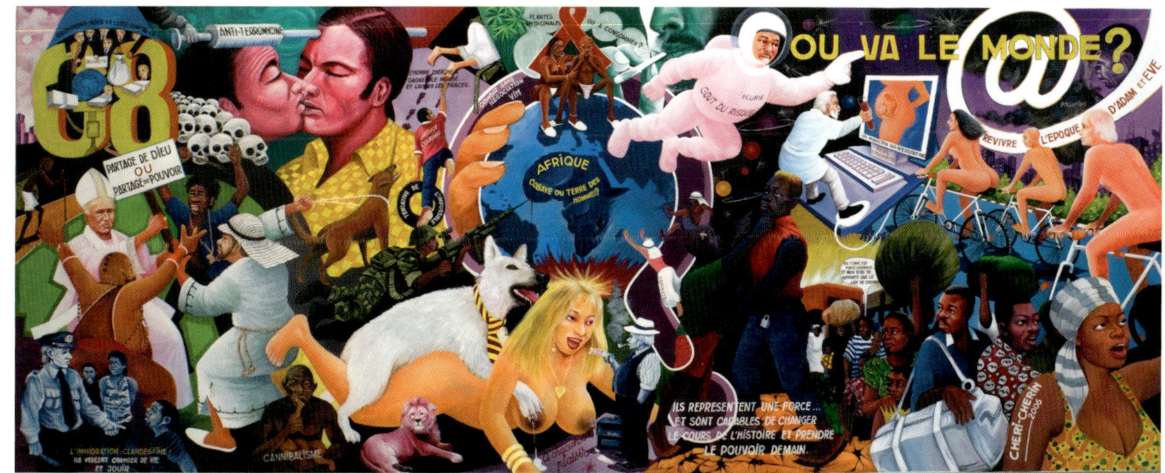

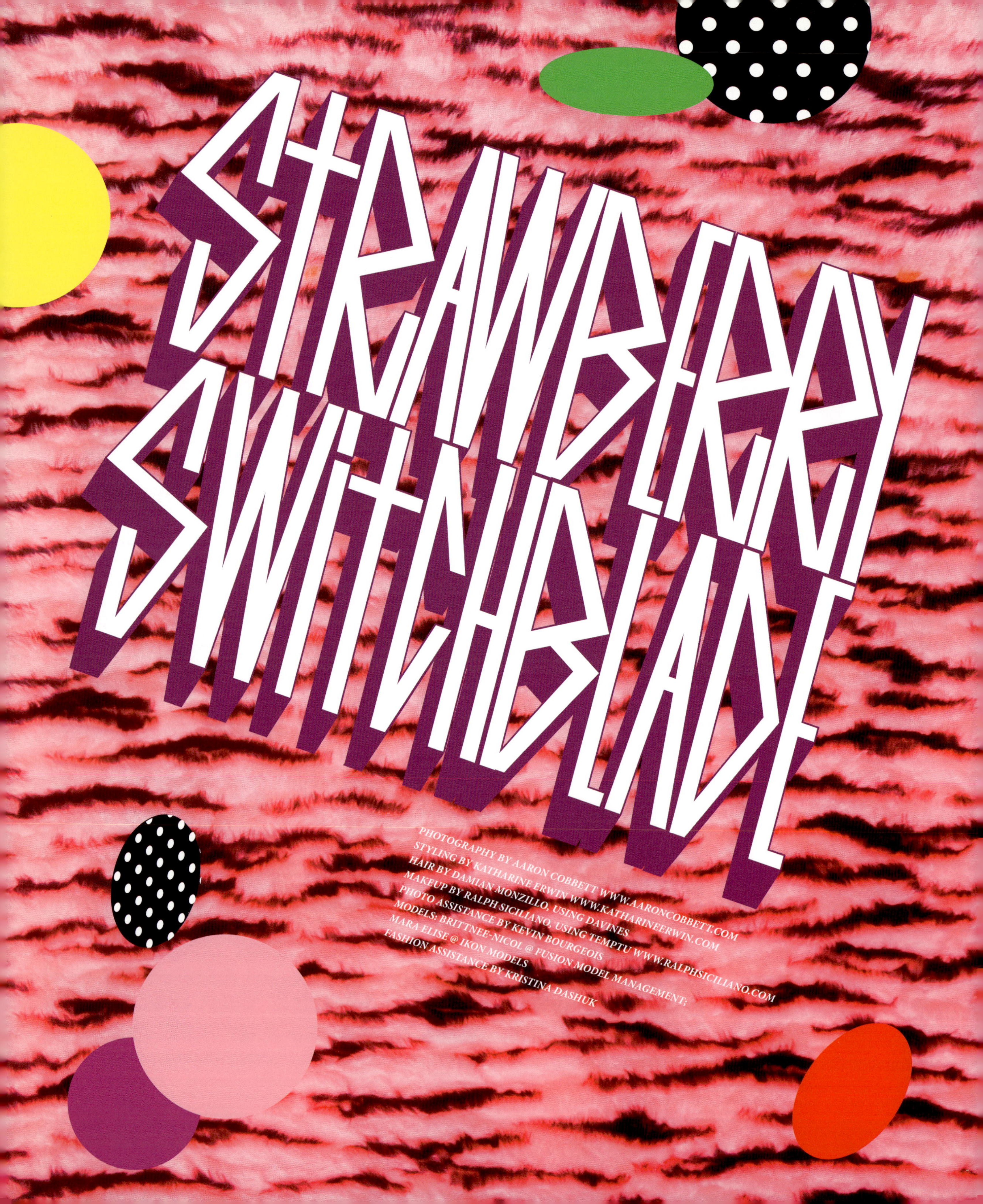

STRAWBERRY SWITCHBLADE
PHOTOGRAPHY BY AARON COBBETT WWW.AARONCOBBETT.COM
STYLING BY KATHARINE ERWIN WWW.KATHARINEERWIN.COM
HAIR BY DAMIAN MONZILLO, USING DAVINES
MAKEUP BY RALPH SICILIANO, USING TEMPTU WWW.RALPHSICILIANO.COM
PHOTO ASSISTANCE BY KEVIN BOURGEOIS
MODELS: BRITTNEE-NICOL @ FUSION MODEL MANAGEMENT;
MARA ELISE @ IKON MODELS
FASHION ASSISTANCE BY KRISTINA DASHUK

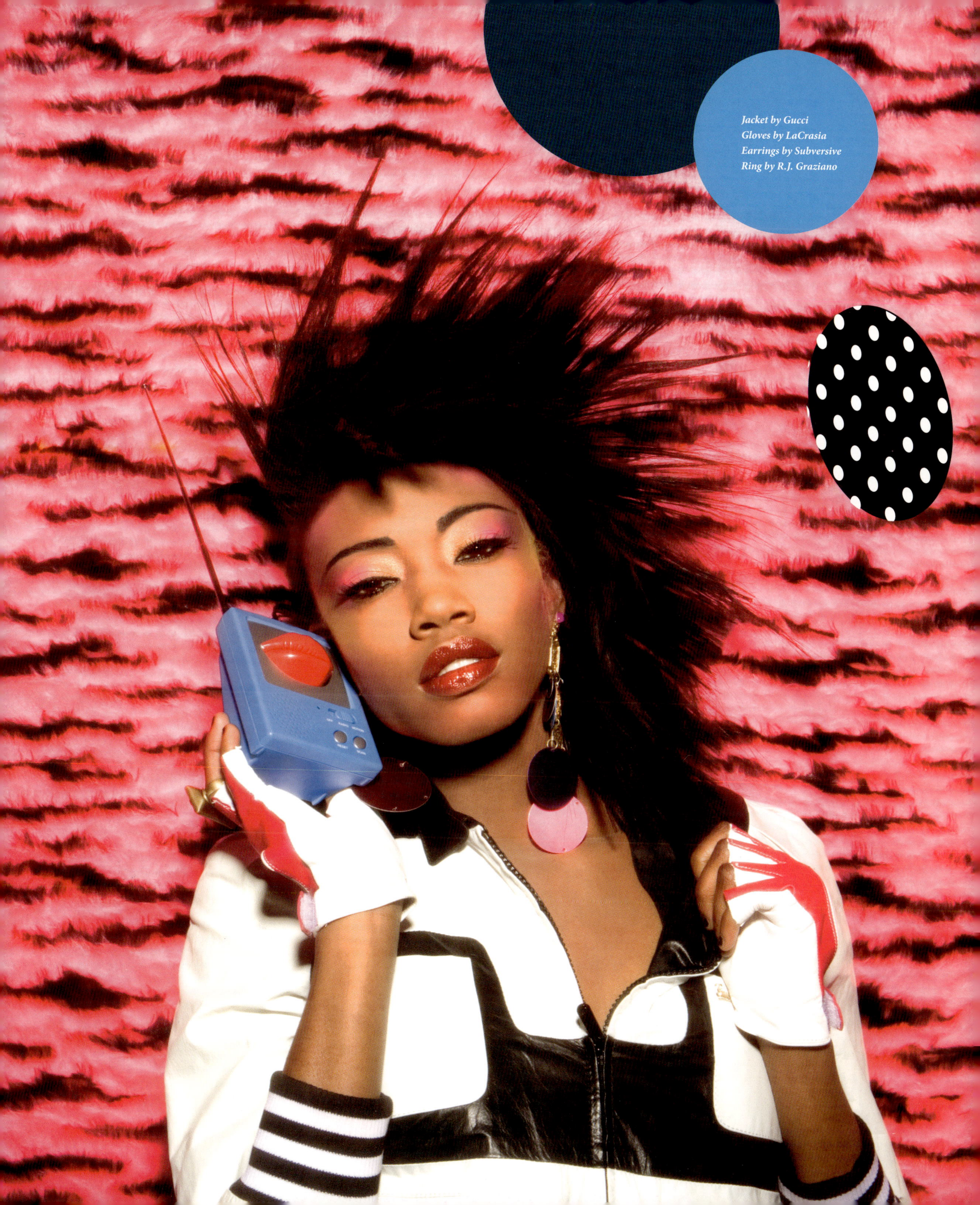
Jacket by Gucci
Gloves by LaCrasia
Earrings by Subversive
Ring by R.J. Graziano

Jacket by Gucci
Shorts by Louis Vuitton
Belt by AC Designs and Sen
Shoes by Giuseppe Zanotti
Stockings by Hot Topic
Gloves by LaCrasia

Jacket by vintage Ozbek
Top by Aurelio Costarella
Shoes by Fendi
Belt by Alessandro Dell' Acqua
Pink belt by Aurelio Costarella
Stockings by Wolford
Earrings by Tarina Tarantino

Dress by Heatherette
Shoes by Bastion
Gloves by LaCrasia

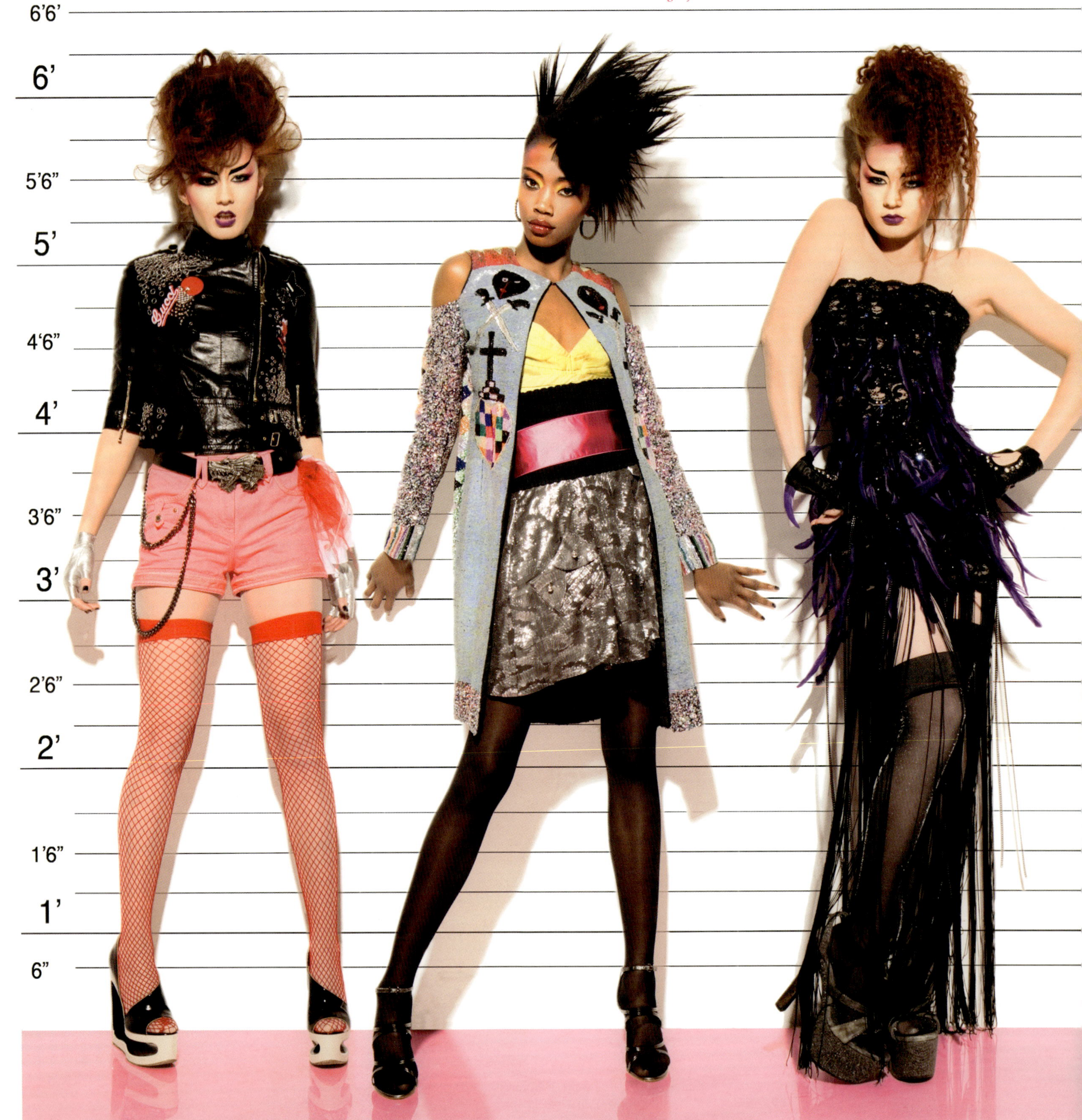

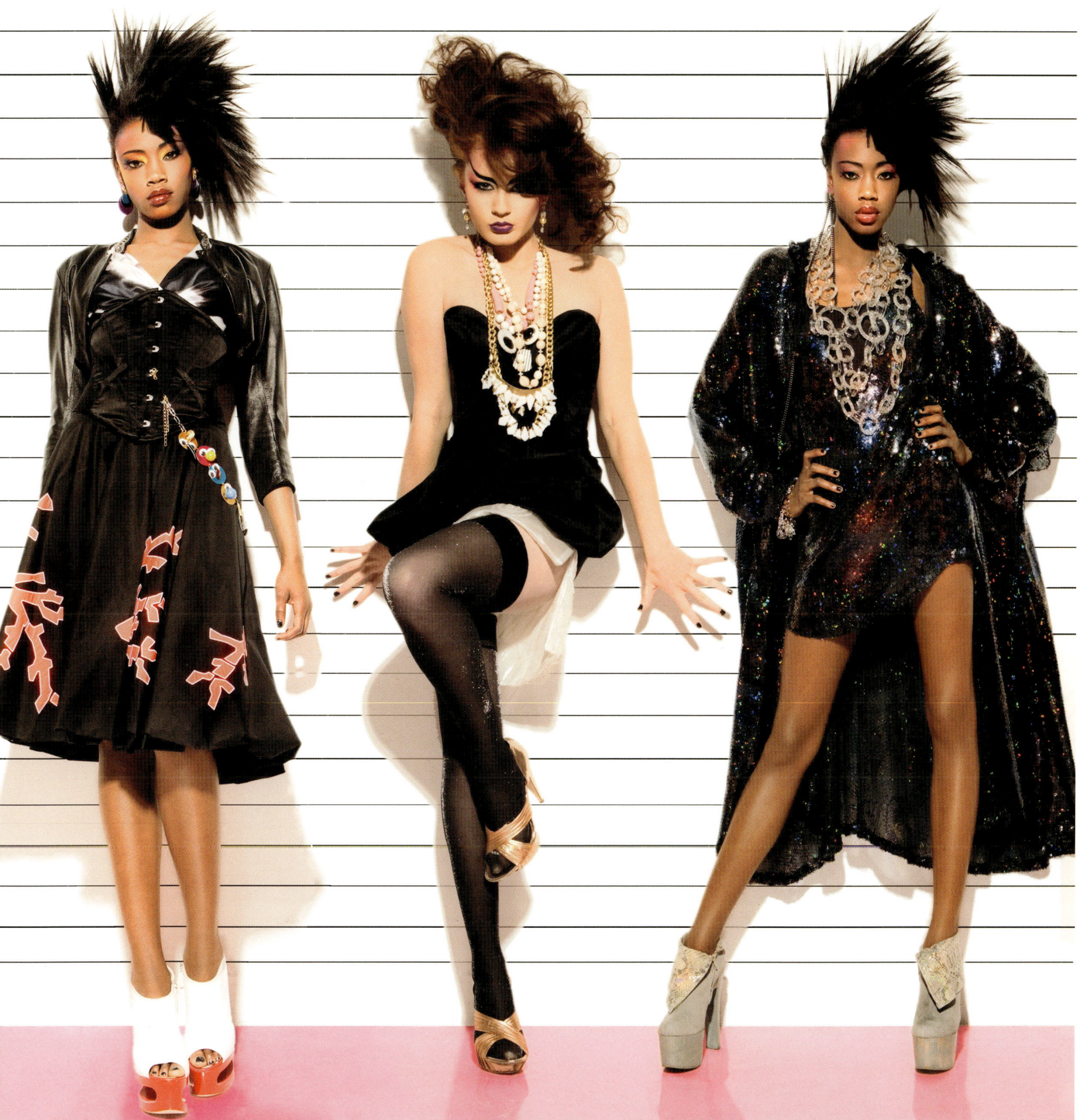

Jacket by vintage Ozbek
Shirt by Max Mara
Skirt by Gucci
Shoes by Giuseppe Zanotti
Corset by Aurelio Costarella
Earrings by Subversive
Chains as a belt by Subversive

Dress by Aurelio Costarella
Skirt by Alessandro Dell' Acqua
Shoes by Sergio Rossi
Necklace and earrings by Subversive
Stockings by Wolford

Dress and jacket by vintage Ozbek
Shoes by Bastion
Necklace by Subversive
Bracelet by Tarina Tarantino

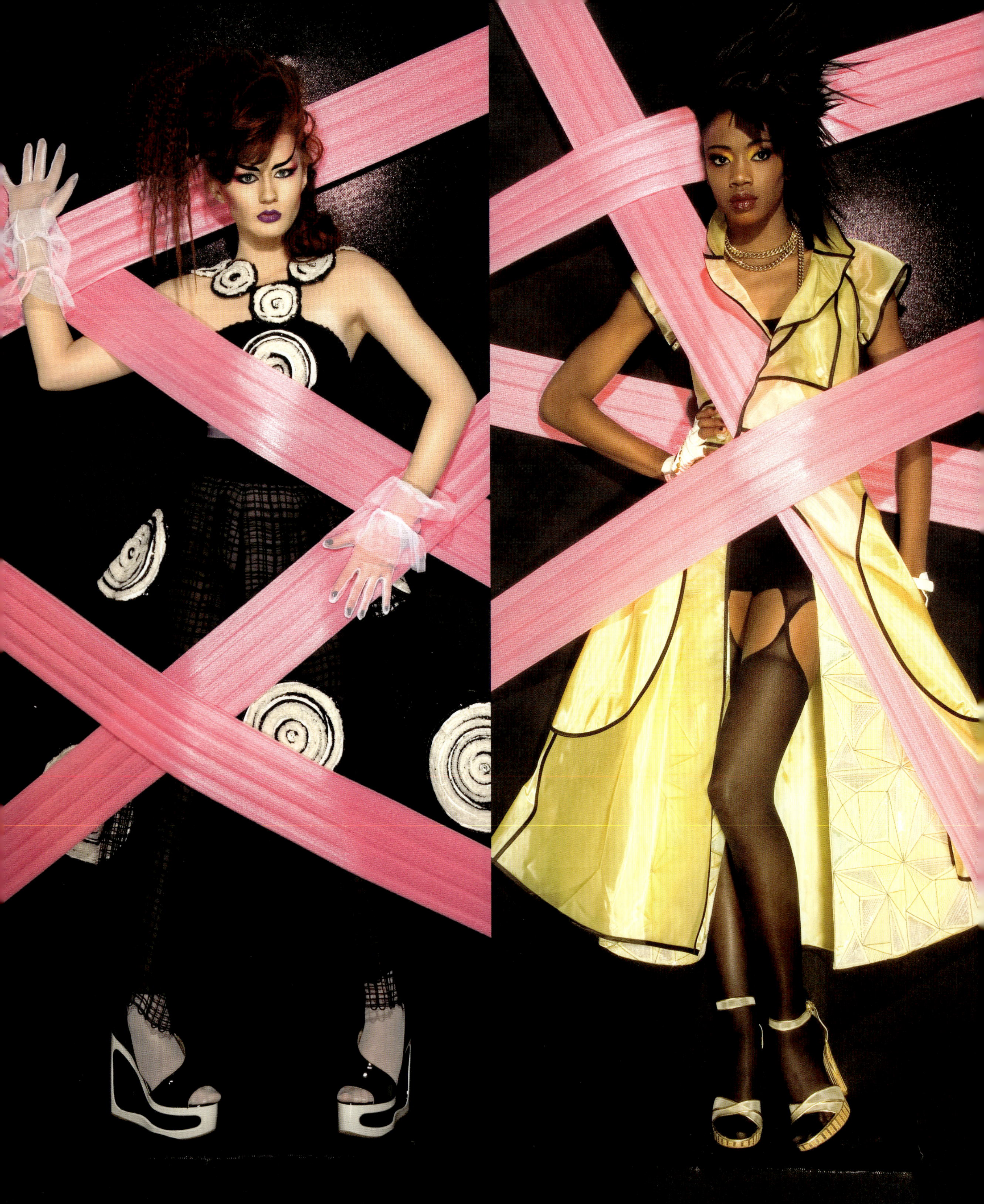

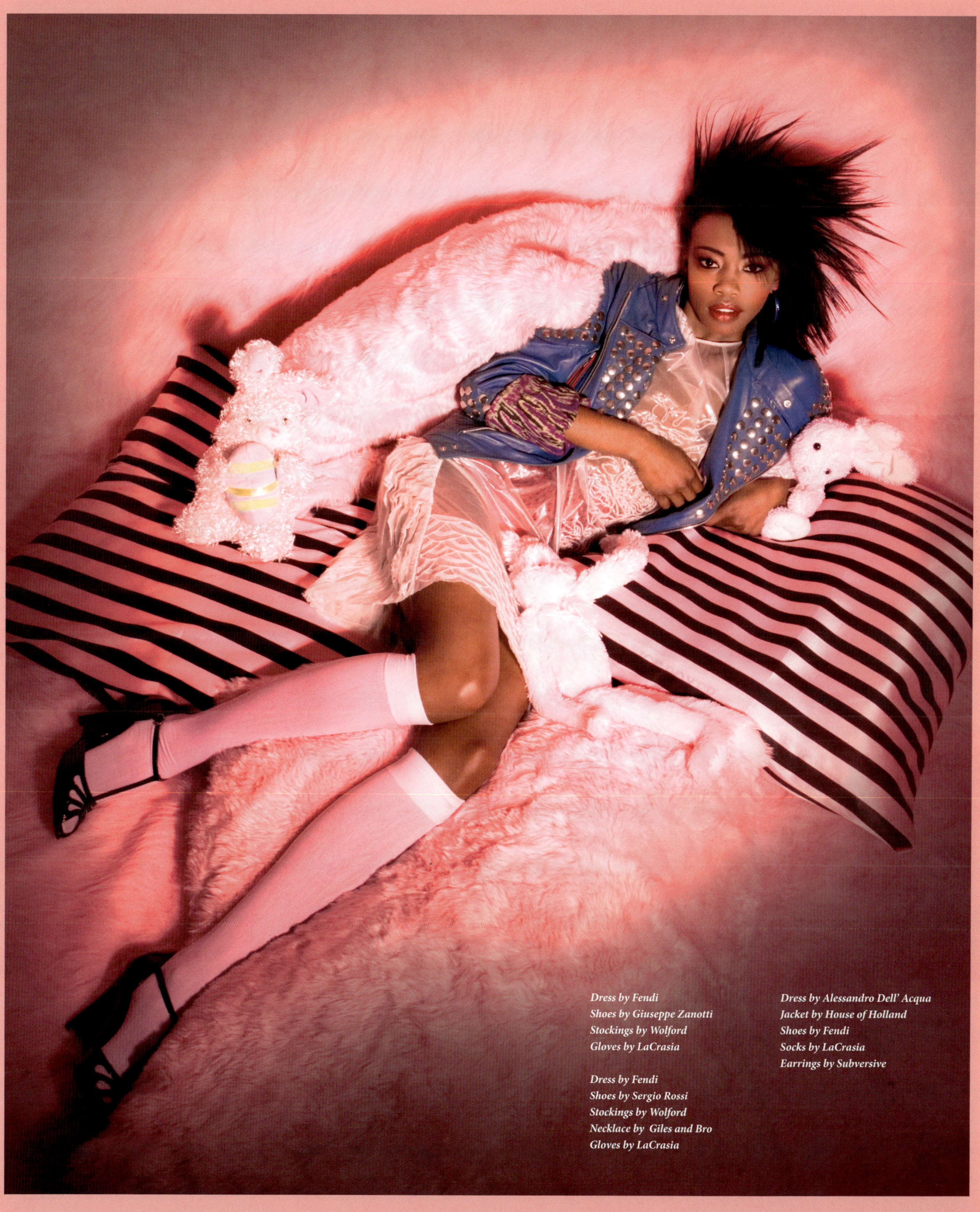
Dress by Fendi
Shoes by Giuseppe Zanotti
Stockings by Wolford
Gloves by LaCrasia

Dress by Fendi
Shoes by Sergio Rossi
Stockings by Wolford
Necklace by Giles and Bro
Gloves by LaCrasia

Dress by Alessandro Dell' Acqua
Jacket by House of Holland
Shoes by Fendi
Socks by LaCrasia
Earrings by Subversive

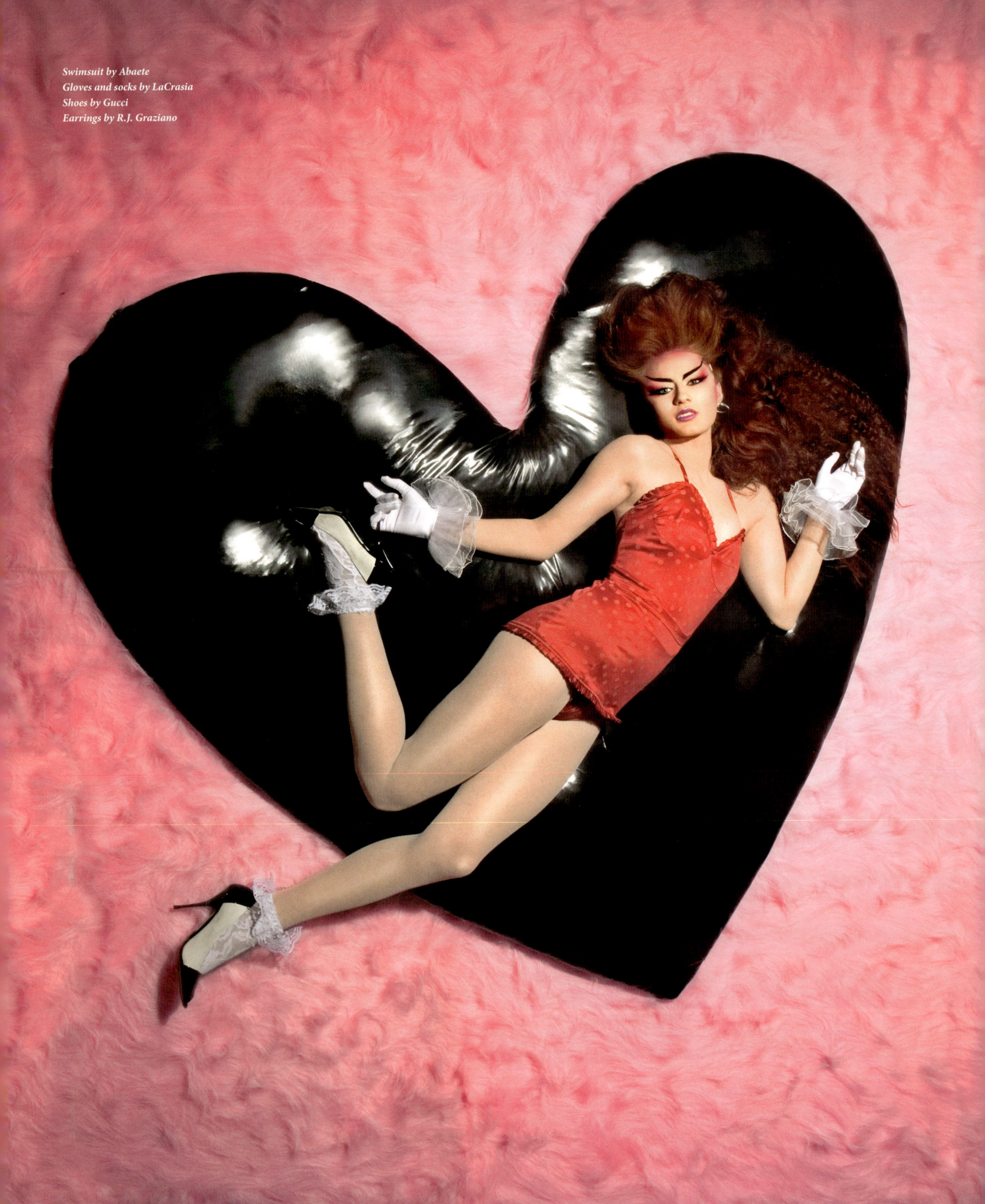
Swimsuit by Abaete
Gloves and socks by LaCrasia
Shoes by Gucci
Earrings by R.J. Graziano

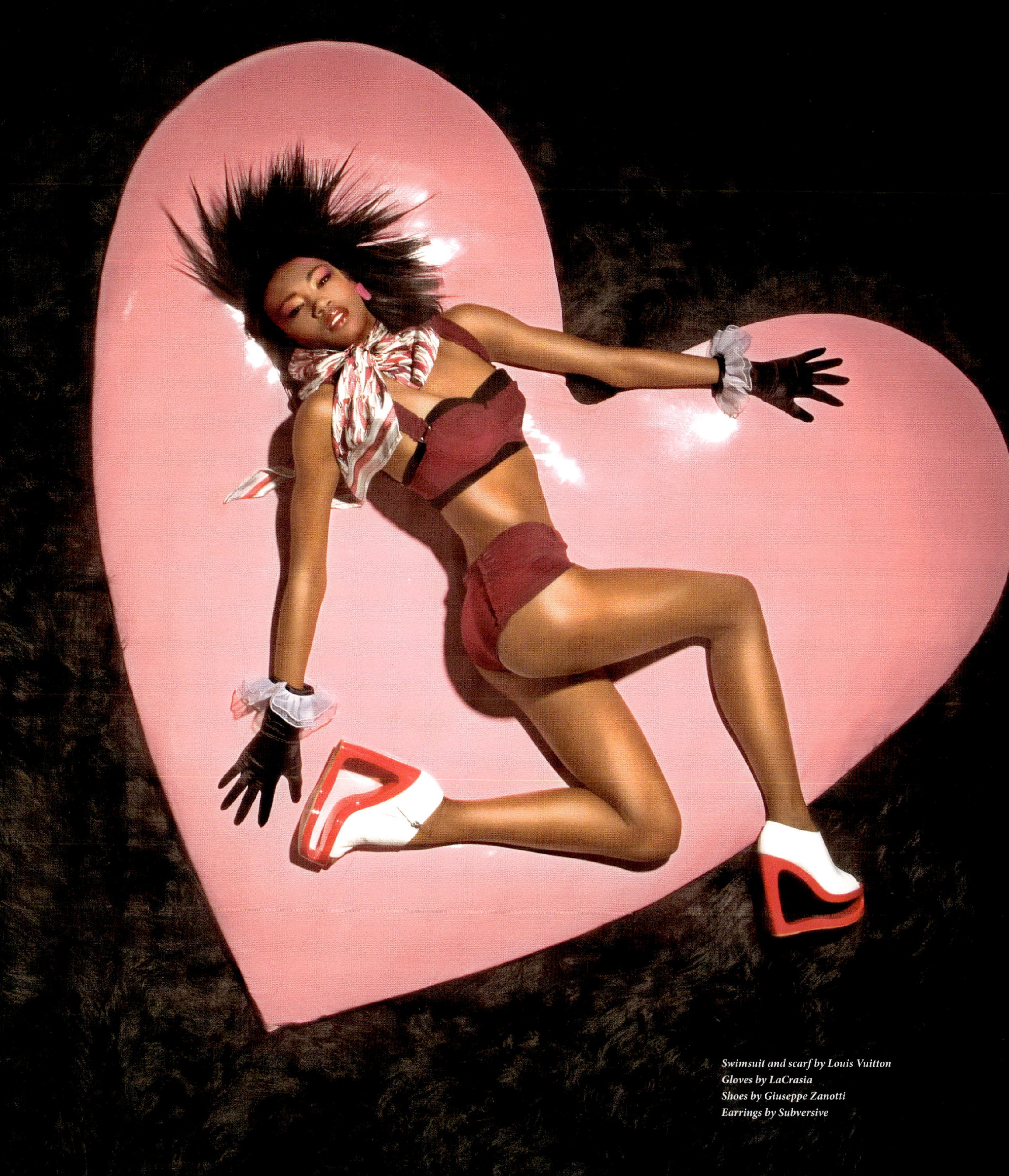

Swimsuit and scarf by Louis Vuitton
Gloves by LaCrasia
Shoes by Giuseppe Zanotti
Earrings by Subversive

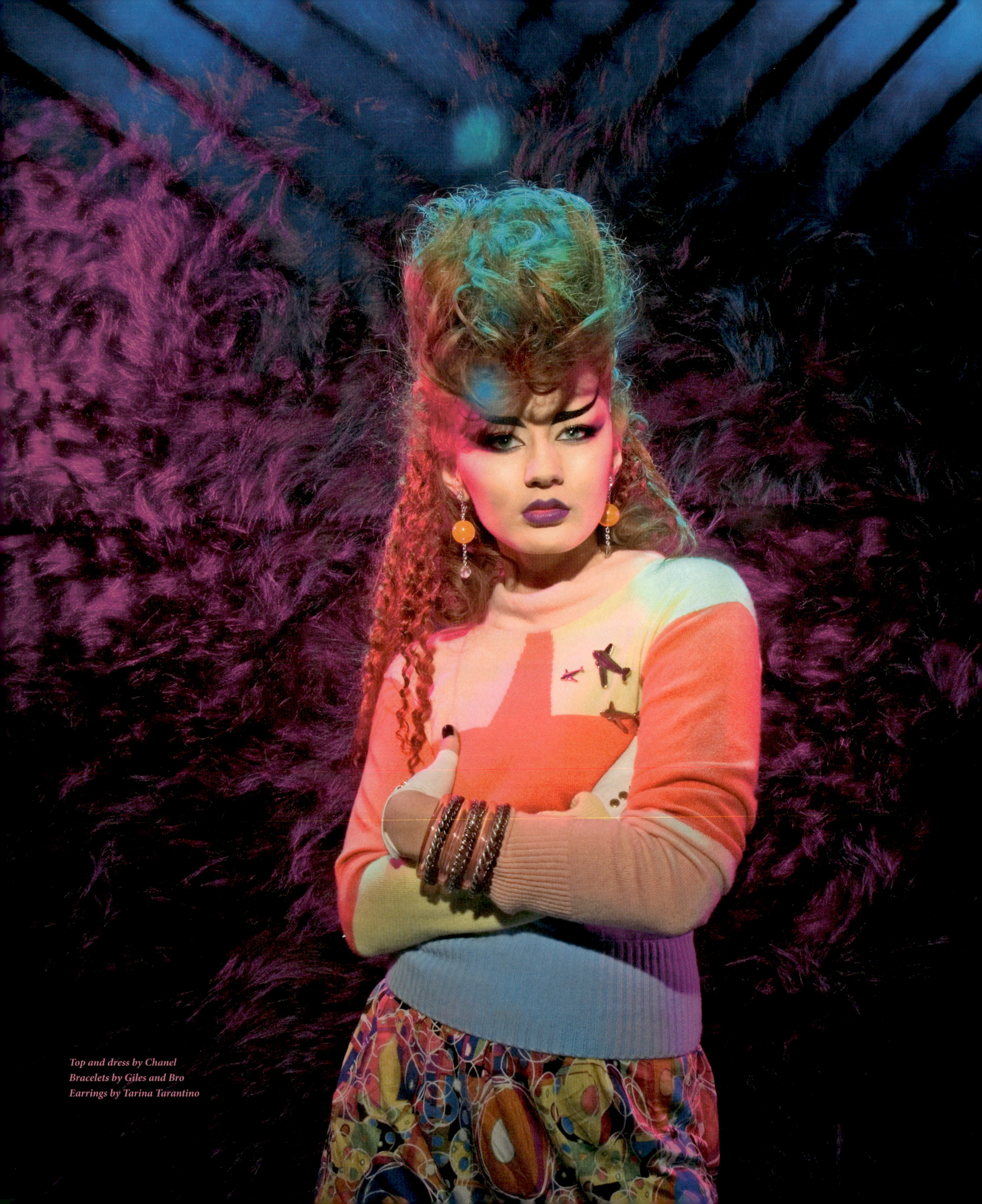

Top and dress by Chanel
Bracelets by Giles and Bro
Earrings by Tarina Tarantino

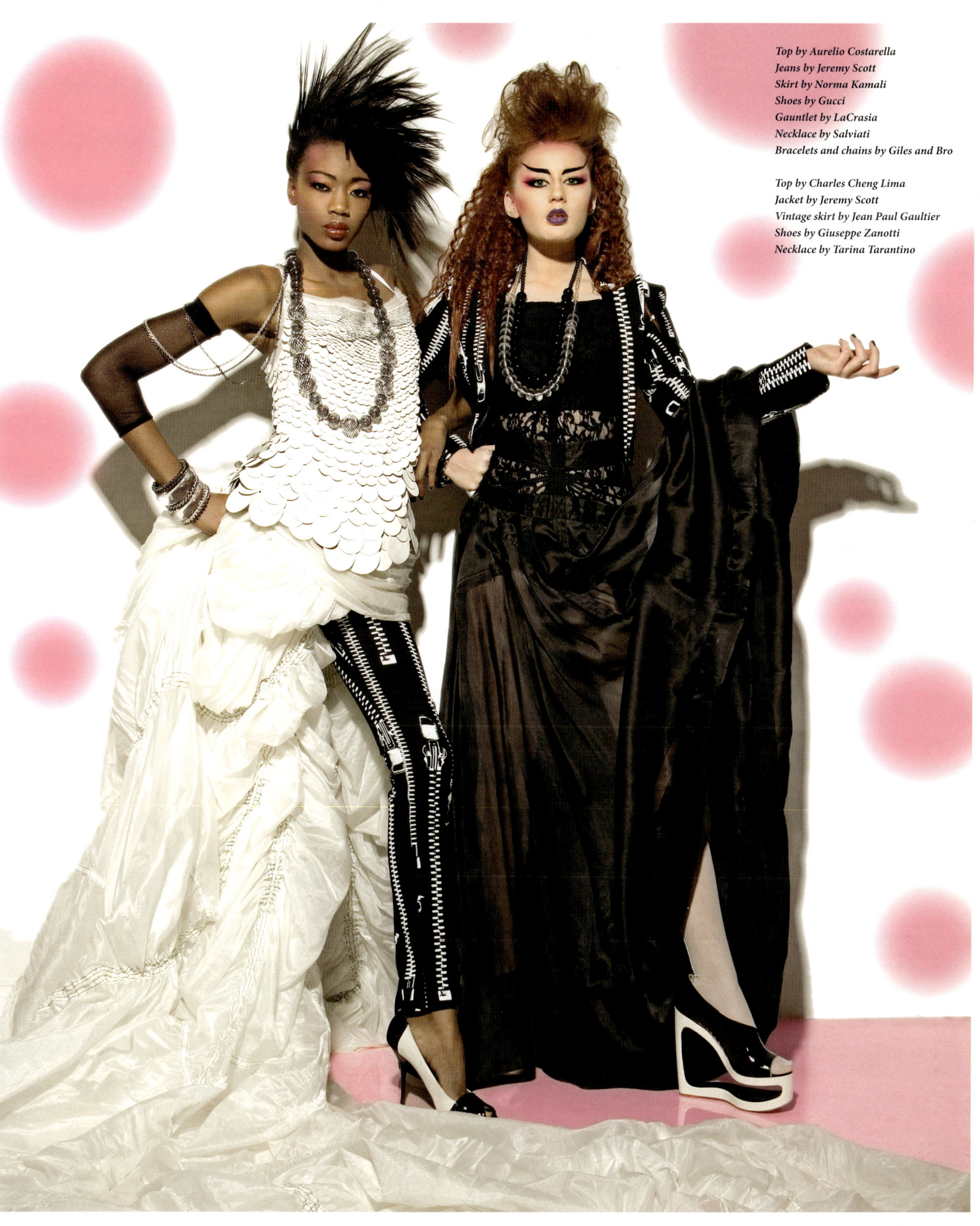

Top by Aurelio Costarella
Jeans by Jeremy Scott
Skirt by Norma Kamali
Shoes by Gucci
Gauntlet by LaCrasia
Necklace by Salviati
Bracelets and chains by Giles and Bro

Top by Charles Cheng Lima
Jacket by Jeremy Scott
Vintage skirt by Jean Paul Gaultier
Shoes by Giuseppe Zanotti
Necklace by Tarina Tarantino

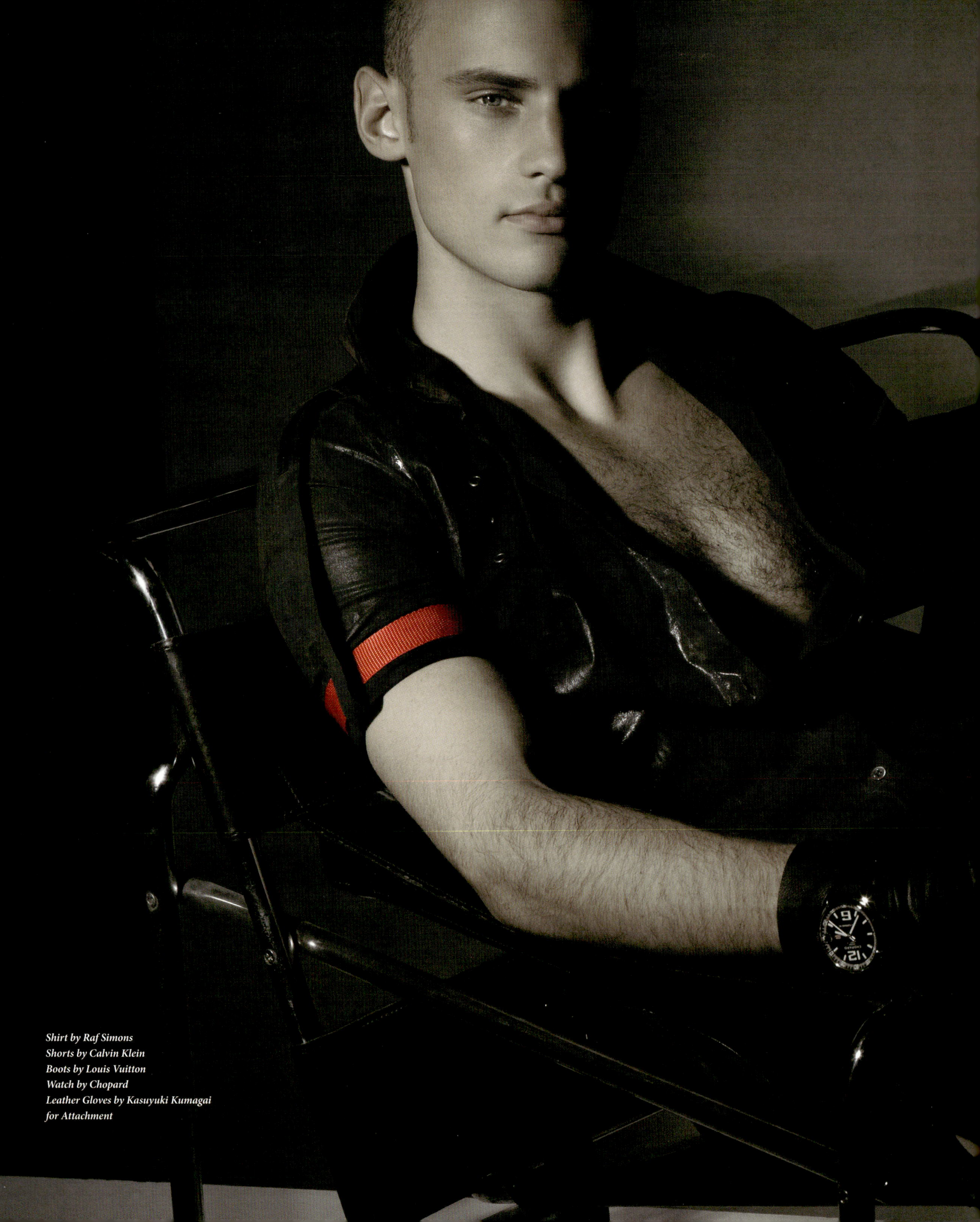

Shirt by Raf Simons
Shorts by Calvin Klein
Boots by Louis Vuitton
Watch by Chopard
Leather Gloves by Kasuyuki Kumagai
for Attachment

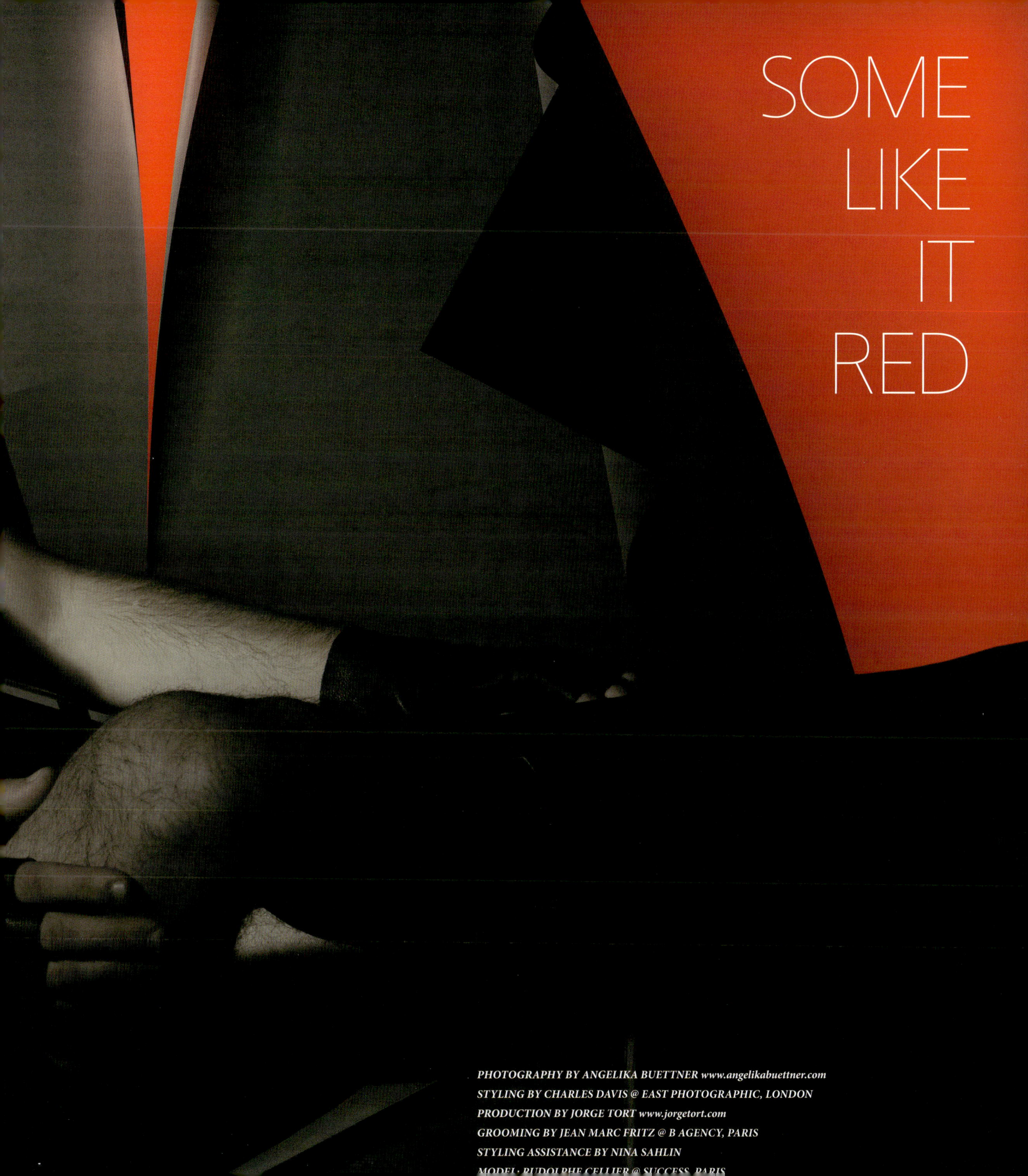

PHOTOGRAPHY BY ANGELIKA BUETTNER www.angelikabuettner.com
STYLING BY CHARLES DAVIS @ EAST PHOTOGRAPHIC, LONDON
PRODUCTION BY JORGE TORT www.jorgetort.com
GROOMING BY JEAN MARC FRITZ @ B AGENCY, PARIS
STYLING ASSISTANCE BY NINA SAHLIN
MODEL: RUDOLPHE CELLIER @ SUCCESS, PARIS

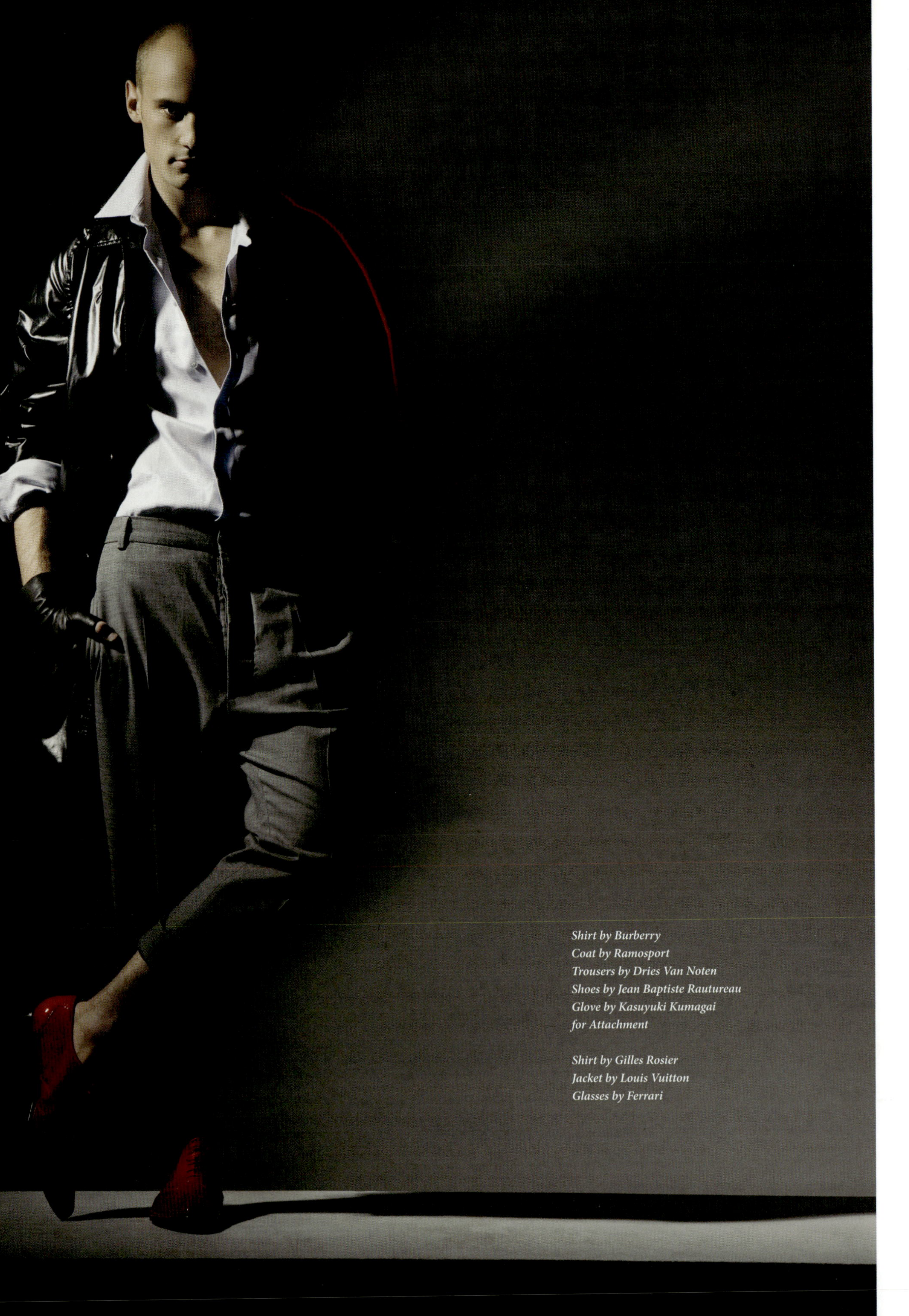

Shirt by Burberry
Coat by Ramosport
Trousers by Dries Van Noten
Shoes by Jean Baptiste Rautureau
Glove by Kasuyuki Kumagai
for Attachment

Shirt by Gilles Rosier
Jacket by Louis Vuitton
Glasses by Ferrari

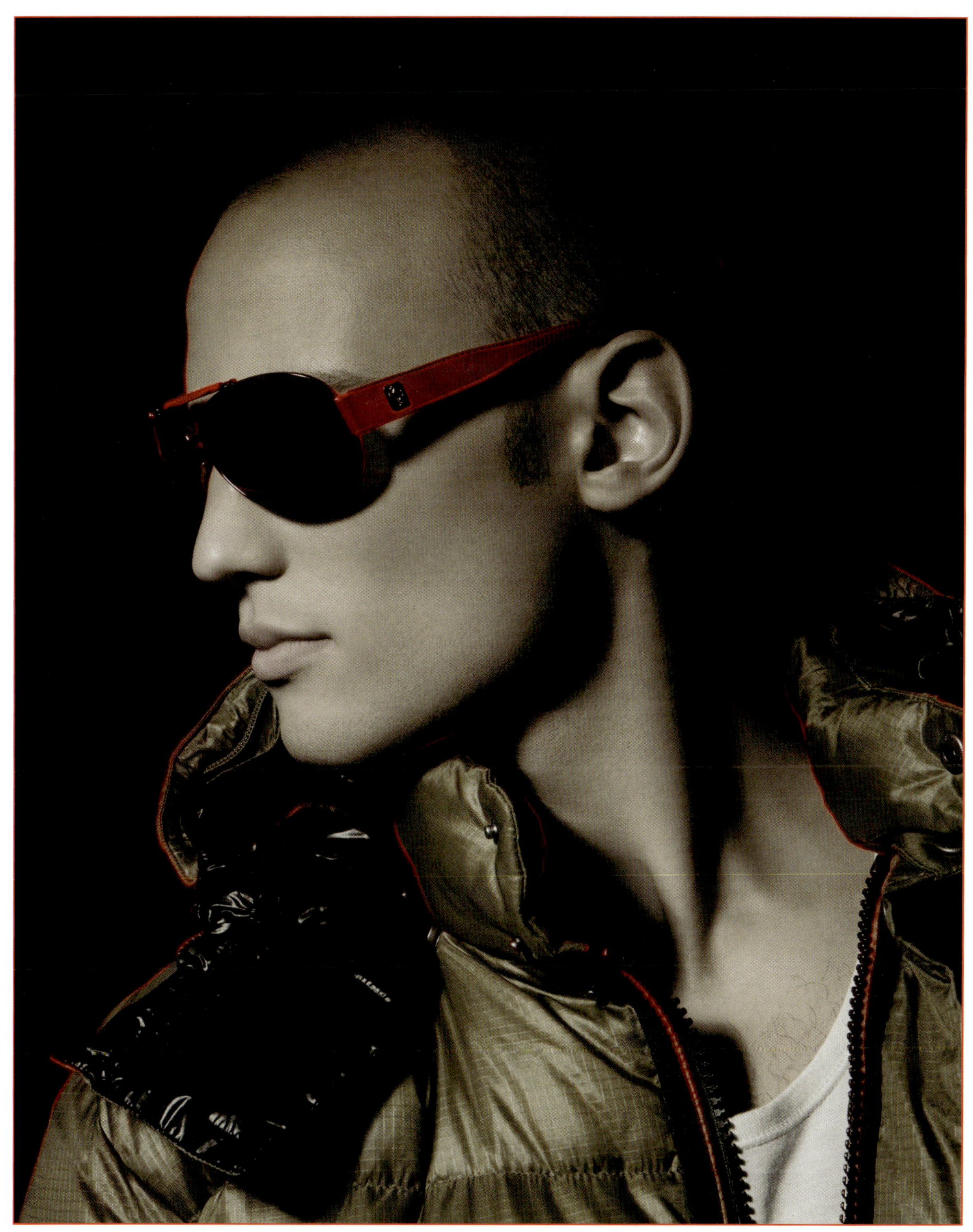

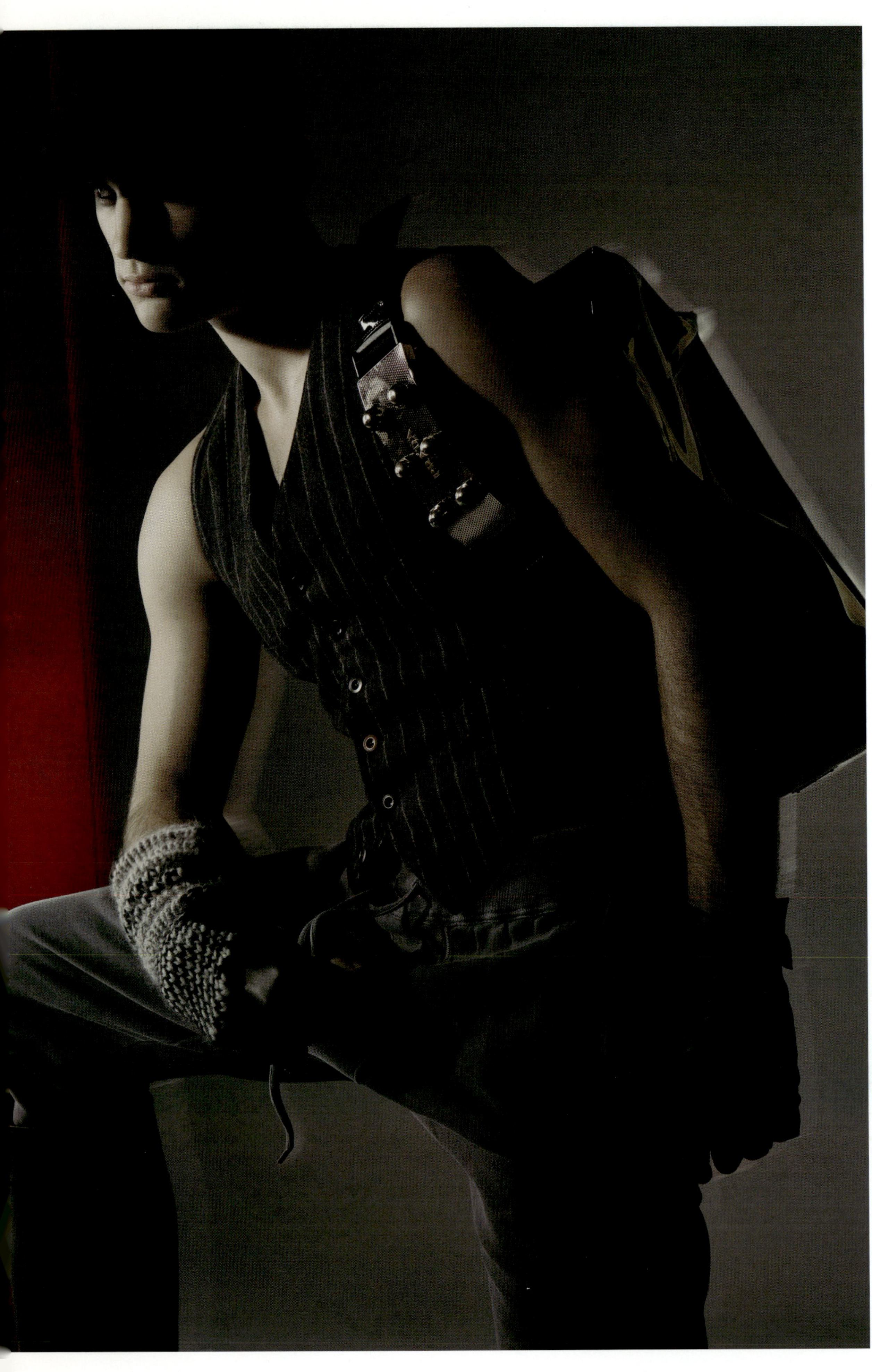

*Vest by Paul Smith
Pants by Dsquared
Cap and long knitted
glove by Rogan Homme
Leather glove by
Kasuyuki Kumagai
for Attachment
Boots by Louis Vuitton
Bag by Prada*

*Shirt by Wendy and
Jim Homme
Scarf by Junko Shimada
Gloves by Kasuyuki
Kumagai for
Attachment*

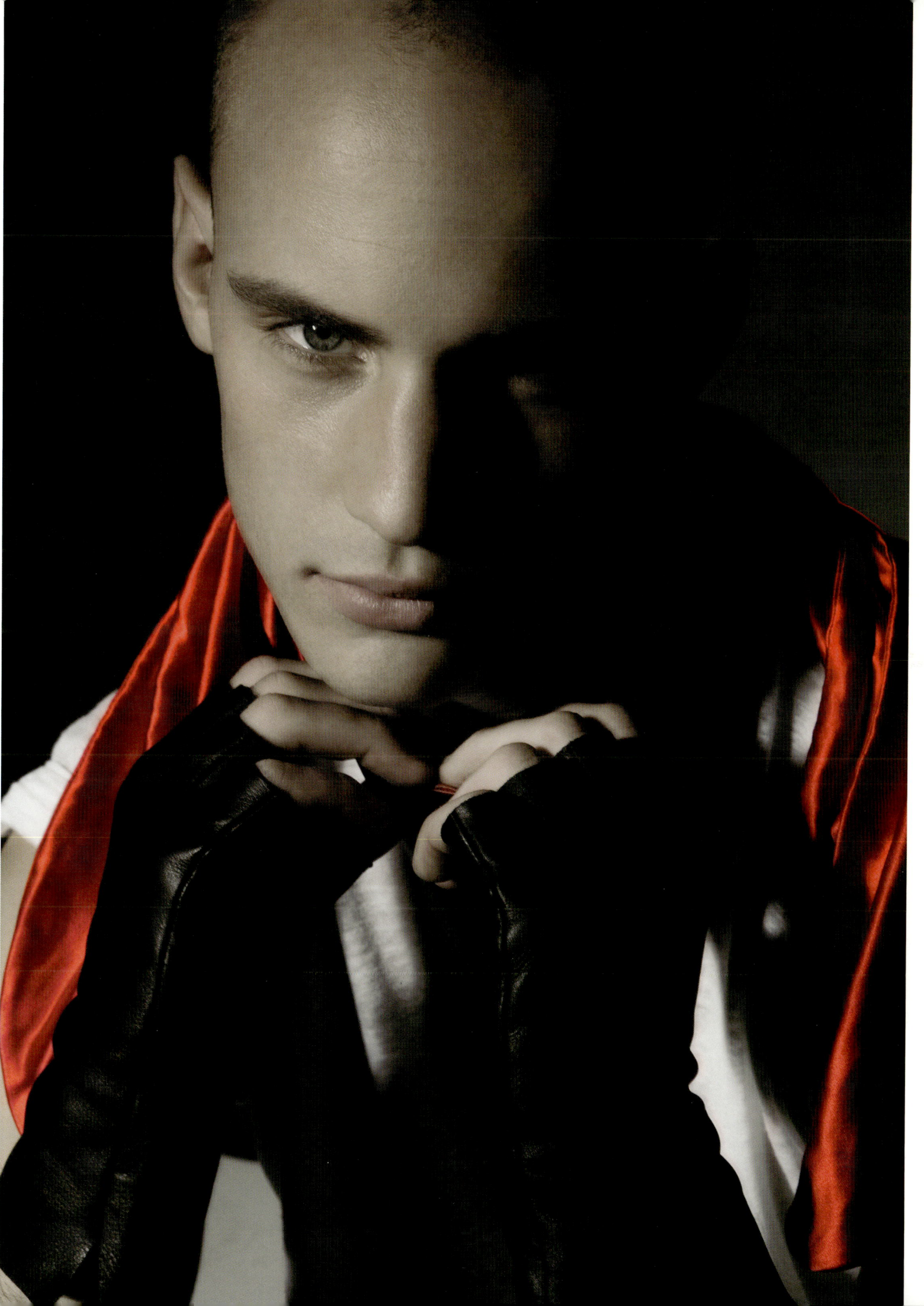

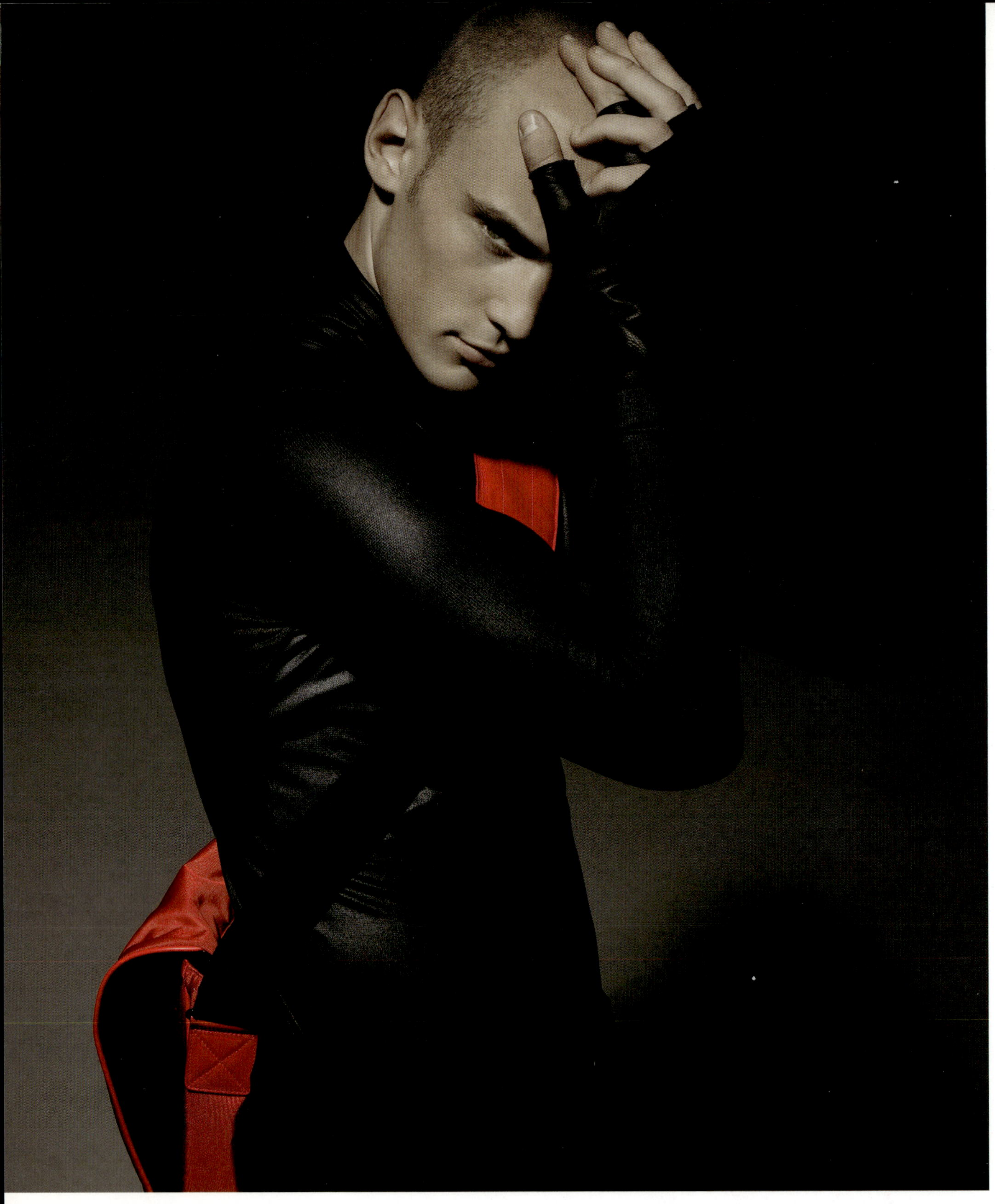

Shirt by Raf Simons
Pants by Wooyoungmi
Red bag by Y3
Gloves by Kasuyuki Kumagai for Attachment

Hooded Jacket by Dsquared
Trousers by Postweiler Hauber
Scarf by Paul Smith
Underwear by Athena Homme
Gloves by Kasuyuki Kumagai for Attachment

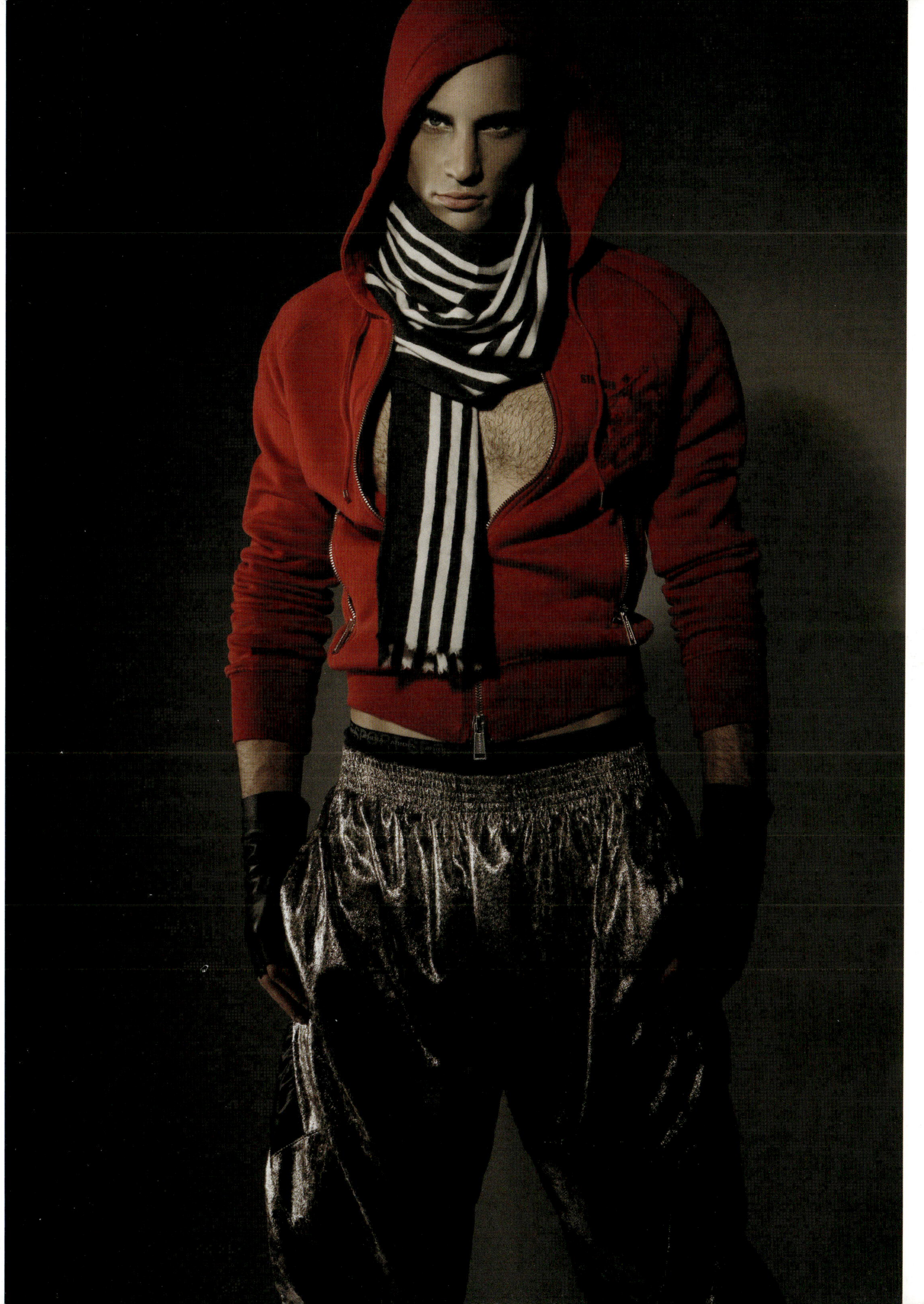

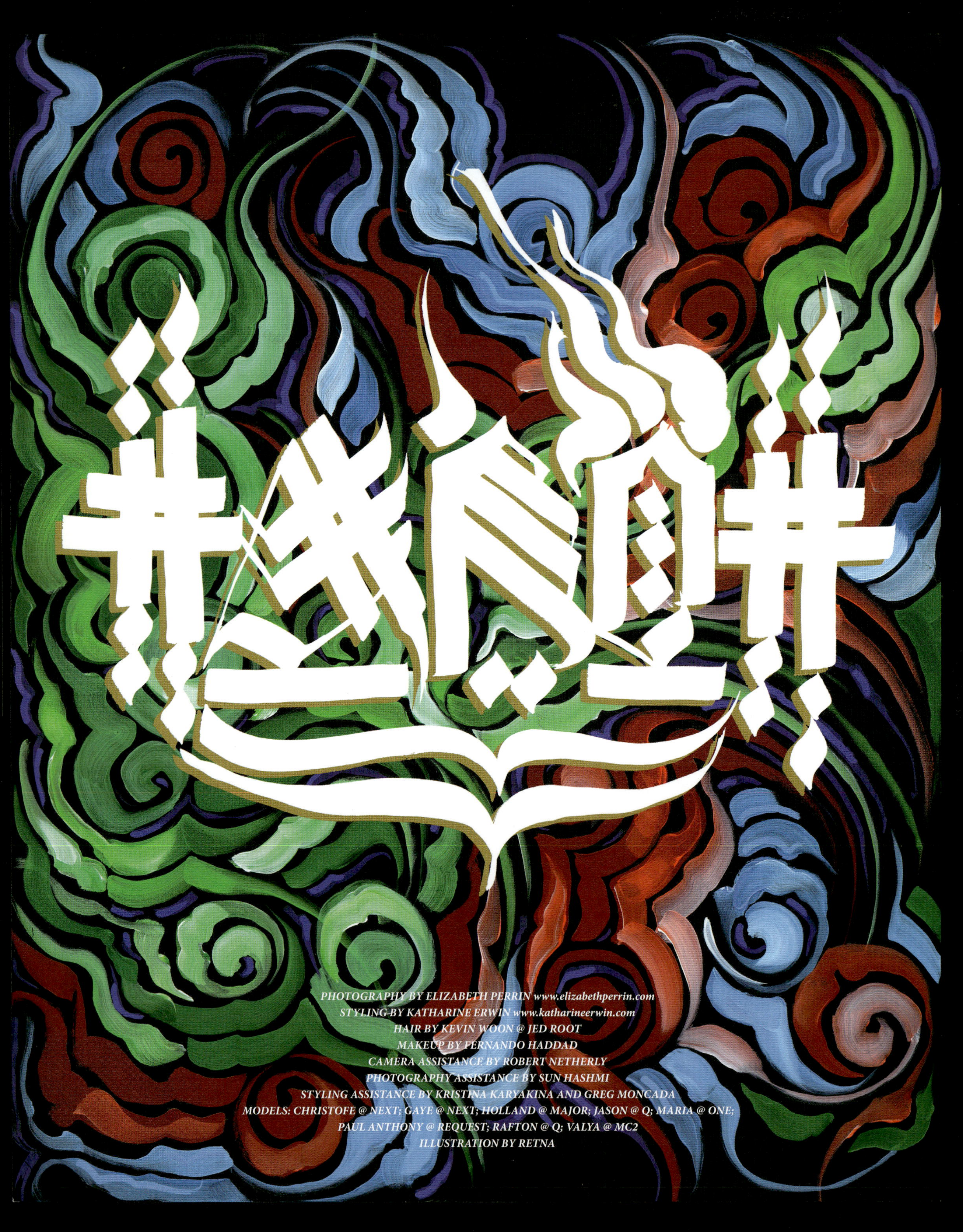

PHOTOGRAPHY BY ELIZABETH PERRIN www.elizabethperrin.com
STYLING BY KATHARINE ERWIN www.katharineerwin.com
HAIR BY KEVIN WOON @ JED ROOT
MAKEUP BY FERNANDO HADDAD
CAMERA ASSISTANCE BY ROBERT NETHERLY
PHOTOGRAPHY ASSISTANCE BY SUN HASHMI
STYLING ASSISTANCE BY KRISTINA KARYAKINA AND GREG MONCADA
MODELS: CHRISTOFE @ NEXT; GAYE @ NEXT; HOLLAND @ MAJOR; JASON @ Q; MARIA @ ONE;
PAUL ANTHONY @ REQUEST; RAFTON @ Q; VALYA @ MC2
ILLUSTRATION BY RETNA

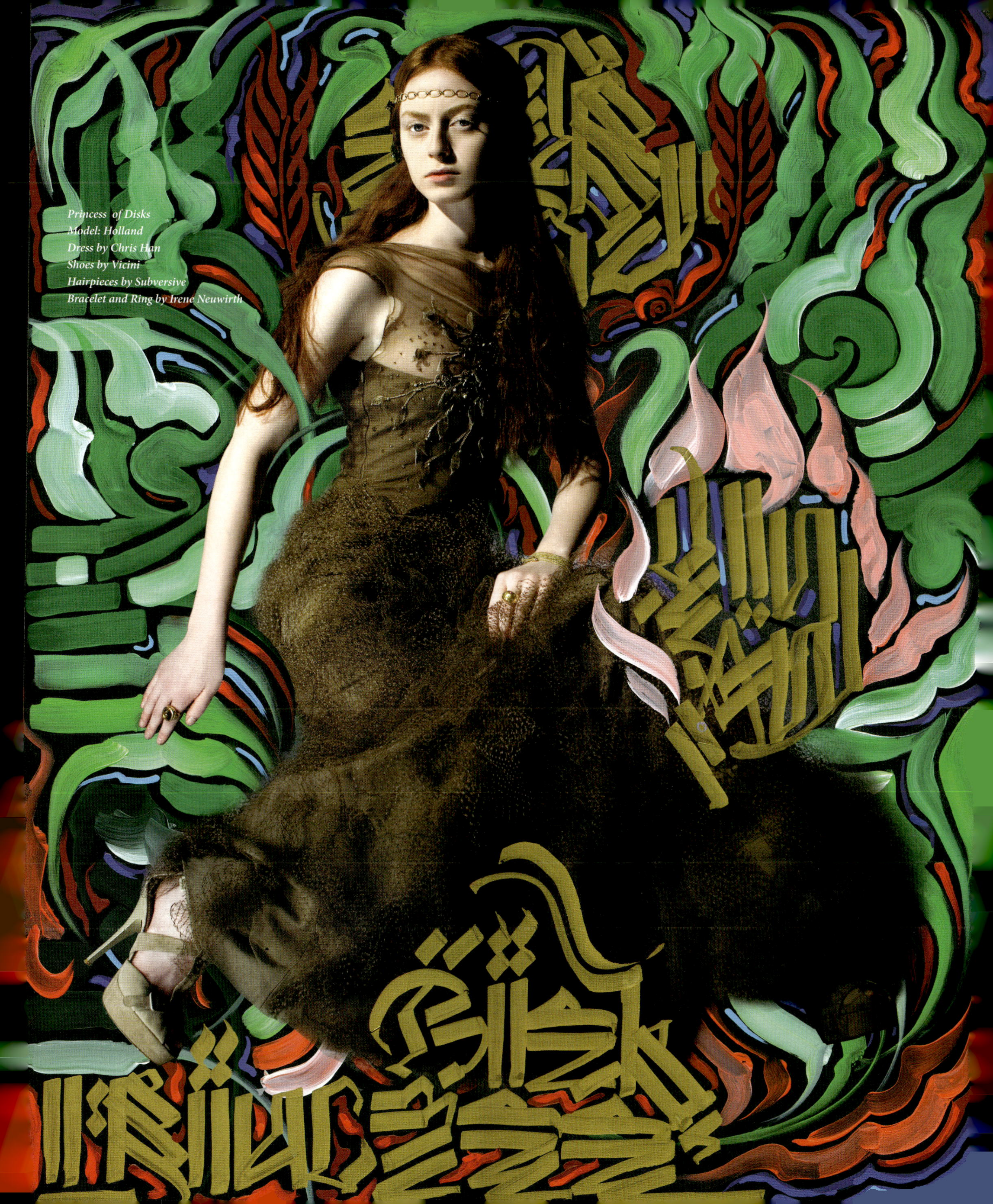
Princess of Disks
Model: Holland
Dress by Chris Han
Shoes by Vicini
Hairpieces by Subversive
Bracelet and Ring by Irene Neuwirth

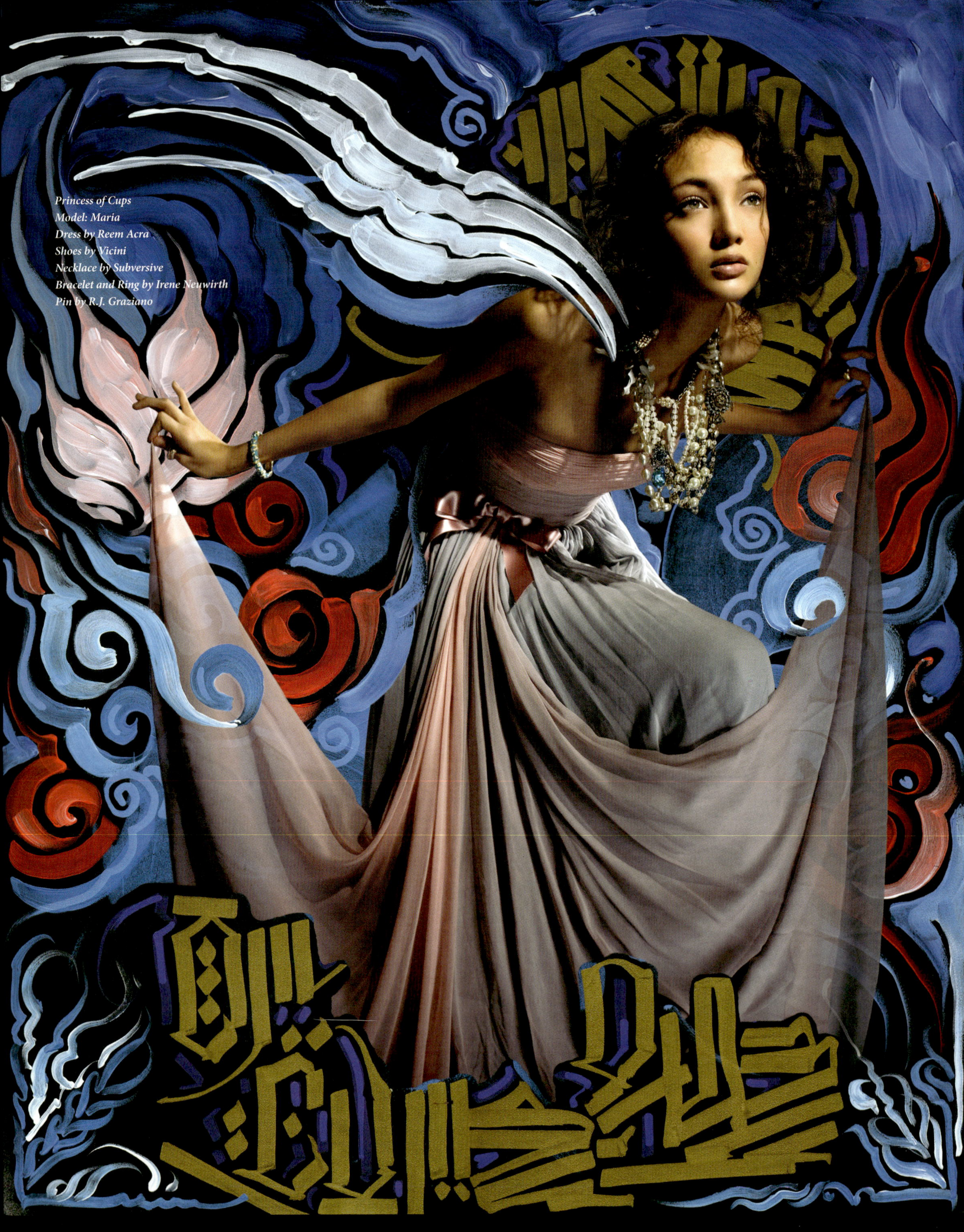

Princess of Cups
Model: Maria
Dress by Reem Acra
Shoes by Vicini
Necklace by Subversive
Bracelet and Ring by Irene Neuwirth
Pin by R.J. Graziano

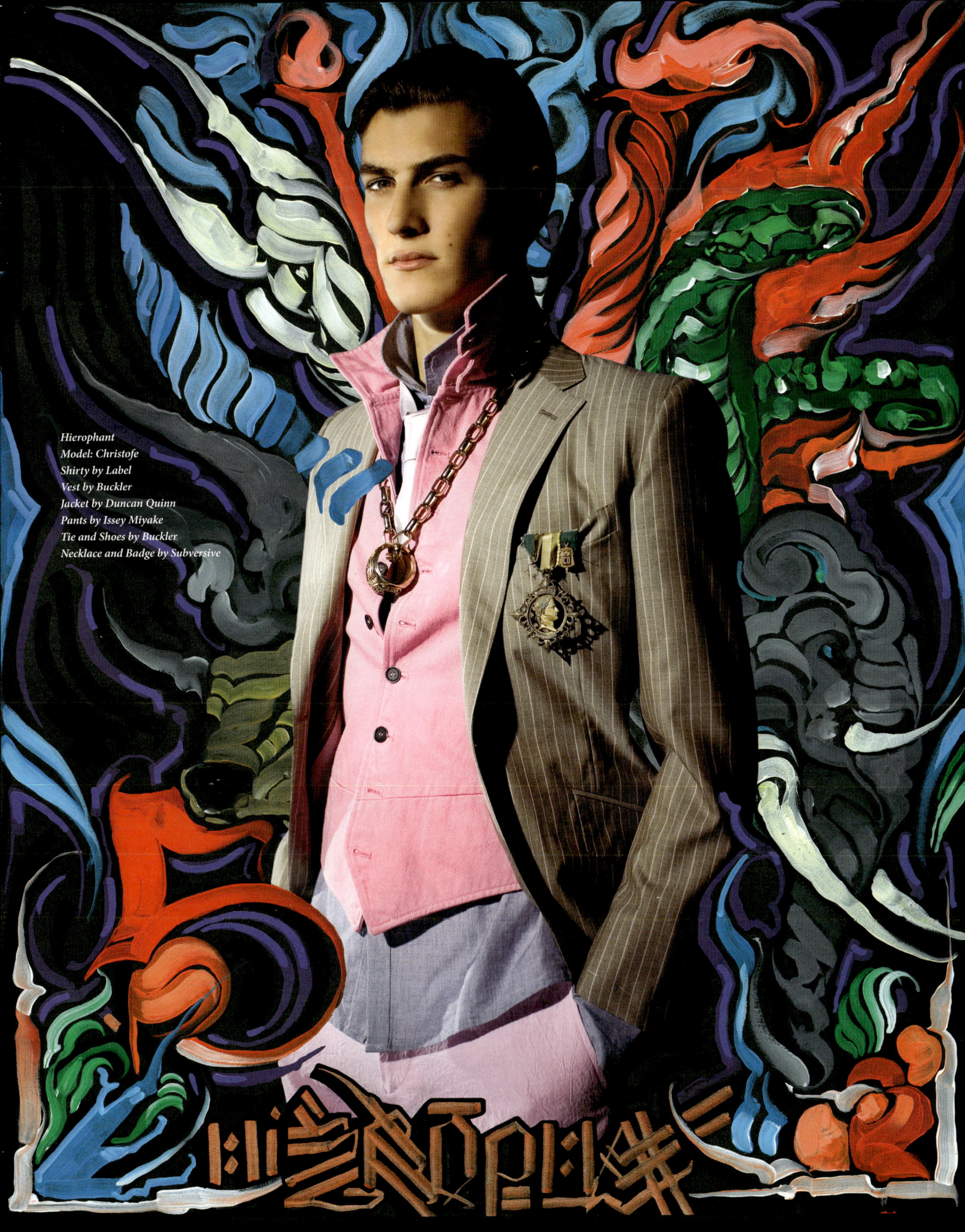

Hierophant
Model: Christofe
Shirty by Label
Vest by Buckler
Jacket by Duncan Quinn
Pants by Issey Miyake
Tie and Shoes by Buckler
Necklace and Badge by Subversive

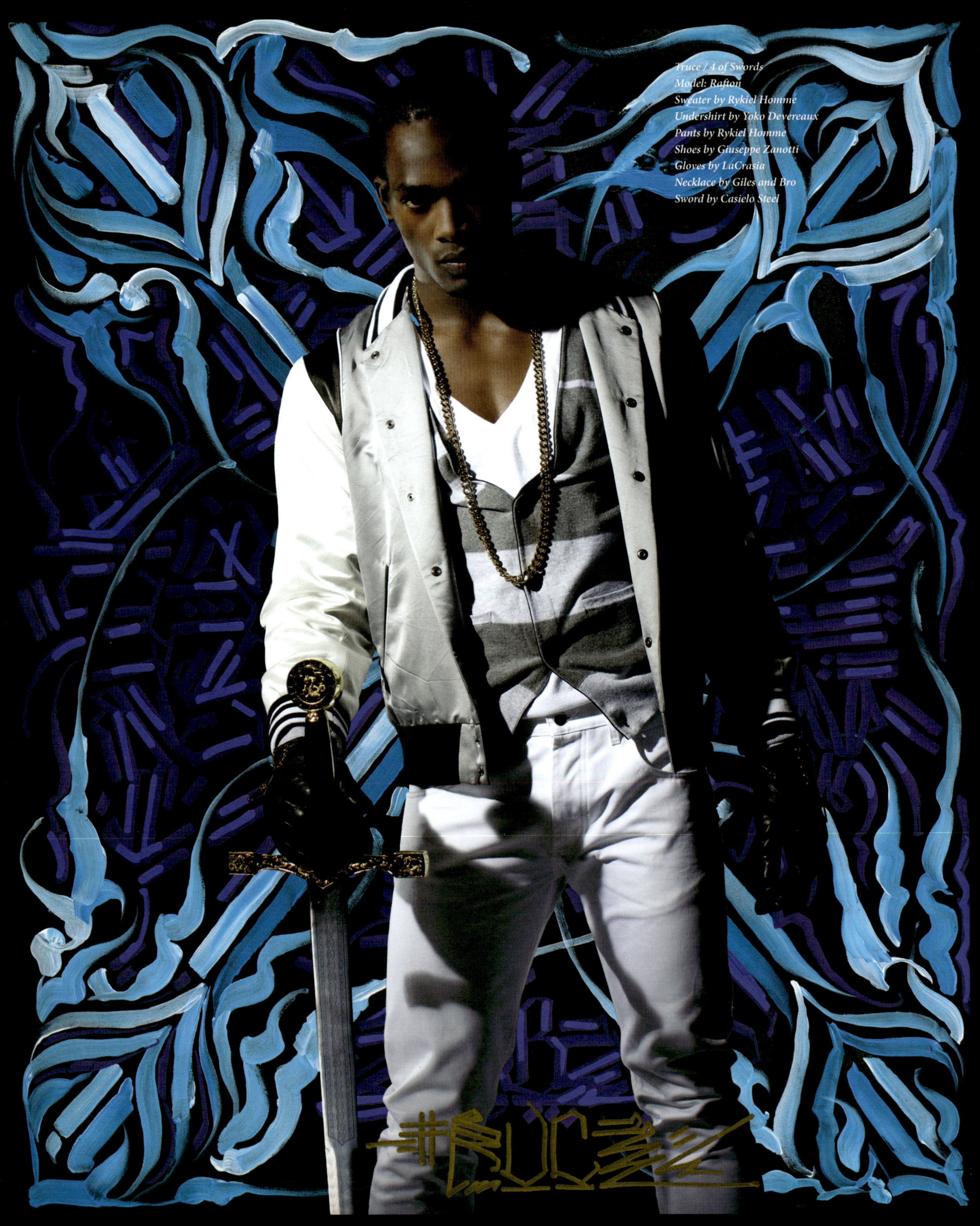

Truce / 4 of Swords
Model: Rafton
Sweater by Rykiel Homme
Undershirt by Yoko Devereaux
Pants by Rykiel Homme
Shoes by Giuseppe Zanotti
Gloves by LaCrasia
Necklace by Giles and Bro
Sword by Casielo Steel

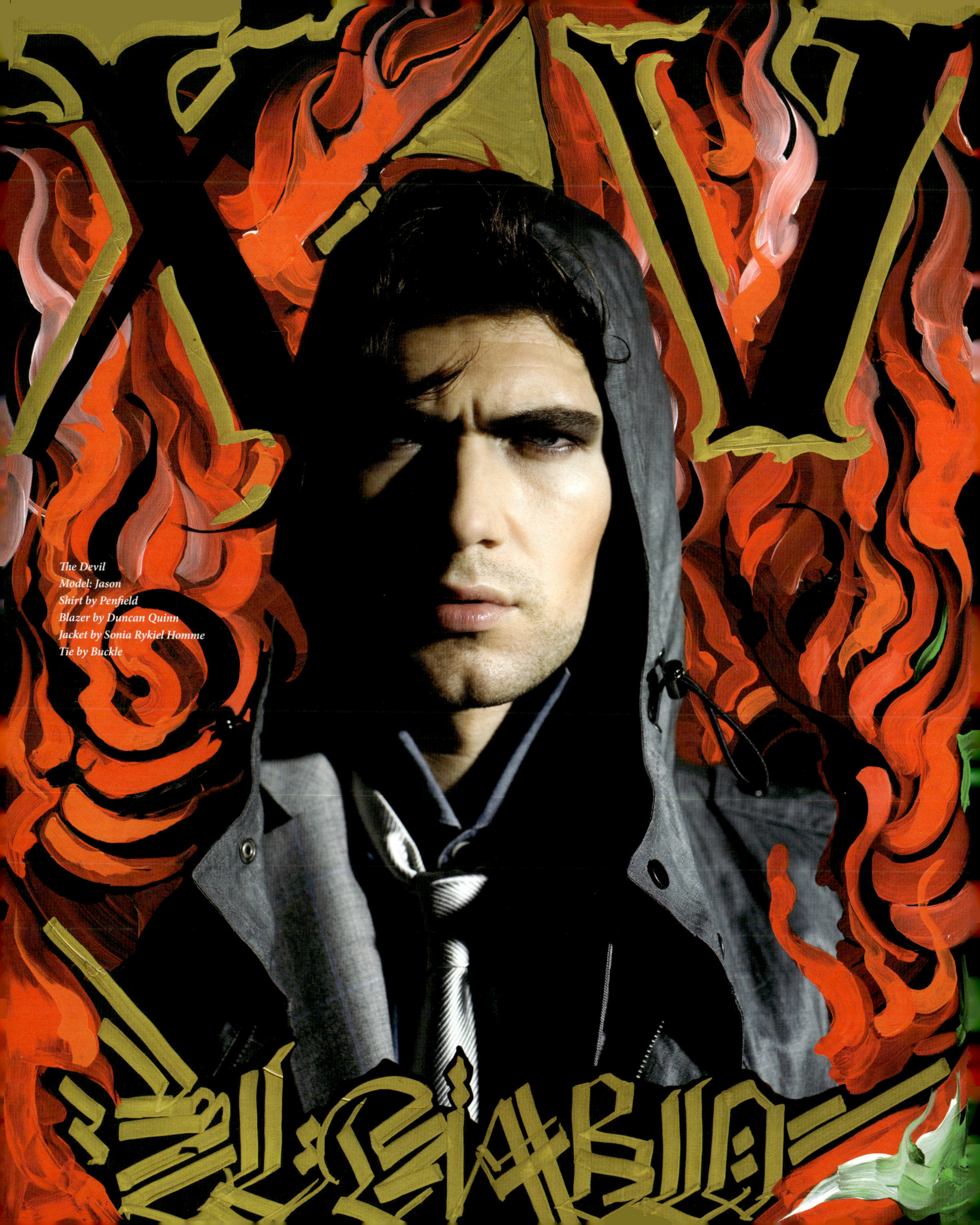

XVI
The Devil
Model: Jason
Shirt by Penfield
Blazer by Duncan Quinn
Jacket by Sonia Rykiel Homme
Tie by Buckle
EL DIABLO

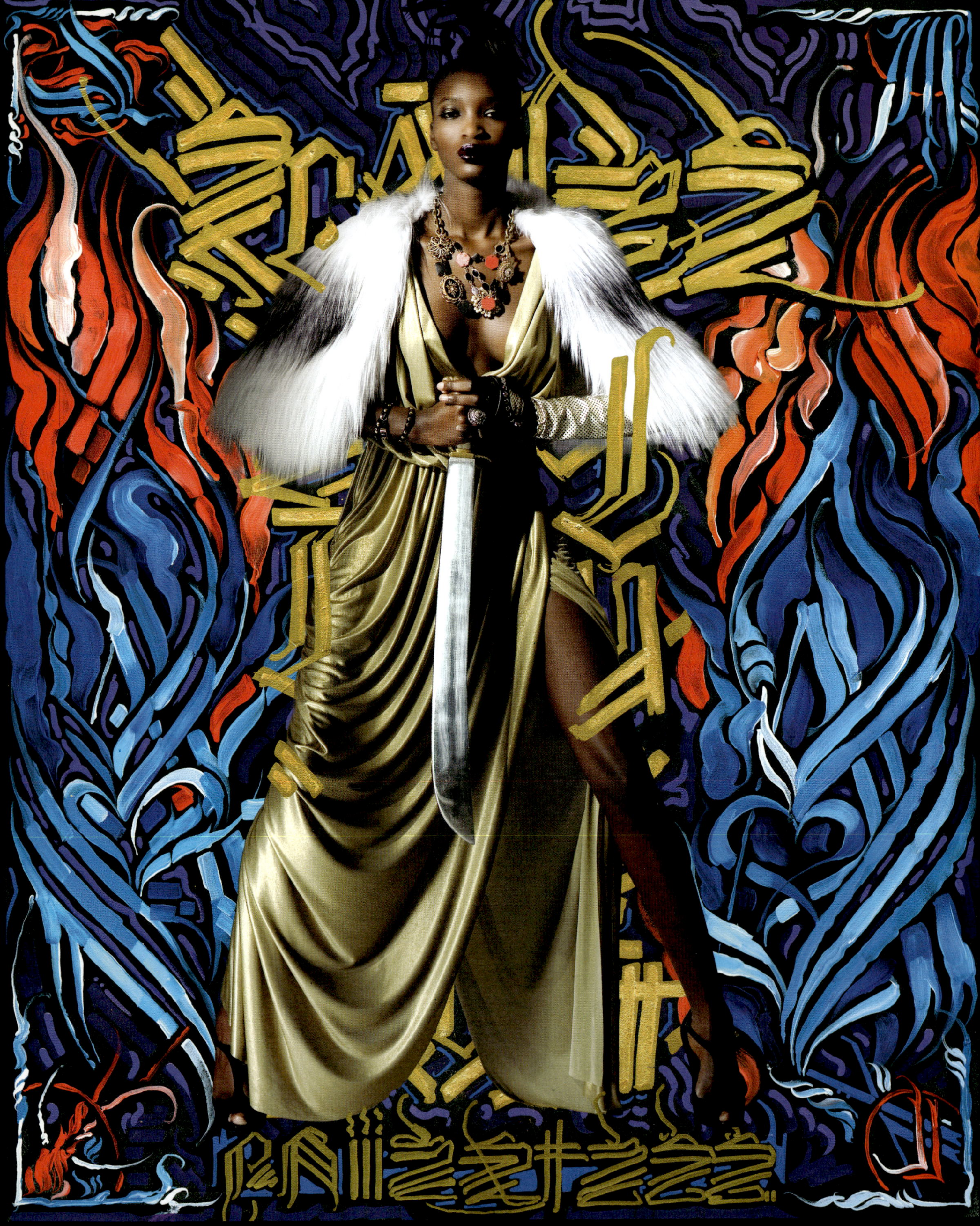

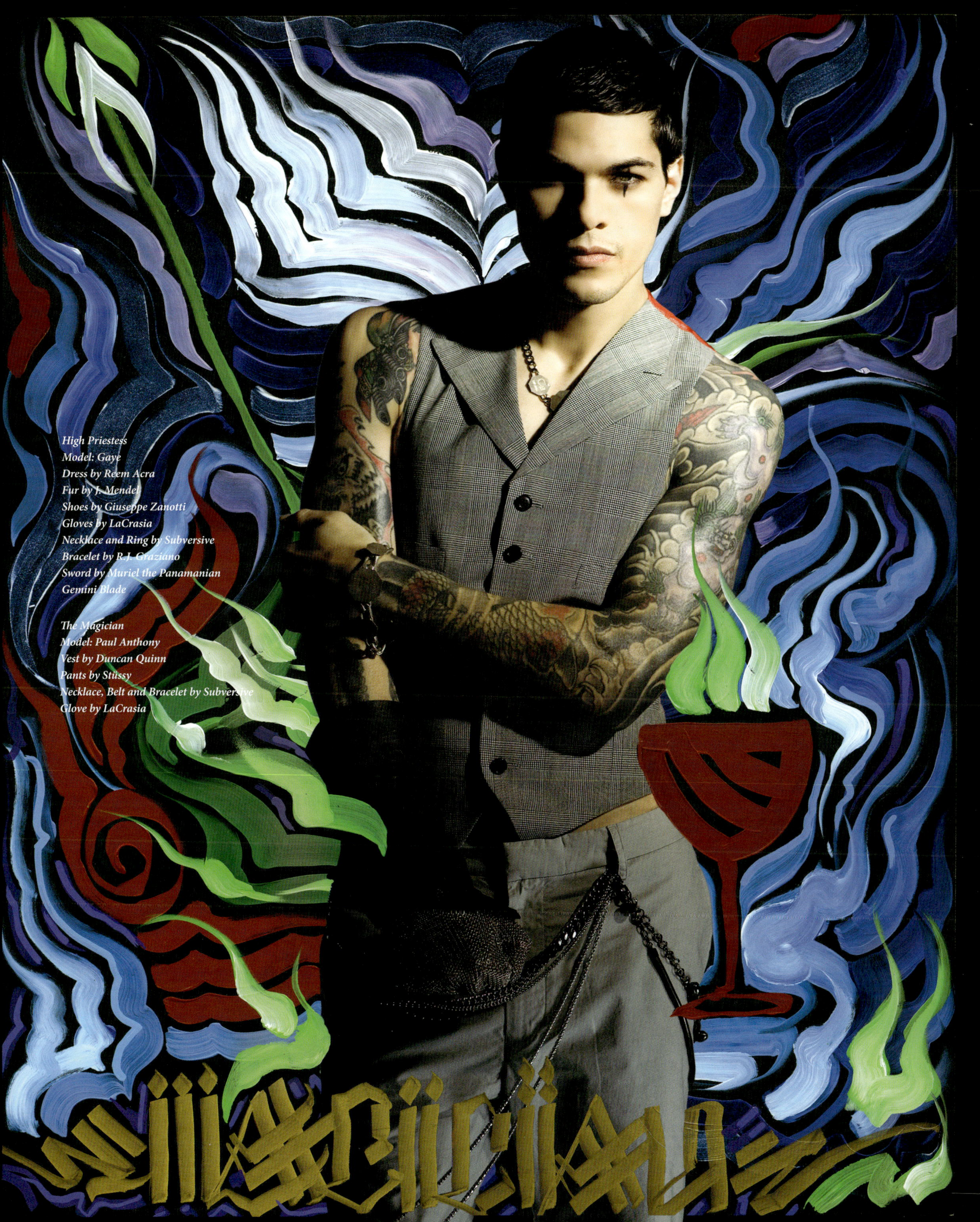

High Priestess
Model: Gaye
Dress by Reem Acra
Fur by J. Mendel
Shoes by Giuseppe Zanotti
Gloves by LaCrasia
Necklace and Ring by Subversive
Bracelet by R.J. Graziano
Sword by Muriel the Panamanian
Gemini Blade

The Magician
Model: Paul Anthony
Vest by Duncan Quinn
Pants by Stüssy
Necklace, Belt and Bracelet by Subversive
Glove by LaCrasia

SHOP TALK

Abaeté
Cantaloup, NYC
212.249.3566

Adidas
Adidas, Santa Monica
310.393.0638

Agent Provocateur
Agent Provocateur, L.A.
323.653.0229

Alessandro Dell' Acqua
Alessandro Dell' Acqua, NYC
212.253.6861

Aurelio Costarella
Funky Lala, NYC
212.260 2865

Buckler
Buckler Store, NYC
212.255.1596

Burberry
Burberry, Beverly Hills
310.550.4500

Calvin Klein
Saks Fifth Avenue, NYC
212.753.4000

Chanel
Chanel, NYC
212.334.0055

Charles Chang Lima
Neiman Marcus, Beverly Hills
310.550.5900

Chopard
Chopard Boutique, NYC
212.223.2304

Chris Han
Mao PR Showroom, NYC
212.226.8510

Christian Louboutin
Louboutin, NYC
212.396.1884

Dior Homme
Dior Homme, NYC
212.421.6009

Dries Van Noten
www.driesvannoten.be

DSquared
DSquared2 Inc., NYC
212.244.5070

Duncan Quinn
Duncan Quinn, L.A.
323.782.9205

Fendi
Fendi, NYC
212.767.0545

Ferrari
The Ferrari Store, Beverly Hills
310.657.9800

Giles and Brother
Odin, NYC
212.475.0666

Gilles Rosier
www.gillesrosier.com

Giuseppe Zanotti
Giuseppe Zanotti Design, NYC
212.650.0455

Gucci
Gucci, NYC
212.826.2600

Heatherette
www.heatherette.com

Hot Topic
Hot Topic, L.A.
323.462.2590

Irene Neuwirth
Barney's New York, NYC
212.826.8900

Issey Miyake
Issey Miyake, NYC
212.439.7822

J. Mendel
J. Mendel, NYC
212.832.5830

Jean Baptiste Rautureau
www.jeanbaptisterautureau.fr

Jean Paul Gaultier
Jean Paul Gaultier, Las Vegas
702.770.3490

Jeremy Scott
www.jeremyscott.com

Junko Shimada
www.junkoshimada.com

LaCrasia
LaCrasia Gloves, NYC
212.803.1600

Louis Vuitton
Louis Vuitton, Beverly Hills
310.859.0457

Max Mara
Max Mara, NYC
212.879.6100

Norma Kamali
Nordstrom, NYC
212.247.3021

Paul Smith
www.paulsmith.co.uk

Penfield
www.penfield-usa.com

Postweiler Hauber
www.potsweilerhauber.com

Prada
Saks Fifth Avenue, Chicago
312.944.6500

Raf Simons
Barney's New York, NYC
212.826.8900

Ramosport
www.ramosport.com

Reem Acra
Reem Acra, NYC
212.308.8760

R.J. Graziano
Nordstrom, NYC
212.247.3021

Rogan
American Rag, L.A.
323.935.3154

Sergio Rossi
Sergio Rossi, NYC
212.956.3303

Sonia Rykiel
Sonia Rykiel, NYC
212.396.3060

Stüssy
Stüssy, NYC
212.995.8787

Tarina Tarantino
Tarina Tarantino, L.A.
323.651.5155

Wolford
Wolford, Beverly Hills
310.277.8112

Wooyoungmi
www.wooyoungmi.com

Yoko Devereaux
Yoko Devereaux, Brooklyn
718.302.1450

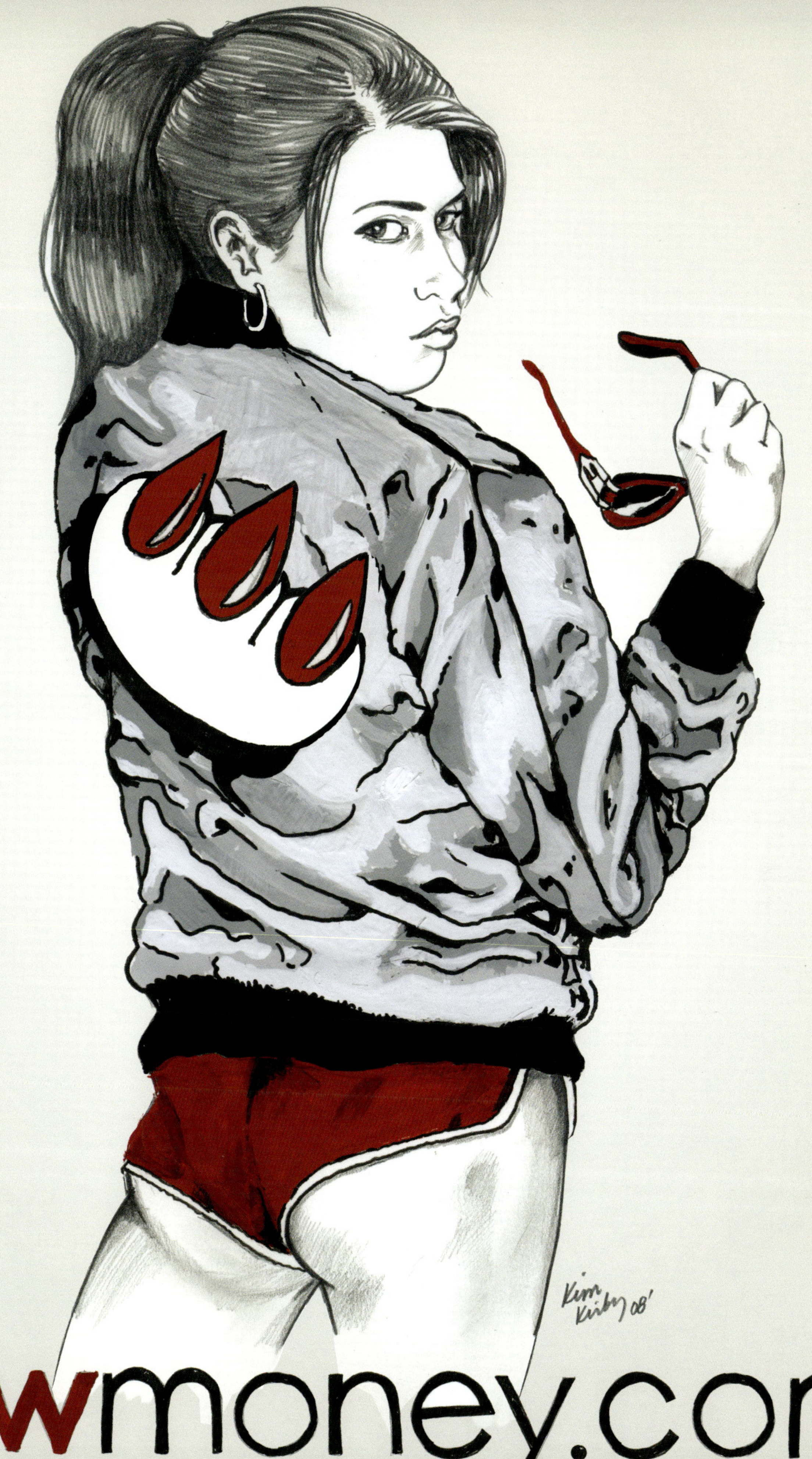

clawmoney.com

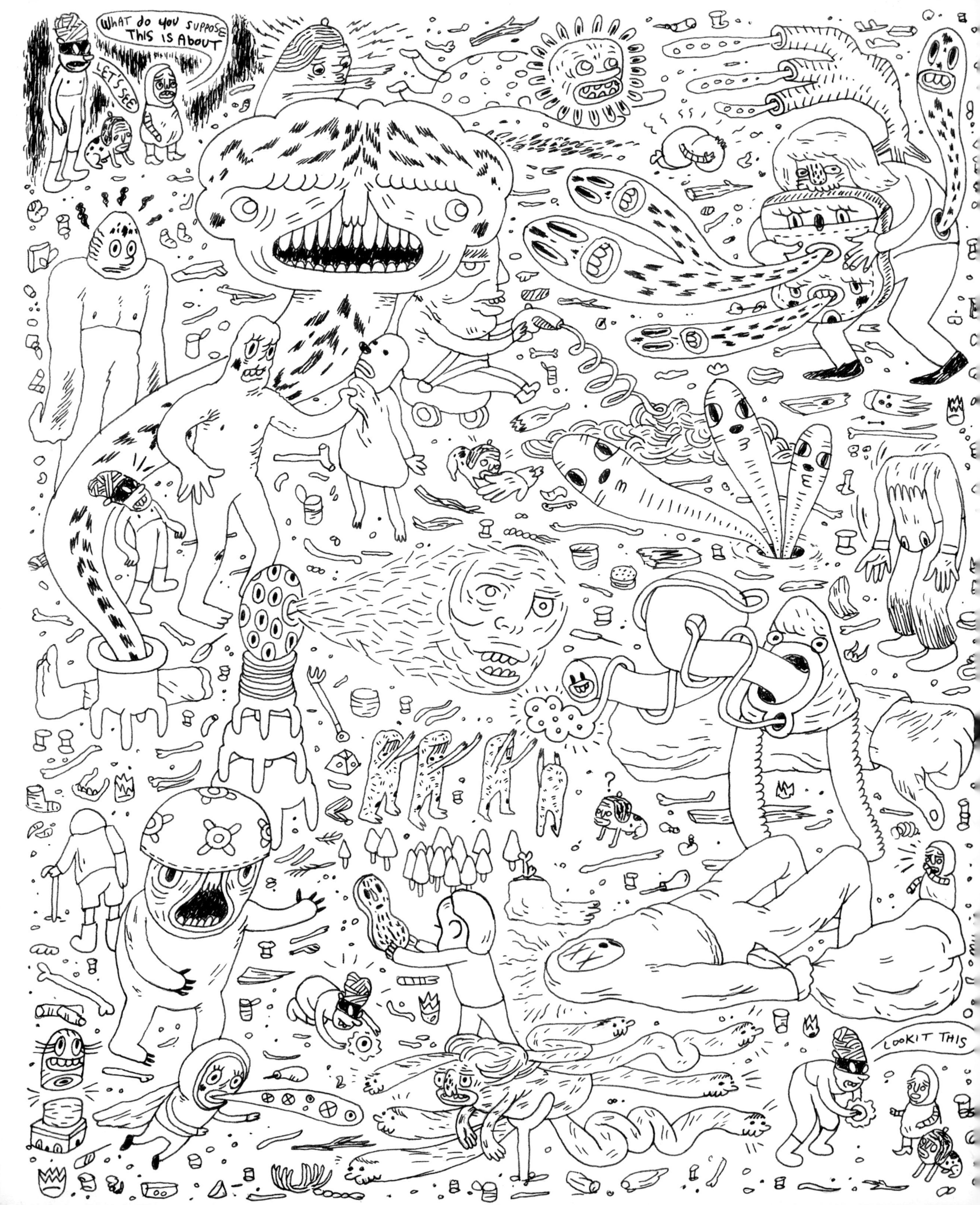

WHAT DO YOU SUPPOSE THIS IS ABOUT
LET'S SEE
LOOKIT THIS

COMIC BY MAX HUBENTHAL

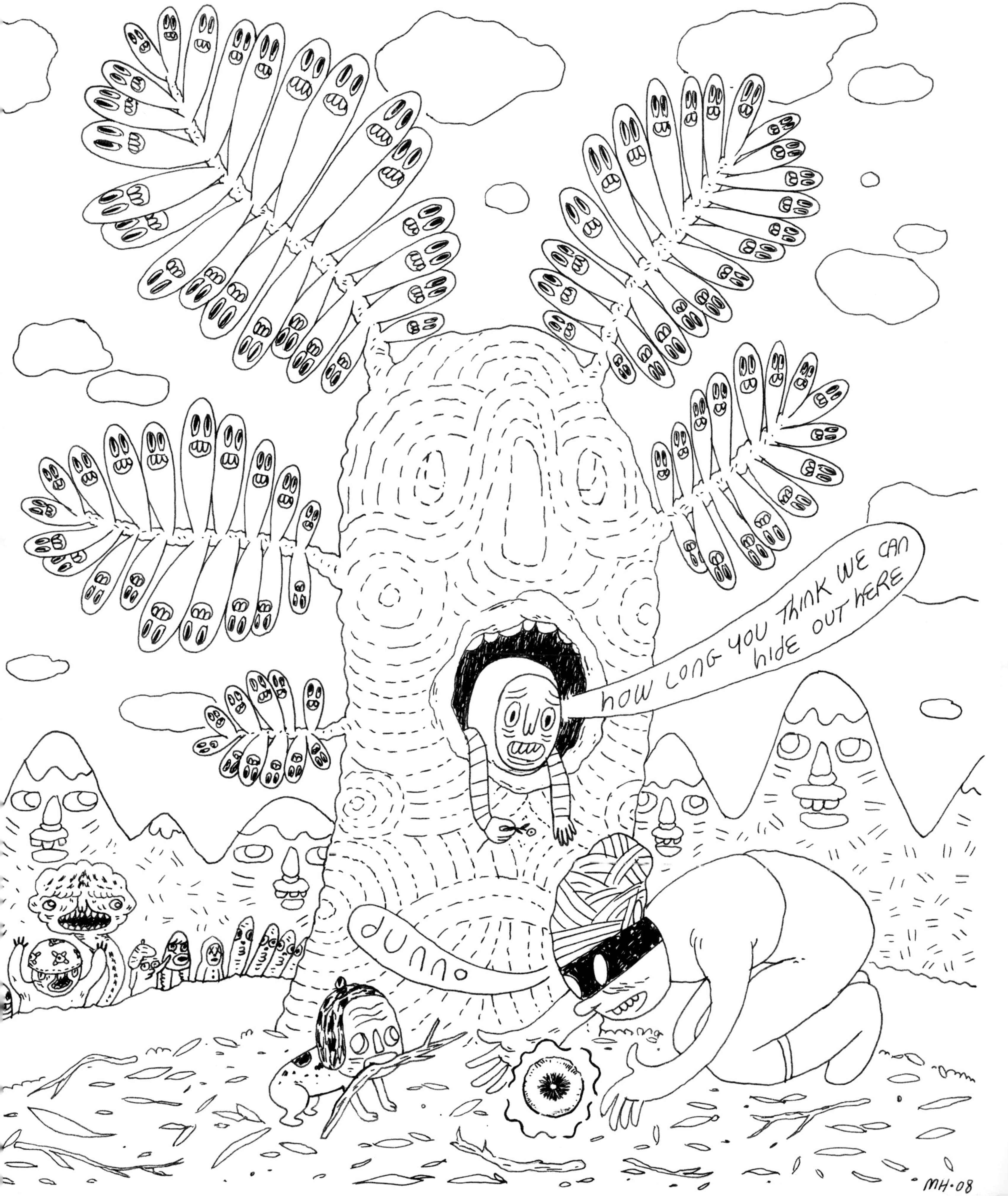

how long you think we can hide out here
dunno
MH·08

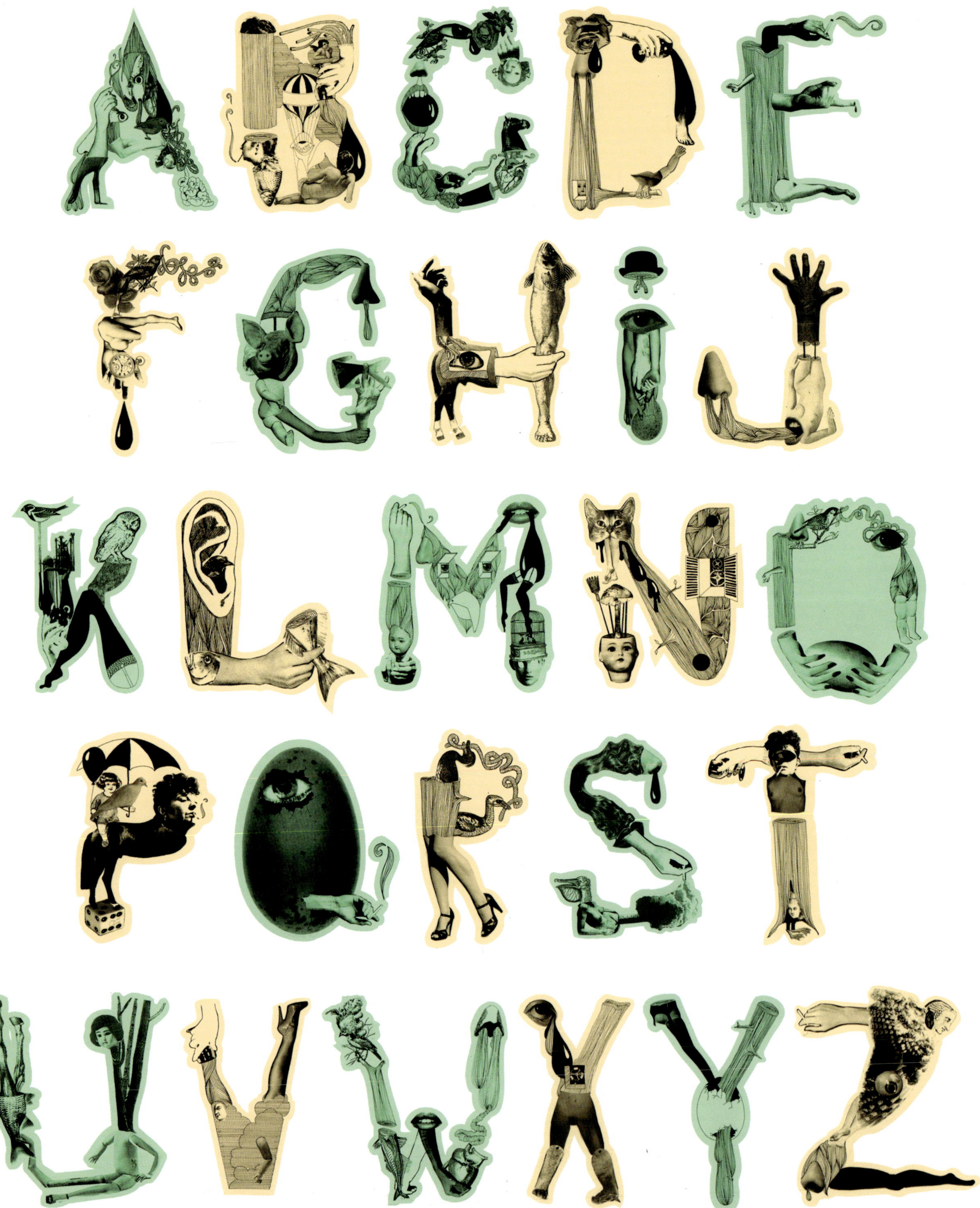

BY THERESE VANDLING